GREAT AMERICAN AIRCRAFT
OF WORLD WAR II

GREAT AMERICAN AIRCRAFT
OF WORLD WAR II

4 1 3 3 5 7

B7 R

BISON BOOKS

First Published in 1983 by
Bison Books Corp.
17 Sherwood Place
Greenwich, CT 06830
U.S.A.

ISBN 0 86124 116 9

Printed in Hong Kong

CONTENTS

B·17
FLYING FORTRESS

H. P. Willmott

Below: A preserved B-17.

INTRODUCTION

'Ten-place, landplane monoplane, long-range high-altitude low-wing bomber.' The official description takes eleven words to define an aircraft that won international renown as the 'Flying Fortress.' It was a name that embraced many variants of an aircraft conceived eleven years before the end of World War II. The aircraft has many grounds for its claim to fame, but longevity of service is perhaps the most important. The Flying Fortress was certainly one of the very few aircraft that saw continuous service throughout the war despite having first flown as early as 1935. Admittedly the variants that were in service in 1945 – mostly B-17s of the F and G Marks – were significantly different from the first prototype and production models; throughout the war successive B-17s showed consistent improvements in both Marks and in-production Marks. However, at a time when the aviation industry was continuously pushing back the frontiers of knowledge with every year producing aircraft faster, more reliable and longer-ranged than the year before, the B-17 still managed to hold its own until the end of the war. By 1945 although still in production it was somewhat obsolescent, but that the aircraft saw continuous and unbroken service under war conditions speaks highly of an original design that allowed so much

modification and change to be worked into the airframe. No other aircraft in World War II showed such adaptability and durability as the B-17.

A glowering pugnacious profile – machine guns snarling aggressively from a massive but not inelegant silhouette – helped the fame of the B-17. She was magnificently photogenic, especially when seen in formation. When alone against a brilliant azure sky or with her sisters, vapor trails marking their progress high above the clouds, the B-17 presents a superb subject for the camera. But the aircraft can also claim renown through the fact that the Mark G was built in greater numbers than any other single Mark of bomber. It is a record that is never likely to be broken. More B-24 Liberators than Fortresses were built, but no single Mark or variant could ever match the 8680-strong batch of B-17Gs built during the last two years of the war. Overall some 12,731 B-17s of all types were built, including prototypes and preproduction models. This total was easily exceeded by the Liberator, but this chunkier, more stolid aircraft could never match the grace of the Fortress or its claim to have been the first American bomber to enter the European Theater of Operations. Nor could it deny the Fortress the fact that the weight of the

II

Above: In the foreground a Fortress III of the Royal Air Force in the company of a Fortress with **USAAF** markings. In fact both served with the RAF. The 19141 carries British camouflage and both British and American markings.

USAAF's campaign of strategic bombing against Germany was carried by the B-17. The B-17 was the workhorse of the American air effort in Europe. Of the 47 Bombardment Groups that served with the 8th Air Force, the main American strategic bombing force in Europe, 29 were equipped wholly or mainly by the B-17. In carrying out the campaign of strategic bombing of Germany the Flying Fortress showed a tremendous resilience and ability to absorb punishment which frequently allowed it to make it home to base. That being said, however, it must be noted that nearly forty percent of all Fortresses built – over 5000 aircraft – failed to return from missions. It is perhaps inevitable that part of the fame of the aircraft must rest on the macabre fact that so many of the dead of the USAAF were lost when serving in the B-17.

Such are the bases for the claim to fame of the Boeing B-17 bomber, which it achieved despite the fact that it was not superior to many aircraft that enjoyed none of the limelight that came to the Fortress. The de Havilland Mosquito, for example, carried a bomb load not inferior to many B-17s; the B-24 was at least its equal and the Avro Lancaster could carry a bomb load three times the size of a normally-loaded Fortress. Such considerations are not of primary relevance and to argue the respective merits of one aircraft against another is seldom a worthwhile pastime, unless one happens to be an aircraft-manufacturer seeking a contract. Because of its strengths and despite its weaknesses the B-17 achieved lasting fame on account of a formidable fighting record in virtually every theater of war. Perhaps its record is only blemished by the tragedy that it shared with the whole of the American concept of strategic bombing. Because it failed to achieve all its objectives, the effectiveness of strategic bombing was doubted or neglected. Strategic bombing successfully distorted German production by diverting scarce resources from the critical fronts and ultimately achieved the ruination of the enemy's economy. The sad fact was, however, that strategic bombing could not achieve the single-handed defeat of the enemy as the more extreme of the prewar, air power enthusiasts had claimed. The simultaneous and total defeat of the enemy on land and at sea has tended to obscure the nature of the Allied strategic air victory and the tactical effect this had on the successful prosecution of the war on land.

H. P. Willmott

CONCEPTION

Above: The seemingly effortless grace and elegance of the B-17.
Below: The Fortress' sturdiness, strength and sense of rugged
reliability is clearly portrayed. The massive redesign of fuselage
and tailpiece, incorporated from the Mark E onward, added to the
aura of power of the B-17.

The origins of the B-17 are confused because the whole of the career of the aircraft is linked intimately to the whole idea of strategic bombing. For the most part the roots of the B-17 are to be found in the dismal experience of World War I and the organizational arrangements of the American services in the interwar period. The indecisiveness of the war at sea and the prodigal useless sacrifice that characterized land battles between 1914 and 1918 led many men of different nationalities to consider the possibility – and indeed the desirability – of bringing about the defeat of an enemy by destroying his means of waging war. This involved the destruction of his means of production (and distribution) and the breaking of civilian willingness to sustain a war effort. This could be achieved by conducting a strategic air offensive aimed at the heartland of the enemy. This concept could only be successful if heavy bombers, in massive numbers and with massive payloads, could be concentrated for sustained operations.

Such an offensive was planned for 1919 by the British, the only combatant of World War I at that stage able to deploy a substantial long-range bomber force with heavier-than-air machines. In the event, given the state of German industry and morale in 1918, an offensive of this nature could not have proved anything of value, the war ending before the British had a chance to carry out their intentions. The idea of strategic bombing therefore remained untried and hence not disproved, making it very attractive to many people. But granted the fact that aviation was still relatively in its infancy the best and most earnest efforts of such men as Hugh Montague Trenchard in Britain, Giulio Douhet in Italy and William Mitchell in the USA not unnaturally failed to secure widespread acceptance for this radical notion of making war. For much of the interwar period the independent air forces of Britain and Italy encountered very great difficulty in preserving themselves as independent forces, clearly identifiable from the traditional services. Though successful in their rear-

guard actions, independent air forces remained the Cinderella of the services, with little money directed to them and with little stress placed upon the construction of bomber forces.

In the USA the ideas of strategic bombing, despite – and perhaps because of – the fiery efforts of Mitchell, failed to impress themselves upon a nation bent on isolation, cocooned by geographical remoteness from the fear of enemy attack and secure in its traditionalist reliance on the Navy – now American and not British – to safeguard national security. Accordingly, American aviation was divided between the Army and the Navy, the latter's interest naturally focusing on the revolutionary concept of the aircraft carrier. Within the Army all aircraft, reconnaissance planes, fighters and bombers became part of the Army Air Corps. The overriding idea of the AAC was tactical, not strategic. Its role was seen as providing support for ground forces over the battlefield, not carrying out a strategic offensive against an enemy homeland. But the nature of air warfare was such that the AAC was made a Major General's command and given a senior representative on the General Staff. The political post of Assistant Secretary of State for War, with special responsibilities for air matters, was created by the Coolidge administration with the approval of Congress.

In view of the flimsiness, unreliability, limited range and offensive power of aircraft before the 1930s, such an arrangement seems eminently sensible. But in the long term it was certain to be doomed as aircraft performance improved and the capacity of land-based aircraft grew more quickly than the power of carrier-borne aircraft. In 1931 recognition of this was given by an arrangement made between the Chief of the General Staff, General Douglas MacArthur, and the Chief of Naval Operations, Admiral Platt. By this arrangement the AAC was rescued from the obscurity to which it had been relegated and the financial parsimony to which it had been subjected by its being made responsible for all land-based air defense of the United States and her territories overseas. In order that the AAC could undertake this role an aircraft with a 200mph speed and a 2000lb bomb load was authorized. The more alert members of the AAC were not slow to appreciate that this arrangement and the aircraft involved presented possibilities for the development of a strategic air force with bombers to match. The Navy, on the other hand, was extremely slow to realize the full consequences of an action that permitted the AAC to usurp successfully part of the traditional, jealously guarded role of the Navy.

Nevertheless there were many problems of operating over the sea and attacking enemy shipping with which the AAC was totally unfamiliar at this time. These difficulties led to the creation in 1935 of a quite separate organization, General Headquarters Air Force (GHQAF), to supervise and coordinate all air action supposedly subordinate to the Navy in maintaining the seaward defenses of the United States. The Navy was growing increasingly concerned by the trend of events and after the long-range interception of an Italian ship by GHQAF aircraft, in 1938 secured the restriction of GHQAF activity to within 100 miles of the American coast. The Navy feared that its role would be taken over by the AAC and was anxious to emasculate GHQAF – the opportunity to achieve the latter presented itself with the incident involving

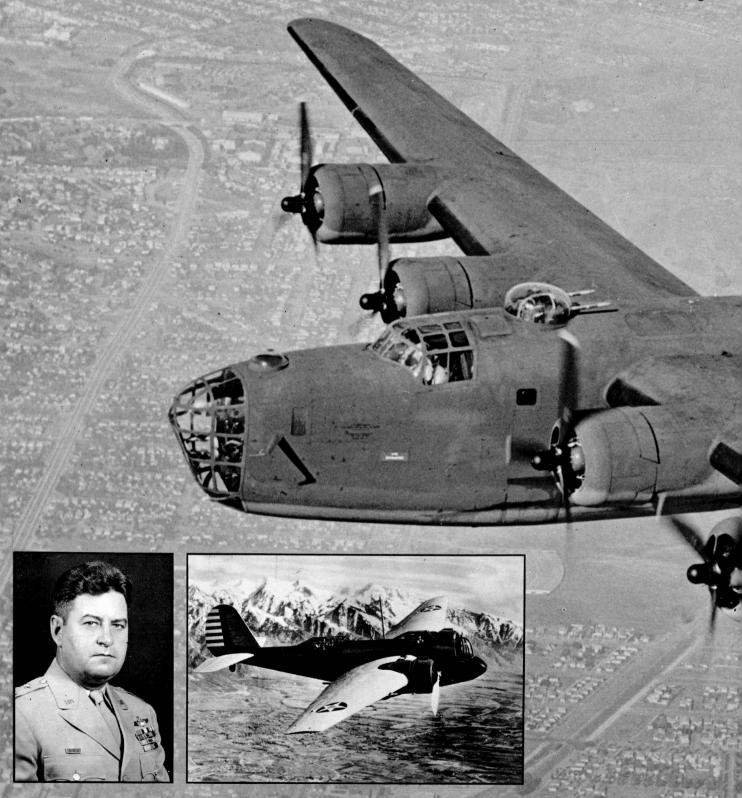

the Italian ship. By 1938, however, such a restriction was totally unrealistic. Either the Navy operated all coastal aircraft itself or the range restriction had to be abolished. It was only sensible to intercept an enemy at the greatest possible range. Perhaps the most significant fact about the new arrangement was that the whole incident was triggered off, and the subsequent row over the role of land-based aviation brought to a head, by three preproduction experimental aircraft designated the Y1B-17. These were the forerunners of the B-17. In the aftermath of the incident the head of GHQAF, Brigadier General Frank M Andrews, was removed from his post because of his staunch and continued advocacy of the concept of strategic bombing.

One of the earliest and clearest indications of the trend of events that were to show the impracticality of the 1931 arrangement – which confirmed the Navy's hesitations regarding the role of land-based aircraft – came in 1934 when ten B-10 Martin bombers of the AAC flew nonstop from Alaska to Seattle. These bombers were steel-framed, twin-engined monoplanes, and their single action really highlighted the question of whether it was wise to trust in a concept of continental defense that was based on slow surface ships. Even with carriers the Navy had no comparable ability, yet in 1934 the AAC invited tenders for an aircraft whose specifications demanded an ability to make a direct flight from the United States to Alaska, Panama or Hawaii. To a 5000-mile range were added demands for a speed of 200mph and a payload of 2000lb.

Previous to this the Boeing Aircraft Company had produced a series of aircraft, mostly transports, that had made the company pioneers in the field of long-range aircraft with a good freight-carrying capacity. With the Model 247 transport Boeing had secured a considerable lead over all its rivals, but even Boeing hesitated when the specifications of the new aircraft demanded by the AAC were appreciated. The specifications were extremely exacting, but Boeing began to draw

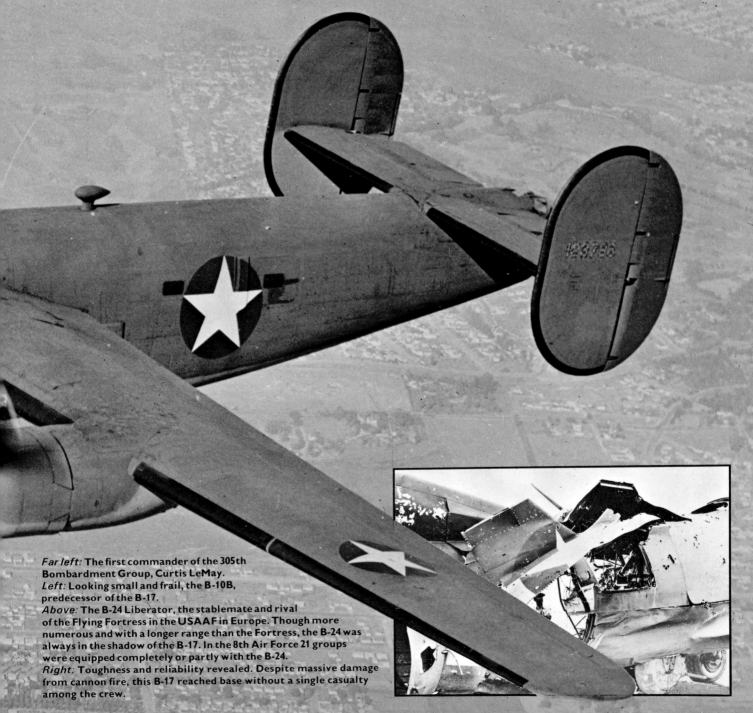

Far left: The first commander of the 305th Bombardment Group, Curtis LeMay.
Left: Looking small and frail, the B-10B, predecessor of the B-17.
Above: The B-24 Liberator, the stablemate and rival of the Flying Fortress in the USAAF in Europe. Though more numerous and with a longer range than the Fortress, the B-24 was always in the shadow of the B-17. In the 8th Air Force 21 groups were equipped completely or partly with the B-24.
Right: Toughness and reliability revealed. Despite massive damage from cannon fire, this B-17 reached base without a single casualty among the crew.

up plans for such an aircraft. Hardly had work begun on what Boeing designated the Model 294 when the AAC requested submissions for a replacement for the B-10. The Boeing firm thus faced a very delicate choice. It risked falling between two stools if it tried to compete for both contracts. It knew that if it failed to secure orders then there was no possibility of financial remuneration from the government for the work that had been done. On the other hand Boeing was well aware of the fact that follow-up contracts could prove extremely profitable.

By the time Boeing formally decided to enter the race for the new multi-engined bomber to replace the B-10 at its Board of Directors' meeting on 26 September 1934, preliminary planning and development work had been in hand for some time. The first piece of metal cutting took place in August, some six weeks before the Board decided to risk $270,000 of the company's money in the venture. The work that had been done on the Model 294 – which flew on 18 October 1937 as the XBLR-1 – had served to convince Boeing that the new bomber on which they were working, called the Model 299, had to amalgamate the best features of the 247 and 294. This involved giving the Model 299 four engines. In making this choice Boeing opted for a design that radically differed from those being submitted by its only serious rivals, Martin and Douglas, both of whom were relying on the conventional two-engined version for their designs.

On 16 July 1935, just eleven months to the day when the first part of the aircraft had been built, the Boeing competitor for the most lucrative contract offered the American aviation industry since the end of World War I was rolled out of her hangar on Boeing Field, Seattle. By contemporary standards she was enormous, and the impression she created was equally large. Weighing some 21,600lb empty and provided – but not armed – with numerous machine-gun positions, she was immediately (but mathematically incorrectly) dubbed, 'The Fifteen-Ton Flying Fortress.' The name, of course, stuck, but the weight was to be greatly exceeded in time by the later variants of this aircraft. The sheer impact of Model 299, on production redesignated X-13372, can be gauged by a direct comparison with the B-10 bomber she was intended to re-

place. The B-10, carrying a four or five-man crew in an aircraft whose span was 70ft 6in and whose length was 44ft 8in, was less than half the weight of the X-13372. Her twin engines gave her a top speed of 210mph and she had a range of about 700 miles with a 1000lb load. With extra fuel the range of the B-10 could be extended to about 1200 miles. The X-13372, on the other hand, measured 103ft 9in by 61ft 10in and could carry a crew of eight, four of whom would be machine gunners. Her tests revealed her to possess a maximum speed of 236mph at 10,000ft and a service ceiling of 24,600ft. Her maximum range was 3000 miles, some 600 miles beyond what was considered to be her normal operating range, and she was capable of carrying a load four times that carried by the Martin. In every respect the X-13372 had exceeded all the requirements made of her by more than considerable margins. In April 1934 the AAC had demanded an aircraft with a 2000-mile range, a payload of 2000lb and a top speed of 220mph at 10,000ft. It was not for nothing that one of the first AAC officers to see her was heard to comment that the X-13372 was an airborne battle cruiser.

The power, speed, punch and range of a battle cruiser were present indeed in the X-13372, but she also shared the battle cruiser's graceful lines and awesome beauty. She had superbly clear rounded lines that gave her an easy elegance enabling what was a very large tailpiece to rest on the top of a wide wing area and circular sectionalized fuselage with unassuming indifference. To add to the streamlined effect, the undercarriage was retractable. This again set her apart from the B-10 and most other military aircraft of the time. By every possible standard in the X-13372 Boeing had produced an extremely advanced and formidable aircraft, well ahead of its time and of any competitor for the AAC order. Confidence in the Boeing camp must have been very high when the X-13372, under the control of the firm's chief test pilot, Leslie R Towers, took to the air for the first time shortly before dawn on 28 July 1935.

The maiden flight went well. Like all her successors the X-13372 proved an extremely easy aircraft to fly. She handled easily, though she was subject to some wing turbulence, but she was stable and quick to respond to the controls. Her first

Above: Boeing's first experiment with a heavy bomber, the **XBLR-1**. It first flew in 1937 as the **XB-15** and saw service as the **XC-105** as a cargo and personnel transport. Length 87ft 7in, Span 149ft, Weight 70,706lb, Range 5130, Speed 200 mph.
Below: The **B-18**, the rival to the X-13372.

Above and left: The YB-17, later renumbered the Y1B-17. The group photograph shows a formation of Fortresses in service with 2nd Bombardment Group, GHQAF. It was as part of this unit that much of the pioneering work with the B-17 was done, the aircraft breaking many speed records without loss.

flight and the subsequent series of ground and air tests to which she was subjected by Boeing (before going to the AAC) all proved eminently satisfactory and at 0345 hours on 20 August with Towers again at the controls, she rose to the skies for what was to be her toughest test to date. She was setting out for the AAC evaluation center at Wright Field, Dayton, Ohio, in an effort to convince the airmen that this was the aircraft they needed. On her way to Dayton, before the AAC tests had even started, the X-13372 achieved a remarkable piece of 'one-upmanship' that gave her a decided edge over her rivals. She arrived at about 1700 hours, having covered the 2100-mile journey in nine hours at an average speed of 232mph. This made the would-be Boeing bomber faster than any front-line fighter in American service at that time, a point of satisfaction to all at Boeing but of no small concern to the AAC and the service chiefs. In her subsequent trials the aircraft proved more than equal to any task set her and far superior to her rivals, but on 30 October during a routine test, with Towers and Major Peter P Hill at the controls, the X-13372 stalled and crashed on takeoff. The aircraft was burned out and both Towers and Hill died as a result of the burns they had sustained. In this accident neither pilot error nor mechanical failure had played a part. Because of its massive tail, the X-13372 had been fitted with a spring locking device to prevent damage to the flaps and rudder being caused by the wind while the aircraft was on the ground. This lock had not been removed prior to takeoff.

Nevertheless, despite the fact that the X-13372 was not in any way responsible for its own loss, it was not unnatural that the accident should have dampened enthusiasm for such an advanced aircraft. Critically, Boeing had no second aircraft with which to complete the AACs series of tests, and this left the way open for Boeing's only serious rival, the Douglas B-18, to secure the order for 133 aircraft. It cannot be doubted that the accident had cost Boeing the chance to bring home this production contract but it must be said that Boeing, in some ways, had hardly helped its own cause by producing in the X-13372 such an advanced aircraft. At over $260,000 per aircraft, the Boeing submission was more than three times more expensive than the B-18. This was a very important consideration at a time when the services were conscious of the need to get value for money. The price of high sophistication, as manifest in the X-13372, was high, and when this went hand in hand with an aircraft that crashed during trials (irrespective of reason), the likelihood of a favorable contract being secured was rather slim. But the AAC, despite giving out the contract to Douglas, had been sufficiently impressed by the X-13372 to give an order for thirteen preproduction models and a fourteenth airframe in order to carry on evaluation trials. This order was given on 17 January 1936. The thirteen aircraft were designated YB-17. This was amended in November to Y1B-17 in order to indicate the funding arrangement of the aircraft.

Just as the initial development of the X-13372 had taken eleven months, so the development and production of the Y1B-17 took the same time. Appropriately, in view of the fact that 1936 was an Olympic year – the Games ironically being held in Berlin – the motto of the new batch of aircraft might well have been, 'Faster, Higher, Stronger.' The Y1B-17 showed that Boeing had not rested on its laurels but had used the time since the first prototype to make many improvements with the new batch of aircraft. By being nearly 7ft longer and a ton heavier than the X-13372, the Y1B-17 had room for one more crew member and had rearranged the flight deck in order to place the pilot and the copilot alongside one another. This was common in civil aircraft; it was not

normal in military aircraft at this time. Undercarriage and armament improvements had been worked into the new aircraft, but the most striking features of the Y1B-17 were its enhanced speed, endurance and lift capability. In the place of the X-13372s four Pratt and Whitney Hornet R-1690-E nine-cylinder radial air-cooled engines, each capable of 750hp, were four 930hp Wright Cyclone GR-1820-39 (G2) engines. These gave the slightly heavier aircraft a top speed of 256mph at 14,000ft. With an extreme range of 3400 miles – an improvement of 400 miles – the Y1B-17 had a service ceiling of 30,000ft. Like the X-13372 the Y1B-17 had a normal bomb load of 4000lb; this could be doubled though only at the cost of considerably reducing her operational range.

Undoubtedly some aeronautical geniuses must have been present at the birth of the B-17. However, on 7 December 1936, just five days after the first flight of a Y1B-17, the first of the new aircraft nose-dived on landing as a result of the brakes seizing. Despite this inauspicious start – which prompted a congressional inquiry – the Y1B-17 subsequently prospered. The first was delivered to the AAC in January 1937. Subsequently as they were produced and delivered from Boeing the AAC retained a single aircraft at Wright Field for experimental work and detailed the remaining eleven to join a new organization, the 2nd Bombardment Group, GHQAF.

GHQAF and 2nd BG on the one hand and the Y1B-17 on the other hand might well have been made for each other. Despite its official role GHQAF, under the direction of Andrews, was primarily interested in strategic bombing; GHQAF wanted to test the concept. GHQAF had to build up the concept and the force needed from base roots because there was no fund of knowledge on which to draw and GHQAF had no real idea of what was involved, either organizationally or operationally. It did not know, and there was no means of knowing, what could and could not be expected from aircraft, and there was no certainty that the Y1B-17 might provide some of the answers or be the answer itself. GHQAF was basically groping in the dark. It wanted to deploy two groups, one on the Pacific coast and the other on the Atlantic. In this manner the primary function of GHQAF – the sorting out of problems involved in the provision of air power over the sea against an enemy invasion force – could be discharged, but for the moment the 2nd BG, with its experimental Y1B-17s, had to suffice. But in this aircraft, all service models of which were fully concentrated with the group by August 1937, GHQAF found that it had an aircraft that could be realistically tested, albeit under peacetime conditions, as a bomber.

The results of the tests to which the Y1B-17 was subjected by GHQAF were astounding. The 2nd BG registered nearly 10,000 flying-hours and almost 2,000,000 miles in all-weather flying without a single accident. Its flights took it over all parts of the USA in the course of which the Y1B-17 broke the existing east-west and west-east records with ease (12 hours 50 minutes and 10 hours 46 minutes respectively). In February 1938 in a goodwill gesture for the inauguration of the new president in Argentina the Group flew from Miami to Buenos Aires, staging through Lima in Peru. The 5036-mile flight was covered in less than 27 hours in the air. It was an impressive performance that showed the intercontinental capability of the aircraft. Everything that the Y1B-17 was asked to do she did superlatively – including the interception of the Italian ship that sparked off the row between the US Navy and GHQAF and cost Andrews his job, GHQAF the role to which it aspired and the Y1B-17 its future – or so it appeared at the time.

Two sets of circumstances were to save Andrews, GHQAF and the Y1B-17. The first was the remarkable Y1B-17 itself. In

Above: **The airframe that was developed into a unique aircraft, the YB-17A, later the Y1B-17A and B-17A. The first heavy bomber with superchargers.**

the spring of 1938, a fully-laden Y1B-17, packed with instruments to collect data on performance, was flying in low overcast conditions over its base at Langley Field when it encountered exceptionally rough air. The aircraft, piloted by Lieutenant William Bentley, was thrown into a stall and into no less than nine spins before Bentley was able to regain control of his aircraft and bring it safely in to land. The result of this unpremeditated event was to make the AAC look a second time at the aircraft it had on its hands. By any standard the wings of the aircraft should have been ripped off as a result of forces the aircraft had never been designed to resist. The instruments aboard and subsequent calculations showed that the aircraft had indeed withstood stress far greater than that allowed for by the designers. Rivets had popped and the wings had been bent as a result of these unanticipated acrobatics, but the aircraft had survived and was able to be repaired. The AAC was quick to take the lesson. The airframe that had been ordered for ground tests on the stress level that could be absorbed by the aircraft was immediately fitted out as an aircraft. Redesignated Y1B-17A (Number 37369), it flew for the first time on 29 April 1939.

This aircraft in its turn proved to be as much an advance over the Y1B-17 as that aircraft had been over the X-13372. What set the Y1B-17A apart from her stable companions were four Moss–General Electric turbo-superchargers fitted to the tops of her new 1000hp Cyclone G-1820-51 (G5) engines while the fairings over the nacelles were removed. These engines and the superchargers made the Y1B-17A nearly 50mph faster than the Y1B-17, allowing her to break the magical 300mph figure for the first time. Her effective maximum speed, however, was 295mph at 25,000ft. She had a service ceiling of 38,000ft and a range of 3600 miles. In one test she was to set a record that by aviation standards was to last a long time. She lifted an 11,000lb bomb load over a distance of 620 miles at an average speed of 233mph. Under normal circumstances she could carry a 4000lb payload, but for operational purposes it was envisaged that she would carry a 2500lb bomb load over 1500 miles. With the Y1B-17A the AAC really had a strategic bomber of unrivaled power, indeed an aircraft worthy of her name. It was with considerable gratitude that the AAC formally took possession of the aircraft on 31 January 1939.

The timing of the delivery could hardly have been better for the cause of strategic bombing because by this stage the second of the two factors was being called into play. The natural march of events was beginning to move in favor of the idea of strategic bombing and the heavy bomber concept.

Certainly the massive improvement in aircraft performance had been a major factor in making many see the idea of strategic bombing in a new light. But what had really begun to break down opposition to the bomber and strategic bombing in the American political and military hierarchy had been the abject capitulation of the British and French in the face of German threats at Munich in September 1938. The US administration realized only too well that Anglo-French spinelessness in large part derived from their consciousness of their inferiority to the Luftwaffe. That the power of the German Air Force had been greatly exaggerated by a grossly inflated figure was of little account. The British and French had been haunted by the prospect of their cities being razed if they attempted to go to the aid of Czechoslovakia.

The administration was also aware of the trend of events in the western Pacific where the Japanese were building up their armaments at the greatest possible speed while being involved in a lurid and violent conquest of China. Nanking in China and Guernica in Spain, both cities being devastated by virtually unopposed bomber forces, were examples that no American administration could afford to ignore. It was not that the USA itself felt threatened, but Washington was beginning to consider seriously the deterrent effect that possession of major strategic bombing forces might have on would-be aggressors. Neither the administration nor the electorate wanted war or sought any change in the isolationist policies that had been pursued since the days of Woodrow Wilson, but by 1939 the purse strings were beginning to be loosened and much of the service resistance to the idea of strategic bombing was beginning to ebb. It was at this time that the Liberator, the aircraft that was to share with the Fortress the task of strategic bombing in the ETO, was ordered. With the trials and evaluation of the Y1B-17 and Y1B-17A complete, these aircraft were redesignated the B-17 and B-17A respectively while orders were given for 39 production models, designated the B-17B. The first of these new aircraft took to the air on 27 June 1939 and all 39 were to be delivered into commission between July 1939 and March 1940. They were not to know that they were to be followed in the next five years by a further 12,677 Fortresses and five main Marks which were to operate in many services of different nations and in many and varied theaters of war.

DEVELOPMENT-B, C A

With the B-17/B-17A the AAC had an aircraft that seemed capable of carrying out the role of a strategic bomber. Technically this was true, for the aircraft was reliable, fast and well armed. But the concept of bombing to which the AAC was committed was daylight operations against precision targets by heavy bombers that relied on high speed and strong defensive firepower to resist fighter interceptors. Time and events were to show that such hopes were to be highly exaggerated, but in the period 1939–41 the AAC never fully appreciated the difficulties inherent in bombing operations. It was aware that advanced though the X-13372, Y1B-17 and Y1B-17A had been when first they flew, further development and modification would be needed for the B-17 concept to operate effectively. The process of continuous change between Marks and production of individual Marks was therefore very rapid with three improved versions of the B-17/B-17A appearing in an evolutionary procession in 1940 and 1941. Thereafter the various changes, first embodied in the B-17E, were more fundamental and revolutionary in character.

Seemingly the B-17B was very similar to the B-17/B-17A. As the first batch of aircraft specifically ordered by the AAC to fulfill an operational role, the B-17B in fact showed many small but very significant changes from its predecessors though its overall performance was very little different from that of the B-17A. The most obvious changes were the altered settings for the turbo-superchargers and a considerable improvement in the nose arrangements to give both cleaner lines and more space to the navigator and bomb-aimer. The cost of this was the removal of the nose blister, the original transparent cone with a bubble-mounted machine gun being discarded in favor of a new Plexiglas fairing. In place of the ventral cutout below the nose where the bomb-aiming panel had been located in the B-17A, the B-17B carried a flat on which was mounted the celebrated Norden gyro stabilized bombsight. (Subsequently

Above: **After extensive modification the B-17C entered service as the Fortress I with the Royal Air Force, but its combat record was not very impressive.**

this bombsight, which was claimed to be highly accurate at an altitude of 30,000ft, was to be linked to the autopilot by means of automatic flight control equipment. The first occasion on which this arrangement was used operationally was on 18 March 1943.) The rudder and flaps of the B-17B were enlarged in order to improve the handling characteristics of the aircraft while a hydraulic braking system replaced the pneumatic type employed on previous Marks.

Even while the production of the B-17B was in hand orders were given out for a further 38 aircraft of a new improved type. This was the B-17C, the first flight of which took place on 21 July 1940. This was a matter of a mere seven weeks after the operational deployment of all the completed B-17Bs and even before the new B-17C first flew a further order for another 42 improved aircraft, the B-17D, had been issued. The increasing tempo of orders and the qualitative and quantitative improvements in the AACs demands all served to emphasize the

ND D MARKS

growing concern felt by the administration over events in Europe. These orders also had one other effect; they paved the way for the much larger B-17E construction program.

The most striking feature of the B-17C was its increased weight (fully loaded it was nearly 50,000lb) and a greatly improved performance, largely brought about by another major engine improvement. Boosted 1200hp Wright Cyclone GR-1820-65 (G-205A) engines, with turbo-superchargers below the engines, gave the B-17C a top speed of 323mph at 25,000ft though she had a slower rate of climb at takeoff than the B-17B. The higher performance of the Mark C also owed something to improved aerodynamics. The waist-gun blisters were removed in favor of flat gun panel windows which were shifted slightly rearward in order to give the waist gunners better fields of vision and arcs of fire. The dorsal gun position was similarly treated, all three gun positions having to shed their protective windows when entering combat. The ventral gun position was also redesigned to form a smooth 'bathtub' which though longer and larger than previous ventral fittings was more harmonious and graceful than previous ventral arrangements. The nose gun was removed and replaced by

Above: **One of the new B-17Cs enters service with the US Army Air Corps on 29 July 1940. Even before it flew, orders for a new Mark had been given.**

two separate guns mounted inside the nose cone but angled through each side of the fuselage. To complete the armament changes both ventral and dorsal positions were given twin 0.5in Browning machine guns.

With the B-17D Boeing made minor though important alterations to the basic B-17C. The new aircraft could be outwardly distinguished from the Mark C only by its re-designed engine cowlings and cooling shutters which were incorporated in an effort to overcome problems caused by engines overheating as a result of their prolonged climbs to operational altitude. Internally, however, the changes were more significant. Boeing revised the electrical circuits of the Fortress and with the Mark D introduced self-sealing fuel tanks and improved armor protection for the crew. Subsequently many of the B-17Cs were recalled and subjected to conversions in order that they incorporate many of these improvements.

Below: **One of the first B-17Ds. This version showed many small advances over the Mark C, but was the last before a major redesign of the airframe.**

WAR AND THE B-17E

The B-17Ds were the last of the original B-17s. Up until that Mark all Flying Fortresses had exhibited certain basic characteristics: smallness of numbers built, minor alterations of silhouette and small (or relatively small) changes in internal arrangements, armaments and specialist pieces of equipment. The cumulative effect of all these measures was by no means negligible, but with the B-17D the qualitative improvements were beginning to level out; the aircraft in the form it had attained was really incapable of much more development. If the B-17 was to undergo any further improvements then they could only be achieved by a revolutionary recasting of certain design features that had to be concentrated upon modification to the airframe.

Normally the impetus toward revolutionary redesign of a weapon or piece of equipment stems from the experience of combat. In part certain of the changes worked into the B-17D resulted from such a source, but one of the remarkable features in the history of the development of the B-17 is that while the B-17E differed in so many ways from her earlier sisters as to be revolutionary – indeed almost another aircraft – the changes were in large part not dictated by combat evaluation but by Boeing's anticipation of criticism and advice. In fact the first of the B-17Es flew on 5 September 1941 – three months before the enforced entry of the USA into the war. By the time war came the production lines were fully engaged in building an aircraft that was largely immune from the weaknesses of earlier Marks, at that time being ruthlessly exposed by the

Japanese Zero-sen fighter. It was ironic, in a way, that the sacrifice of the B-17Bs, Cs and Ds in the opening months of the Pacific War did not result in major redesign features; the changes had already been put into effect before the outbreak of war. Such was Boeing's flair and ingenuity in being able to anticipate problems.

The B-17 saw combat even before the Americans entered the war, but that combat experience came too late to affect the B-17E. In March 1940 the British purchasing mission in Washington obtained the permission of the Roosevelt administration to secure the first twenty B-17Cs to come off the assembly lines. The purchase was covered by the open deception that these aircraft were to be used for training duties only by the Royal Air Force, but in fact it was understood that the British would make their combat analysis available to the Americans. In view of the fact that in September 1939 the USA only had 23 operational Fortresses and only 53 were delivered in 1940, the American decision, though not disinterested, was extremely generous and all that could be reasonably expected at the time.

The twenty B-17Cs – and, secretly, their crews and ground maintenance parties – were taken over by the RAF and allocated to No 90 Squadron at West Raynham, Norfolk. The force was concentrated only as late as May 1941, partly because the British insisted upon certain major changes being worked into (what they called) the Fortress I before they accepted delivery of the aircraft and committed it to combat.

Above: One of the first Flying Fortresses to enter active service. A Mark C in service with the RAF as the Fortress I.
Below: This Boeing B-17E was specially rebuilt for General Douglas MacArthur as his flying staff headquarters. It was named 'Bataan' and ferried MacArthur throughout Southeast Asia.

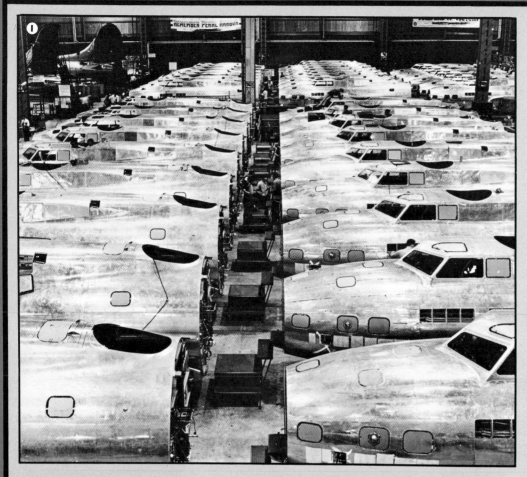

The awesome power of US industry:
1 and 3. Main body assembly line at the Boeing factories in Seattle.
2. The Vega plant at Burbank.
4. The Boeing assembly line for the tailpiece. Note the massiveness of the tailpiece and (absent) rudder, compared to the smallness of the rear fuselage, and the employment of women on production line.
5. Inboard wing section showing engines and fuel tank caps. Outboard wing sections were made separately.

Among the changes about which the British were adamant were the installation of self-sealing tanks and a heavier forward armament. These changes the British considered essential if the aircraft was to have any chance of survival in the hard school of combat over Germany. The RAF had gone to war in 1939 with much the same ideas as the AAC regarding the desirability and practicability of daylight bombing. By 1941 experience had convinced the RAF that not merely were there drawbacks to such a plan of campaign, but that it was prohibitively expensive. The British losses in daylight raids over Germany from the start of the war were crippling to the extent that area bombing of industrial areas at night had been substituted as the only means of carrying out a strategic bombing offensive. Thanks to their own combat experience over Germany and the German defeat in the Battle of Britain in 1940, the British drew the correct conclusion that daylight bombing could not be successful because the bombers, lacking the protection of long-range fighters, could not defend themselves. The British were skeptical of the claims made by the AAC (renamed the US Army Air Force after 20 June 1941) on behalf of the Flying Fortress. The British doubted the ability of the B-17C to fight its way to a target and there was a distinct coolness toward an aircraft that was so big and costly in terms of scarce manpower resources but which possessed so little punch. The American faith in their ability to fight their way to and from a target in formation and en masse was unshaken by

British doubts and warnings, and the RAF did not endear itself to the USAAF by its tactical employment of the Fortress I. It was almost as if the RAF raids with the B-17Cs were deliberately staged to show up the aircraft's limitations rather than its strengths. In RAF hands in 1941 the B-17C showed itself capable of absorbing massive battle damage and still making it home safely at 30,000ft, but very little else. The British used their Fortress Is in very small groups against targets that tended to be very well defended. The resultant losses were heavy and with accidents accounting for several other aircraft, the few survivors were sent either to North Africa (and two to India where incredibly they rejoined a USAAF formation) or to Coastal Command. At this stage in the war for the RAF to assign anything at all to Coastal Command was tantamount to its being condemned as unfit for further service.

The British view of the Fortress was rather damning, but there was justification for many of the criticisms made by the British. The B-17C did tend to shudder at bomb release and was not a good bombing platform. She was vulnerable to head-on fire and attacks from the rear and from below. The Fortress's lack of protection and self-sealing tanks were serious matters, and the speed with which Boeing acted on this indicates the validity of the British criticism. The Americans, on the other hand, were correct in their criticism of British tactics and the evident lack of faith in the aircraft shown by the

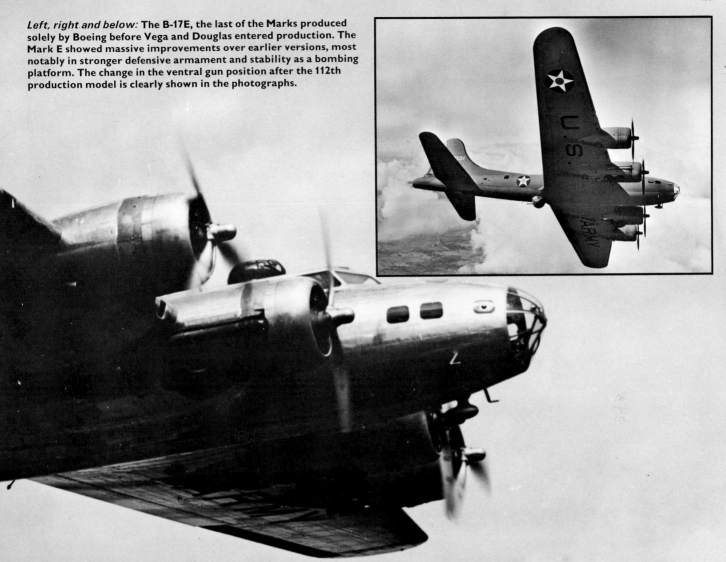

Left, right and below: The **B-17E**, the last of the **Marks** produced solely by Boeing before Vega and Douglas entered production. The Mark E showed massive improvements over earlier versions, most notably in stronger defensive armament and stability as a bombing platform. The change in the ventral gun position after the 112th production model is clearly shown in the photographs.

RAF, but they were far too sanguine in their belief that 'the bomber will always get through.' Experience was to show that the Americans asked far too much of the Fortress; even at its peak the Fortress could not withstand concerted fighter attacks and had only a short life expectancy in skies controlled by enemy fighters.

In fact both the Americans and the British were wrong in their views of strategic bombing. The Americans saw strategic bombing as a means of securing air supremacy; they failed to see that air supremacy had to be achieved before a bombing offensive could be successful. The British, conscious from the start of the war of the bomber's vulnerability, attempted to evade the real issue by seeking the cover of darkness in order to bomb while avoiding heavy losses. In 1941 British night bombing was against specific targets; in 1942 it shifted to general area attacks when it was realized that the degree of accuracy needed for night precision bombing was not possible with the equipment then available. The fact of the matter was that American and British fighters had to oppose German fighters over their own cities before the bombing attacks could begin to inflict significant damage without having to suffer unendurable losses. At this stage of the war, the USAAF was confusing various issues while the RAF was intent on evading them. In 1941, however, without any trace of national bias, it is probably fair and accurate to state that the B-17, while a fine aircraft, was not a good bomber, and that at the

very best the case for it was nonproven. Its combat record can be described as indifferent.

Many of the technical criticisms of the B-17C had been anticipated by Boeing and were being remedied in the new order of B-17Es. This aircraft proved to be extremely significant in the development and history of the B-17 on purely technical grounds, as well as on two other grounds. Firstly, it was ordered in unprecedented numbers. To a world numbed by the sheer scale of American output in the course of World War II, an order for 512 aircraft might not seem very much, but in pre-Pearl Harbor days this was a massive order. It must be remembered, moreover, that at the time the order was placed only 119 earlier variants had been built or were being built. What was really important about the order was the fact that it was based more on an act of faith and hope than solid judgment on the part of the Army Air Force.

Secondly, in order to build aircraft in such numbers the USAAF was led to demand a complete reorganization of production. Exclusive manufacture of the Flying Fortress was taken out of the hands of Boeing and placed in the hands of a consortium of Boeing, Douglas and Vega. The Boeing factory at Seattle was augmented by another plant built at Wichita, Kansas, while Douglas, the long-standing rival of Boeing, found itself opening a factory at Long Island, California, in order to build an aircraft to take over from the B-17. This pooling of resources was supposed to take effect with the

Mark E production order, but in fact the Douglas and Vega companies both encountered such teething problems – inevitable in setting up complex assembly lines – that the B-17E order was the last to be exclusively completed by Boeing. Only in the long term was the USAAF's arrangement to show its true worth because this pooling of resources did for Flying Fortress production what Henry Kaiser did for Liberty Ship construction.

The combining of the three companies plus the expansion of factory space and production lines left the Americans in a position subsequently to step up production to a level that no other nation could possibly have envisaged, still less matched. The significance of the measure can be seen by the fact that the first B-17F left the production line on 30 May 1942; by the time production on that particular Mark ceased some fifteen months later, 3405 had been built. Of these Douglas and Vega had contributed 605 and 500 respectively. Thereafter production shifted to the B-17G and of the 8680 produced before the order books were closed in April 1945 Vega produced 2250 and Douglas 2395. Between them, therefore, the two secondary companies built nearly 48 percent of all the B-17Fs and B-17Gs constructed. At their peak in March 1944 the three companies between them were producing 130 B-17Gs a week, or twice the weekly loss rate in the ETO. It was about this time that Boeing's Seattle plant touched its record production level of sixteen complete B-17Gs a day. To properly gauge the significance of these figures of overall production in general and that of Vega and Douglas in particular, it is worth noting that between them Douglas and Vega covered what is

euphemistically termed wastage. About 5000 B-17s were lost from all causes during the war, most of them naturally in the last two years of the war in Europe. Douglas and Vega made good these losses. Though this part of the story is not directly relevant to discussion of the B-17E, it must always be remembered that the massive expansion of construction and the numbers of B-17Fs and B-17Gs available to the Americans in 1944–45 were only possible as a result of certain actions taken while the B-17D was being built and before the order for the B-17E was finalized.

In September 1941, when the first of the B-17Es took to the skies, such matters remained in the distant future. For the moment the new Mark held all attention because she represented a definitive break with earlier B-17s. The most striking feature of the Mark E was her totally altered profile. In the place of the long but relatively thin fuselage and huge tailpiece – a phenomenon that led to her being called 'the big-assed bird' – there appeared a much longer aircraft, 73ft 10in in length, with a greatly enlarged rear fuselage. This allowed the already big empennage to be increased still further in order to improve the aircraft's stability at extreme altitude and during bomb release. The increase was incorporated into a massive dorsal fin that stretched forward down the airframe until it was almost on the upper level with the wings. By itself this constituted a thirty percent design alteration of the aircraft. Gone were the long fine lines and seemingly disproportionately large tailpiece; in their places was an alteration that made for a fuller aircraft, by its very appearance more menacing, tenacious and powerful. But even with this dorsal fin the

B-17E retained much of the aesthetic grace of earlier marks. In addition, the alterations provided for a sting in the end of the tail. The wider, stronger fuselage permitted for the first time the location of a manually-powered turret, armed with twin 0.5in Browning machine guns, in the tail of the aircraft. This had the effect of partially eliminating one of the B-17s known and most glaring weaknesses. The vulnerability of the Flying Fortress's earlier variants to attack from the rear had been quickly discovered in combat, but both German and Japanese pilots seemed singularly slow in appreciating the difference between the Mark E and her elder sisters.

Other major, though less obvious changes, were worked into the aircraft. Except for the single nose gun (where retained) all machine guns were standardized with the 0.5in Browning. A twin set of machine guns were installed in a power-operated turret mounted just behind the flight deck and the radio compartment was adapted for the possible mounting of additional guns. The oddest feature of the new gunnery arrangements was the replacement of the ventral bath by a retractable power-operated turret just aft of the wings. This turret was operated by remote control, the gunner firing the guns from a periscopic position in the waist hatch. This novel arrangement proved impractical and was abandoned in favor of a Sperry ball turret, housing gunner and guns, after the 112th production model. This new arrangement was simultaneously worked into the B-17F. The gunner in this seemingly exposed position had to be small, but statistically his was one of the safest positions in the aircraft, despite its apparent vulnerability. One of his occupational hazards,

Above: **An action shot of a B-17E showing four of the Fortress's defensive positions – one ventral position, two dorsal positions and the waist gunner.**

however, was that in many bombers to be fitted with this turret, particularly the early ones, the door frame and the fittings of the turret proved inadequate.

Many other minor variations were worked into the aircraft by Boeing to counter various small problems, but it was the changes to the tail, fuselage and defensive armament that set the B-17E apart from the earlier B-17s. The radical changes resulted in a much stronger and better aircraft, a formidable bomber capable of further modification and improvement.

Below: **The Boeing B-17E of 1941 was first flown on 5 September. Compared to earlier versions the Mark E was longer, had a larger fin area and carried better defensive armament. Armament improvements included dorsal and ventral power turrets and tail-gun position. A total of 512 were built by Boeing.**

THE B-17F AND B-17G

While the B-17E had been a ton heavier than the B-17D and had shown no decline in performance this was not true of the B-17F. Another ton heavier, she was nearly 20mph slower than the Mark E, and roughly the same decline in speed was repeated in the B-17G over the B-17F. Yet despite their increased size and slower speeds both represented substantial qualitative advances over the B-17E and the decline of speed was not too great a handicap. With the operational speed of B-17s fixed at about 180mph any decline of the theoretically maximum speed of the aircraft was not particularly serious.

With the first of the B-17Fs coming off the production line just two days after the last of the B-17Es, some idea of the pace and urgency of American construction can be assessed by the fact that all the B-17F's tests had to be completed within one day before she was operationally assigned. In the spring of 1942, with the Germans and Japanese advancing on all fronts, there was no time for either prototypes or proper testing. Externally the first of the B-17Fs showed little change from the Mark E, but inwardly over 400 alterations were worked into the aircraft. These included self-sealing oil tanks, an improved oxygen system for the crew, more power sources, changes in the layout of the controls and better radio communications. Outwardly the most obvious change was the fitting of a single one-piece molded frameless Plexiglas nosepiece into which was slotted the flat bomb-aiming panel. New more powerful engines, the R-1820-97 with an emergency 1320hp rating, were installed along with carburetor intake dust filters and the wide paddle-bladed Hamilton Standard propellers. These were slightly longer but much broader than the propellers used up until that time. They were installed because they were more effective than the normal model under tropical conditions. The result of these combined modifications was to help push the weight of the loaded B-17F up to 65,500lb and this necessitated the strengthening of the undercarriage and the incorporating of a dual braking system.

One of the side effects of the Boeing-Douglas-Vega link-up was a natural tendency by the firms to work into their products their own idiosyncracies and modifications. It also allowed three sets of ideas to improve the aircraft to be in play at any one time. As a result many changes, peculiar to firms, were installed in B-17s. Mostly these were of a very minor nature, but they nevertheless demanded an involved system of numbering and lettering to show clearly what in-production modifications had been worked into specific aircraft. This, of course, was important in the correct allocation of spare parts for maintenance. Of the many modifications, however, one was of immense importance. In the 76th B-17F produced by Douglas a Bendix power-operated turret with twin 0.5in machine guns was mounted on the chin. This feature had been added as a result of combat experience with the second B-17F produced (No 41-24341). This aircraft had been specially fitted out as a heavy escort to the bombers and not as a bomber itself. Designated the XB-40, she was joined by fourteen Vega-built YB-40s. The standard armament of these aircraft differed from normal Fortresses by having an extra twin-gunned dorsal turret, double machine-gun posts in each

Above: **The B-17F in flight. Rushed into production and into service, the Mark F showed more than 400 alterations over the E version, most of which were internal. This version carried the Bendix chin turret.**

of the waist positions and the Bendix chin turret. The idea behind these aircraft was for them to fly at the vulnerable extreme edges of bomber formations where their seemingly endless supply of ammunition could be used to best effect.

Unfortunately the weakness of the concept was that the escorts were too slow to cover the bombers effectively, particularly after the bombers had unloaded their bombs. In that state the bombers could easily outstrip their heavy escorts, burdened down as they were by abundant ammunition. Just as the tail turret had cut down one of the weaknesses of the B-17, the chin turret went some way to eliminate another. The majority of B-17Fs and all the B-17Gs incorporated the chin guns, but even these were not the full answer to the vulnerability of the Fortress to head-on attack. It was not so much defensive firepower that was weak in the B-17 – quite the reverse – but the aircraft's protection. Despite having some 27 pieces of armor and flak curtains worked into various parts of the aircraft, the lack of armor in the nose and the absence of bullet-proof glass were perennial weaknesses in the B-17. Perhaps the worst of the B-17s in this respect were the Mark Es. Many of the rear gunners were killed by fire not from aircraft they were engaging but from enemy fighters attacking from dead ahead. Their fire, raking the nose, often tore through the length of the fuselage before ripping out the rear turret and its crewman. Admittedly, better armor protection for both aircraft and individual members of the crew improved the situation, but the improvements were never really enough. The truth of the matter was that it was impossible to give the aircraft sufficient armor; it was impossible to produce an invulnerable aircraft.

With the B-17F the Americans had produced an aircraft extremely formidable in performance, defensive firepower, protection and bomb load, and a detailed examination of the ordnance and firepower of the B-17F is appropriate at this stage. Though the bomb-stowage arrangements of the B-17F differed from those used in earlier Marks, the normal bomb load remained 4000lb. But just as it had been possible for earlier B-17s to carry more than 4000lb, it was possible for the B-17F to carry a maximum load of 9600lb. Moreover, because the wings of the B-17F had been specially strengthened it was

Above and below left: Two photographs that show the most obvious external change worked into the F version of the Flying Fortress – the single-piece molded Plexiglas nose housing the bombardier's bombsight. This, of course, did nothing to cut down one of the major weaknesses of all B-17s, their vulnerability to head-on attack. Both Fortresses shown are early versions without a powered chin turret. *Below right:* The Cheyenne-type rear turret helped counterattack from another of the Fortress's most vulnerable quarters. Each gun had about 500 rounds per operation.

possible for her to lift a payload of 17,600lb and, in very exceptional circumstances, 20,800lb of ordnance. This weight of destruction could be lifted only because of the provision of special external racks that could be fitted to the aircraft by their ground crews. Though purpose-built the racks themselves were not factory fitted, but the bomb-release mechanism for the wing racks were naturally built into the aircraft during production. Some 2884 B-17Fs were thus fitted. The problem of massive payloads, except in a purpose-built machine, was that endurance fell away sharply. The heavier bomb loads were incompatible with the range requirements for aircraft attacking Germany from bases in Britain, but were useful in attacking tactical or even strategic targets in German-occupied western Europe. Under normal circumstances the bomb load of a Flying Fortress seldom exceeded 4000lb and in most operations would have been either 2600lb or less. Defensively the ammunition supplied to each aircraft and each gun varied, but it can be reasonably assessed at about 500 rounds per gun. Not altogether surprisingly, the best-supplied gunner was the rear gunner, but in stark terms, no gun on a B-17 carried more than one minute's supply of ammunition.

With the B-17F and its in-production modifications major improvements basically ceased. The B-17G was essentially the same as the later B-17Fs that carried the chin turrets and extra fuel tanks in the outer wing sections. The latter were the so-

Specifications for the B-17G

Wing Span	109ft 9in
Length	74ft 4in
Height	19ft 1in
Wing area	1,420sq ft

Weights:

Empty	36,135lb (16.13 tons)
Equipped	38,000lb (16.96 tons)
Normal Load	55,000lb (24.55 tons)
Maximum Normal Load	72,000lb (32.14 tons)

Power:
Four Wright Cyclone GR 1820-97 (R-1920-65) nine-cylinder air-cooled radial engines with Moss-General Electric turbo-superchargers. Each engine had 1,200hp at takeoff; emergency 1,320hp at 25,000ft. Engines ran at 2,300rpm. Four three-bladed Hamilton Standard propellers, 5ft 9½in in radius.

Fuel:

Normal	2,490 Imp Gallons
Maximum	3,569 Imp Gallons

Oil:
180 Imp Gallons

Range:

Maximum	4,400 statute miles on maximum fuel
	3,300 statute miles on normal fuel

Ceiling:

Service	35,600ft

Speeds:

Maximum	300mph at 30,000ft
Maximum continuous speed	263mph at 25,000ft
Landing	74mph
Rate of Climb	37 minutes to 20,000ft

Bomb Load:
Depending on the types of bomb carried on a given mission the maximum normal load could be 2,600lb or 4,800lb or 6,000lb or 8,000lb. Maximum normal short-range bomb load was 17,600lb.

Armament:
Up to thirteen 0.5in machine guns, mostly concentrated in six positions.

Crew:
Ten

Above: **A Vega-built B-17G.**
Below: **Despite massive damage to the fuselage and outboard engine, the aircraft survived.**

called Tokyo tanks. There were some changes, but they were of a relatively minor nature. The nose compartment was slightly rearranged to allow the navigator marginally more room and the bomb-release mechanisms were slightly improved. The waist-gun windows were glazed over and the guns specially mounted. These last changes were very important for the crew members in the rear of the aircraft. With the later B-17Gs the fields of fire for the rear gunner were widened still further and the gunner was given a new reflector sight as a result of changes made at the Cheyenne Modification Center, Wyoming. These changes allowed the aircraft to be shortened by 5in. Thus, at the end of the war, an aircraft that had begun life as a solitary prototype, X-13372, way back in 1934–35, showed the following characteristics (see opposite).

Impressive though the technical data might be, the Flying Fortress in many ways belied her size. Inside she was a cramped, cold and awkward aircraft, completely unlike the B-29 which was de luxe in comparison. The B-17 demanded only the highest possible physical standards on the part of her crews. Sixty percent of the personnel screened by the RAF in 1941 for their twenty B-17Cs were rejected on medical grounds alone, being unable to withstand the effects of decompression and altitude sickness. Malfunctioning oxygen sets were always a danger, particularly in the earlier versions, with anoxia not uncommon. Frostbite was an occupational hazard for many of the crew, particularly the tail and waist gunners. Until excluded by the glazed windows of the B-17G, hurricane-force winds lashed the insides of the fuselage where temperatures could reach fifty below zero. The rear gunner, trapped on a small bicycle seat and padded knee holds, was particularly badly affected, but waist gunners faced the additional hazard of being thrown together and having their guns and ammunition belts entangled by violent gyrations of the aircraft. The radio room, the only part of the aircraft where a 6ft tall man could stand erect, could be as cold as the rear fuselage, and operators usually had to transmit wearing gloves. Only the five crew members in the nose had any real warmth, but of these only the pilots had any degree of comfort. The flight engineer's position was crouched and on a bicycle seat behind the pilots; that of the navigator, despite successive improvements, was cramped. The bombardier

Below left: **The B-17H, a modification of the B-17G, saw service in the Pacific and Atlantic. It was modified for air-sea rescue work, being fitted with a lifeboat that could be dropped on three parachutes to ditched crews. Note the Flying Boat behind the B-17H.**

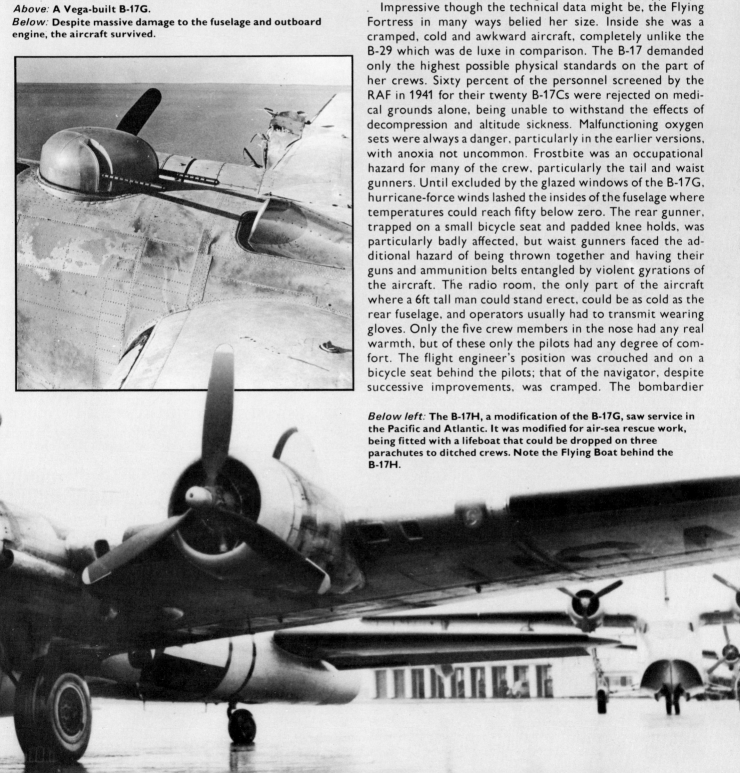

Above: **B-17s were adapted for use in specific roles during the war. Here a B-17G with early warning radar for search purposes.**

shared with the pilots and gunners superb views, but he had to double as a gunner – and this he could not do in the critical run-in over the target.

Overall, none of the B-17s were comfortable aircraft, and movement within the aircraft was never easy. Movement along the rear fuselage, between the waist gunners, was by swaying rope-handled catwalks, and a similar situation prevailed in the bomb bays. Certain parts of the fuselage, particularly into the rear turret, could only be negotiated by the crawl. General movement between various parts of the aircraft seemed to be deliberately impeded rather than aided by the size and awkwardness of doors. But what the aircraft demanded in terms of physical discomfort, she paid back to her crew in rugged reliability. Though they were prone to flames the B-17s showed a remarkable ability to survive attacks that took out huge sections of wings, fuselage and tail. One Fortress survived an operation that resulted in over 2000 bullet holes being counted in its wings and fuselage. Many aircraft survived seemingly hopeless structural damage, while landing on feathered engines was almost a routine occurrence. There were many instances of novice pilots or even untrained crewmen improvising a flight home after the elimination of the two pilots, though this naturally was not that common. The B-17 was easy to fly and capable of absorbing massive damage: on these counts alone she secured and deserved her almost legendary reputation. Though the aircraft had its weaknesses, it is not altogether surprising that its overall robustness and airworthiness resulted in its seeing service in various specialist roles and in no less than eleven services.

Various B-17s, mostly of the later Marks, were converted for specific tasks and some of the older, tired survivors of many missions ended their days ferrying mail for the armies in the field. In the latter stages of the Pacific War many modern B-17s were pressed into service as troop carriers. Indeed, in the early stages of the Pacific War one of the first B-17Es, No 41-2593, was used as the personal transport aircraft of no less a person than General Douglas MacArthur. Many of the other conversions were for cargo transportation (one was for fuel) or for photographic reconnaissance. The 8th Air Force was assigned for a very brief period the 3rd PG, including one squadron of B-17s, but this group never saw service with the 8th and was sent to the Mediterranean. The Fortresses delegated to photographic reconnaissance in fact were considered too vulnerable to be used in combat zones, and most

of their work was done in secondary theaters. Over fifty B-17Gs were converted to one vitally important role that was well out of the mainstream of B-17 activity. Designated the B-17H these aircraft were fitted out with a lifeboat that could be dropped on three parachutes to ditched aircrews. Such aircraft saw service both in the Pacific and in Europe.

Among the more bizarre activities to which certain B-17s were subjected was the BQ-7 project. Many war-weary B-17s were earmarked for experimental purposes, the object of which was to produce a radio-controlled flying bomb. The whole of the interior of the aircraft was gutted and then packed with 22,000lb of Torpex. The aircraft was manned by just two men, a pilot and a radio operator who primed the weapon. Both men had to bale out when their charge was activated. The idea was for the bomber to be guided in to its target by another bomber, but Project Castor, sometimes called Project Perilous, was abandoned after certain spectacular failures. One fully primed B-17 decided to embark upon an independent inspection of a major British industrial area before, oblivious to its controller, it wandered out to sea and self-destruction. Another B-17, out of control, made a crater 100ft wide in the countryside of East Anglia in a detonation that was heard thirty miles away. After these dangerous and unnecessary incidents the project was abandoned. The Allied superiority in conventional weapons was so great that there was no need to persist in work on unconventional weapons; that was something that could be left to the side lacking the strategic initiative.

It is ironic that after the early efforts of the US Navy to stifle the B-17 project, a B-17F should have been tested by the Navy during the war as a patrol bomber. In fact during the postwar years a number of B-17s saw service not only with the US Navy but with the Marine Corps and the Coast Guard. The B-17 also saw service in other foreign forces. The most important recipient, of course, was the RAF and various other Commonwealth air forces. After their unfortunate experiences with the Fortress I (B-17C) in 1941, the British received two more batches of B-17s (simply called Fortress II and Fortress III by the British) that together numbered 170 aircraft. Nearly all saw service either with Coastal Command or in an ECM role, but most finished serving as weather reconnaissance aircraft. Naturally for the purposes of strategic bombing the British preferred to use their own aircraft.

After the war Flying Fortresses saw service in various South American air forces, most notably those of Brazil and the Dominican Republic. In Europe they saw service with the French, Portuguese and Dutch air forces and in the War of 1948–49 for the establishment of the state of Israel some found

Above: **A B-17G-85-DC adapted as a test bed for a T-34 engine.**
Above right: **A B-17G in peacetime at Transpo-Dallas Airport.**
Right: **A ground radio-control unit of the 3225th Drone Squadron.**

their way into the Israeli Air Force. One Fortress actually bombed Cairo en route to Israel-Palestine, neither the crew nor the aircraft ever having been to the land for which they fought. Many, naturally, saw peaceful service. The Fortresses that were forced to land in Sweden were turned over to the Swedish government and SAS used them extensively as passenger airliners. Sweden was not alone in this. Various countries and minor American companies used Fortresses either on feeder or main routes. Mostly, however, the survivors that were kept on after the war were used either as freight carriers or for surveys. A handful are still believed to be in service, but the fate of most Fortresses soon after the end of the European war was simple and straightforward. They were scrapped, in their thousands. Hands of men less able than those that built, maintained and fought them achieved what enemy action had signally failed to achieve in war.

Below: **A Boeing B-17G which was converted into a director-plane for use by 3205th Drone Squadron, is now kept at the USAF Museum, Dayton, Ohio.**

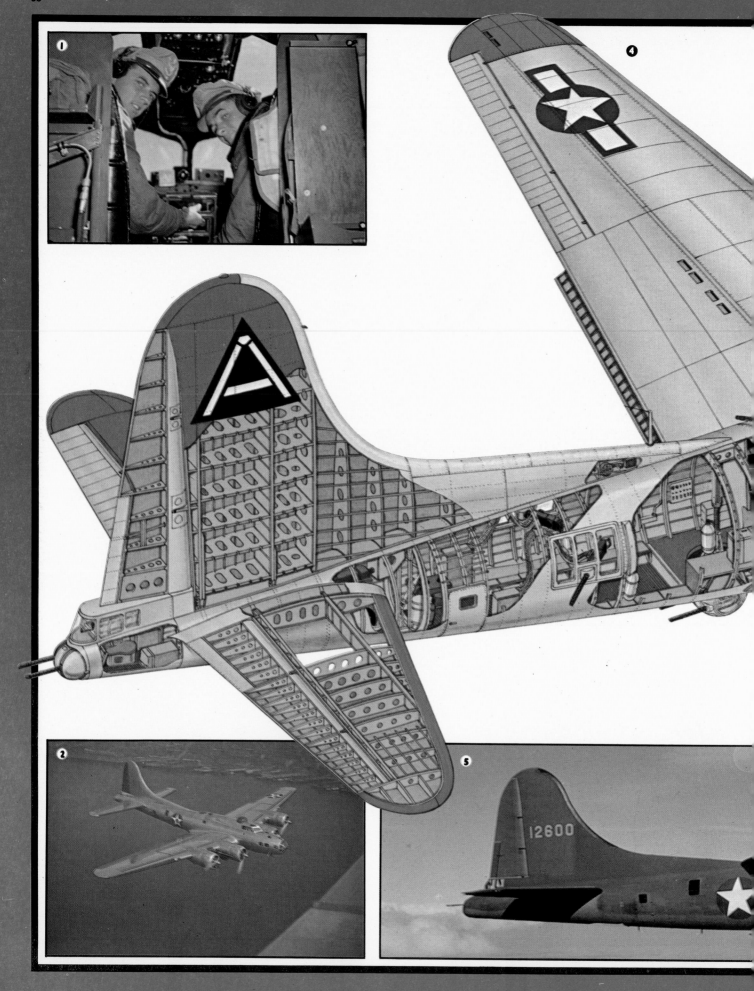

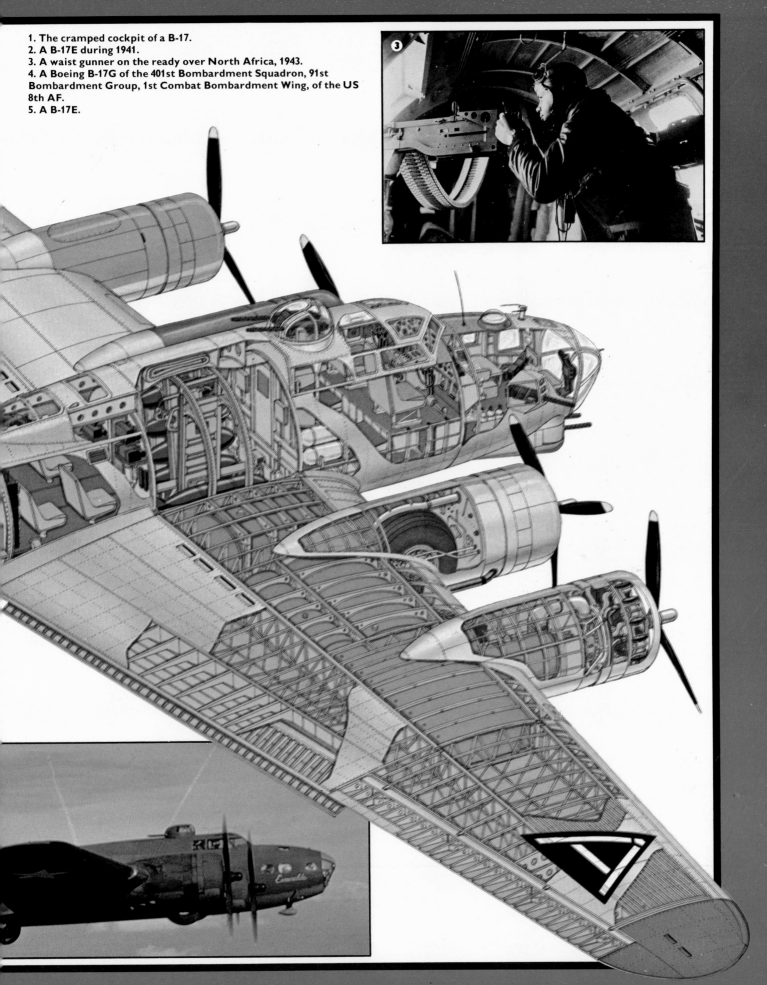

1. The cramped cockpit of a B-17.
2. A B-17E during 1941.
3. A waist gunner on the ready over North Africa, 1943.
4. A Boeing B-17G of the 401st Bombardment Squadron, 91st Bombardment Group, 1st Combat Bombardment Wing, of the US 8th AF.
5. A B-17E.

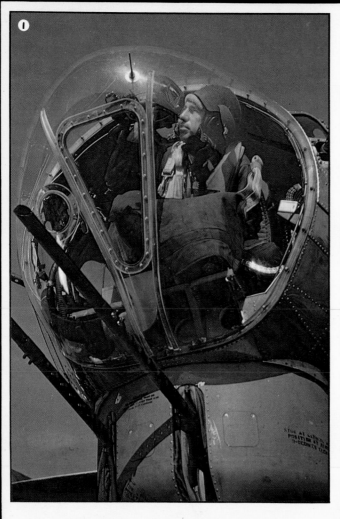

1. Captain Charles Hudson in the nose of his plane.
2. Sergeant Barraza, gunner and radio operator in position at the waist gun.
3. Crew positions in a B-17F.
4. A B-17F of the 324th Bombardment Squadron, 91st Bombardment Group, of the US 8th AF.

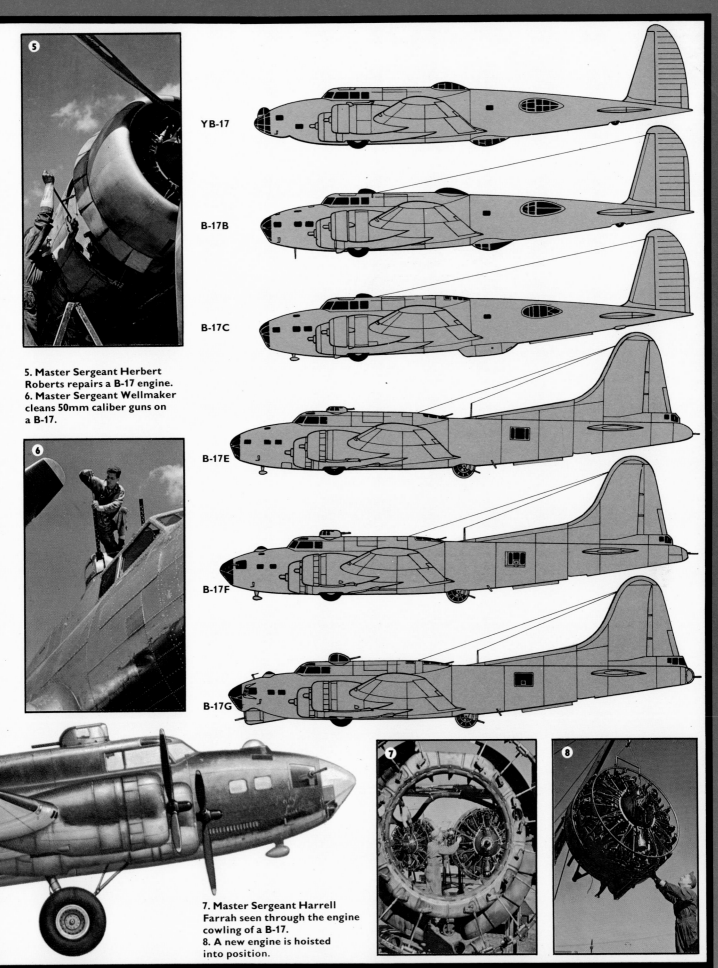

YB-17

B-17B

B-17C

B-17E

B-17F

B-17G

5. Master Sergeant Herbert Roberts repairs a B-17 engine.
6. Master Sergeant Wellmaker cleans 50mm caliber guns on a B-17.

7. Master Sergeant Harrell Farrah seen through the engine cowling of a B-17.
8. A new engine is hoisted into position.

THE PACIFIC CAMPAIG

The coming of war to the USA in December 1941 found the USAAF in the Pacific in no position to counter the well-planned Japanese attack throughout Southeast Asia. Given the weakness of the US Asiatic Fleet (a paper or prestige force rather than a properly balanced fighting force) and the inferiority of the US Pacific Fleet to the Combined Fleet of the Imperial Japanese Navy, the Americans, in the absence of large ground forces, had to rely on air power as their only means of countering Japanese movements once the policy of deterrence had failed to prevent the Japanese from going to war. The problem for the Americans, however, was that even in the air their forces were totally inadequate to meet the Japanese challenge. In December 1941 the USAAF had only 150 B-17s of which only fifty were the combat-worthy B-17Es. Only one-third of all the Fortresses were in the vast expanses of the Pacific. The USAAF had but a motley collection of 131 aircraft on Hawaii. Of this total there were only twelve B-17Cs and Ds, part of the 5th BG. In the Philippines the Army deployed 176 aircraft and two Bombardment Groups, the 7th and the 19th. But the 7th was effectively in cadre form, awaiting reinforcement from the USA, while the 19th was drasti-

Below: **The nine-man crew of a B-17D pose beside their aircraft after a mission at their base at Maceeba, Queensland, Australia. They formed part of the 64th Bombardment Squadron, 43rd Bombardment Group.**

cally understrength. Between them the two groups mustered just 35 Flying Fortresses, none of them B-17Es.

The opening of the war immediately reduced the already low strength of the Fortresses. Five were lost during the opening attack on Pearl Harbor and fourteen were destroyed on the ground when the Japanese launched their first strikes on the Philippines. The brunt of the effort to hold the Japanese fell on the depleted forces in the Philippines because the aircraft on Hawaii were too far away either to be of assistance or to carry the fight to the Japanese elsewhere. Though on 10 December 1941 the B-17s in the Philippines carried out the first American bombing raid of the war – an unsuccessful series of attacks on the Japanese invasion fleet bound for Luzon – a steady attrition forced the Americans to pull all their surviving aircraft out from the Philippines by the end of the month.

The surviving B-17s were withdrawn to Australia where only ten were found fit to resume combat duties. These were rapidly redeployed to Java, since they were the only Allied aircraft capable of offering serious resistance to the Japanese invasion of the Netherlands East Indies. Until the capitulation of the Indies in March 1942 these aircraft, plus reinforcements rapidly sent out from the USA, tried in vain to stem the Japanese advance. By the end of the campaign some eighty B-17s had been concentrated and fought in the theater, 49 in Java

itself. The results achieved by these aircraft were singularly unimpressive. Of the 49 on Java thirty were lost. Nineteen had been destroyed on the ground, but only six had been lost in combat with Japanese aircraft. Of the eighty in the theater, 52 were lost and a further six had to be written off as a result of accidents in Australia. Postwar analysis was to show that in the 350 missions flown by the B-17s in the opening phase of the war only two Japanese ships were sunk, a meager return for much bravery. Not unnaturally the paucity of success was not appreciated at the time, reports of successes being greatly exaggerated and far in excess of actual achievements.

In large part the poor showing of the B-17 in this phase of the war stemmed from factors beyond its control. The Flying Fortress was really in an impossible situation. It was an offensive, strategic weapon, but in 1942 it had to try to be a defensive, tactical weapon. Understrength at the start of the war and suffering unacceptably high losses in the opening phase of hostilities, the reinforcements sent out from the USA – in the form of the 43rd BG – could be used only to bolster the depleted 7th and 19th. Reinforcements were too few in number and too widely spread in area and time to permit their being in a position to exercise some direct influence in the battle area. Some 53 aircraft were dispatched from the eastern seaboard of the USA where the 43rd was based. These aircraft were forced to fly via the Caribbean, Africa and India

to reach their operational areas, and perhaps it is remarkable that of the total only nine never made it. Many of the aircraft sent had come directly from the factories and desperately needed servicing and maintenance, which were not available, when they arrived in Java and Australia. The crews, too, were raw, and it was many months after its arrival in the theater that it can be said that the 43rd was properly constituted. By that time, however, the 7th had been redeployed to India in an effort to try to hold the Japanese advance in Burma while the 19th, taking crews and aircraft from the 7th, reconcentrated in Australia. By the time the rearrangement of the B-17s had been completed, however, the flood tide of Japanese conquest had been largely brought to a halt, though it continued to edge its way forward in certain areas for some time afterward. In May 1942 at Coral Sea American carrier forces had checked the Japanese advance in the Southwest Pacific, forcing the enemy to recast plans for the reduction of Port Moresby and eastern New Guinea. In June the cream of Japanese naval aviation, the carrier forces, was annihilated at the Battle of Midway. Only in the latter battle did B-17s participate, but their intervention was negligible. In both battles it was Ameri-

Below: **The bombing of Hickham Field, Oahu, Hawaiian Islands on the morning of Sunday 7 December 1941. At the time of the Japanese attack on Pearl Harbor only 12 Fortresses were on Oahu, and three are shown.**

can carrier-based aircraft, particularly the dive bombers, that wreaked havoc, not the land-based aircraft.

After Coral Sea and Midway the Japanese attempted to consolidate their initial gains by a series of movements through the Bismarck Archipelago, into the Solomons, their aim being to outflank Australia and to achieve its isolation from supplies and reinforcements drawn from the USA. After these two successes, however, the Americans were in a position to counter such moves with their sea and land forces, landing in August 1942 on the Japanese-held island of Guadalcanal. In this effort the B-17s played a significant role, because by September the USAAF deployed four Groups in the area. To shore up the defenses there the 5th and 11th Groups from Hawaii were deployed to the New Hebrides, the 35-strong 11th arriving in New Caledonia in July. These forces formed part of the hastily-constituted 13th Air Force. Those forces in Australia were part of the 5th Air Force. Between them the four groups in September 1942 reached their peak strength of about 155 aircraft. The process of reinforcement had indeed been massive, far higher than these simple figures would suggest. Losses, from all causes, had to be covered, and such was the strain on shipping resources at this critical juncture of the war and such was the crucial importance of time, that many B-17s had to be employed as load-carriers in order to keep their sisters in service. It was paradoxical that the reinforcement of the theater with B-17s came at a time when it had already been decided to phase out the aircraft from the Pacific theater. In the vast area of the Pacific the Liberator, with its slightly longer range, was preferred to the Fortress, and after October 1942 the process of breaking up units and the re-equipment of new and existing formations with the B-24 began. By the beginning of 1943 the Fortresses no longer carried the weight of the American counteroffensive in the air, but it was not until September 1943 that the 5th and 11th Groups flew their last Fortress mission. Even in the Aleutians the limited numbers of Fortresses were gradually reduced to nothing. By November 1943, apart from command transports, only one B-17 remained in service in the whole of the Pacific area. Nevertheless, for all the time the B-17s were on station they carried the fight to the Japanese, mainly in the form of attacks on harbors and shipping. Success, as we have seen, was scant, though the 43rd was heavily involved in the devastatingly successful Battle of the Bismarck Sea (March 1943) which resulted in the annihilation of a Japanese military convoy bound for the upper Solomons. This battle in effect doomed Japanese efforts to hold the area.

For the most part, however, the record of the B-17 was not convincing, though it must be stated that after the introduction of the B-17E, complete with tail gunners, Japanese aircraft showed a healthy respect for the aircraft. In fact the new generation B-17s showed that the new Flying Fortresses could look after themselves in fights with Japanese interceptors. The small-caliber guns used by Japanese fighters made it very difficult for them to shoot down the heavy bomber, while their own lack of armor and self-sealing fuel tanks made them very vulnerable to 0.5in gunfire. Had the B-17s remained in the Pacific then, their success may well have been as great as that of those aircraft that replaced them. But the sad fact of the matter for the B-17 was that throughout its period of service in the Pacific it labored under far too many handicaps to be really effective. Probably the most critical weakness lay in the fact that on all too many occasions the B-17s were forced to go into action in very small numbers. For most of this period of the Pacific War for a squadron to be at fifty percent strength – in effect five or more aircraft – was little short of miraculous. For a whole group to attack with

five aircraft was normal; for a group to attack with anything more than that number really was an exceptional feat. Against land targets such numbers were totally inadequate while to attack shipping in such strength was almost derisory. Even when attacking in formation – an inverted Vee – in order to pattern the bombs in a straddle, the chances of hitting a ship were very small. On far too many occasions the B-17s were called upon to commit themselves to actions at the extreme edge of their endurance, thus lessening the amount of bombs that could be carried and, as a result, lessening the chances of a successful operation. Indeed, in many such attacks it can be quite reasonably argued that had the Japanese been better equipped, particularly with early-warning radar, far heavier losses would have been inflicted on the attacking B-17s than in fact were the case. Even allowing for the defensive firepower of the Fortress and the vulnerability and poor performance of the Zero-sen at high altitudes, the smallness of American attacks always ran the risk of defeat in detail, and perhaps the Americans were fortunate to escape without heavier losses.

Allowance has to be made for other factors when assessing the performance of the B-17 in the Pacific. It was the aircraft's misfortune to be involved in a catastrophic defeat. The B-17 was the major weapon in the aerial armory at a time of chaos and disorganization. It lived a hand-to-mouth existence on rough-hewn jungle strips, without proper maintenance, often having to stage through equally or even more primitive airstrips in order to reach objectives. It had to contend with appalling climatic conditions. The alternating heat and rain, bringing dust and mud in turn, made servicing a nightmare. In the air the bombers could encounter cloud and storms of ferocious violence that stretched the width of the horizon and over which they could not climb. It is not without significance that in seven months of operations the 11th BG lost six Fortresses to enemy action and twelve to the weather. One raid by three B-17s actually resulted in 100 percent losses when the aircraft could not find their way through a weather front and had to ditch in the sea as the fuel tanks spluttered dry. Overall the Pacific experience was an unfortunate one for the B-17, though the odds were heavily stacked against it from the start. As a result it left the area not properly or fairly tested because at no time in its operations had it been able to act en masse strategically. That test, for the B-17, was to be in Europe.

Right: Following a bombing raid on New Guinea, the crew of a Flying Fortress clean the plane's guns.
Below: A B-17C which was preserved after the war.

All pictures: Shots of a B-17G85DL which has been preserved. Some 42 B-17s have survived to the present day and are kept by museums and enthusiasts.

Ten in the air and one on the ground. *Above:* a **B-17F-100-BO** seen against the clouds. *Below far left:* **Two B-17Bs together in peacetime.** *Left center:* **Six B-17Fs form up in staggered Vees.** *Right center:* **A B-17C in flight.** *Right:* **The christening of** *Rose of England* **by Princess Elizabeth.**

THE EUROPEAN CAMP

Even before the American entry into the war in December 1941, Anglo-American strategic discussions had resulted in the decision that the primary Allied effort would be directed against Germany, the most powerful and dangerous of the three Axis powers. In order to defeat Germany the USA promised full land, sea and air participation in the joint Anglo-American effort, but the USAAF had arrogated for itself the role of bombing Germany into surrender. Both the USAAF and RAF Bomber Command claimed that given sufficient aircraft they could conduct a strategic bombing offensive that would bring Germany to her knees though they had very different ideas of how to bring this about. Nevertheless, before the war and before the differences of tactical doctrine became apparent, it was assumed that even while the USA mobilized her full resources for war prior to embarking upon major land and sea operations against the Germans, the USAAF would be able to build up forces quickly in Britain and soon assume a major part in a joint bombing campaign.

Matters did not work out as easily as that. To simplify a rather complicated story one can argue that 1942 was a year largely concerned with training, deployment and initial, limited operations; 1943 was the year of repeated attempts to make the theory of strategic bombing work without adequate resources. In 1944 the main effort of the USAAF to make its policies work was frustrated by the need to divert air resources toward support for the forthcoming invasion of France. It was only in the latter part of 1944 and in 1945 that the Americans had the forces needed to conduct a full-scale strategic bombing campaign, and by that time it was really too late to prove that the concept was workable. Air enthusiasts who had claimed that strategic bombing could end a war by itself and do away with the need for such mundane matters as invasions and land battles always had to contend with the unpalatable fact that the American air offensive against Germany had to be halted several times, most notably in October 1943, after the bombers had taken unacceptably high losses. In

1943 in fact the Germans were destroying the British and American strategic bombers far more rapidly than they could be replaced, and far more quickly than they could inflict commensurate and significant damage on Germany. To put the matter simply: in 1943 the Luftwaffe beat the bombers; strategic bombing failed. Subsequently, the air enthusiasts had to contend with the equally awkward fact that two out of every three bombs dropped on Germany in the course of the war fell after the Normandy invasion – for which, if their arguments had been correct, there would have been no need.

There was, however, a reverse side to this rather bleak coin. What remained hidden from the Allies during the years of war was the fact that their campaigns had a cumulative effect, and what they had said bombing would achieve was in fact achieved, but over a much longer time scale than had been anticipated. The true effectiveness of bombing was obscured in the end by the rapidity and totality of Germany's defeat. Hitler's armies fought their last battles almost without fuel as a result of Allied air attacks; they fought over a country whose economy lay in ruins as a result of many factors, but the most obvious and important was the carnage wrought from the skies. It must be noted that strategic bombing achieved the neutralization and isolation of the industrialized Ruhr. In normal circumstances this would have been rightly hailed as a remarkable achievement, but the fact that within one week of its isolation the Ruhr was surrounded and mopped up by land forces took the edge off the air forces' success. It more or less went unnoticed in a series of successes that by that time had reached avalanche proportions. Success really came too late to justify fully the concept of strategic bombing.

The activities of the B-17 and the concept of strategic bombing were intimately related and to understand them both, and

Below: **Two B-17G 75-BO Fortresses and a combination of Douglas- and Boeing-built B-17Gs practice box-formation flying over southern England.**
Right: **The bombing of Schweinfurt, the raid of 14 October 1943.**

AIGN

to comprehend the part that the B-17 played in strategic bombing, one must first really redefine what the USAAF sought to achieve and then why success proved elusive until too late in the war for the concept to be really successful. The essence of the American case for strategic bombing rested on the belief that, used en masse for mutual protection, heavy bombers such as the Flying Fortress could launch a series of devastatingly accurate attacks on key industrial centers, thus paralyzing enemy production and bringing about the collapse of his war effort. To achieve the required accuracy and scale of destruction the Americans had to use their aircraft in concentrated formations in daylight. Given the primitiveness of air navigation, night bombing could not hope to strike the key centers singled out by the Americans for destruction. The British had tried night precision bombing between 1940 and 1941; they realized its inherent inaccuracies and abandoned such tactics in favor of general attacks on built-up areas in February 1942.

The Americans, however, had certain very good reasons for wanting to go their own way. The American airmen were astute enough to realize that in any war economy there were certain very vulnerable bottlenecks which could be crippled by heavy air attacks. Among such bottlenecks they identified the submarine construction yards, the aircraft industry, the ball-bearing industry, oil, the synthetic rubber and military vehicles industries. Subsequently the Americans were to appreciate the value of sustained attacks on the transportation network. The Americans knew that if their attacks were to be successful then targets such as these had to be attacked during the day. In addition, the USAAF was adamant in its advocacy

Above: **B-17s of the 8th AF line up on their runways for a mission.**
Top right: **Fortresses of the 15th AF hit Ploesti oil targets, 24 April 1944.**
Bottom right: **Major General Ira C Eaker and Lieutenant General Carl Spaatz, in London, 1 January 1944.**

of this concept for 'political' reasons. A successful strategic bombing policy alone could justify the independent role the Army Air Force sought. The USAAF desired a genuinely recognized separate identity from the US Army and the US Navy. It also wanted to be clearly separated from RAF Bomber Command; it rightly feared being subordinated to the British effort. This was where the B-17 entered the picture. It was primarily the Flying Fortress, but with the Liberator as the second string, that was the means of putting into effect the policy of strategic bombing..The B-17 was the main means by which the USAAF intended to bring about the defeat of its four enemies – the Germans, the British and the US Army and Navy; and Flying Fortress was the aircraft in which the AAF placed its trust.

The reasons why the Americans failed to achieve the strategic victory over Germany in the manner they anticipated were many and complex, and in this book only certain of those reasons, most relevant to the story of the B-17, will be discussed. A major factor was the extraordinary degree of elasticity in an economy. The German transportation system is a microscopic example of the problem that the Americans faced. The Americans had many hesitations about the wisdom of bombing the transportation system. They feared that transportation would prove too resilient, too flexible. They suspected that ways around damage could always be improvised.

In part this hesitation was correct, but only in part. Experience was to show that even so flexible a transport system as that of Germany could be brought to utter ruination, but in general the American fear was well founded. The transportation system can be applied across the board to the whole of German industry. The dispersal of industry across a vast territory, the 'hardening' of specially sensitive centers and the efficiency of German repair and maintenance systems meant that the extent of damage inflicted by bombing was minimized and absorbed far more readily than had been anticipated.

A second factor directly related to this was the lack of co-operation the USAAF received from RAF Bomber Command. Air Chief Marshal Arthur Harris, whose true abilities and worth have never received proper recognition, was correctly skeptical of many American claims, but this hardly justified his pointed refusals to tie in British raids far more closely with the American effort than in fact was the case. Nominally the Allies were to co-ordinate their efforts in order to bomb Germany 'around the clock.' In raids that were supposed to complement one another and to throw the greatest possible strain on German resources, the British were supposed to bomb by night targets that blended with those sought out by the Americans during the day. As early as 25 September 1943 the Deputy Chief of the Air Staff (British) commented critically on the refusal of Harris to bomb certain targets as he had been ordered. These cities were centers of the German aircraft industry, against which American efforts were then directed. For the most part, however, Harris went his own way. This was a major handicap to the American effort, though in fairness it must be said that American complaints against Harris were few. In any case, had the American concepts been valid in the first place, there would have been no need for any form of support from the RAF for American operations.

Another major handicap was the weather. The Americans had been trained for bombing from high altitudes, for which they were equipped with a very good sight. But the vagaries of the European weather frequently resulted in missions being cancelled or aborted or bombs being dropped more or less at random. To be effective strategic bombing had to be continuous because its toll was, by its very nature, attritional. There were many reasons – losses, maintenance difficulties, crew fatigue, the need to change targets in order to retain surprise but still afford relief to those places already attacked – that made it very difficult to maintain the high tempo of operations needed to ensure success. Of all these material factors possibly the most important one remained the weather, which often afforded German industry protection that the Luftwaffe could not provide.

By far the most important factors in the shortcomings of the American concept of strategic bombing lay in the flaws inherent in the theory itself and the weapons with which the theory was supposed to be put into practice. The American idea envisaged a heavy bomber fighting its way to and from the objective. The harsh reality of the situation was that no bomber, however well armed or protected, could hope to operate successfully deep inside air space controlled by enemy fighters. Conditions of air superiority had to be assured if the bombers were to be effective. The bombers themselves could not hope to fight for and secure air supremacy, yet this was in effect what was being asked of them. The Fortress, in formation, was capable of about 180mph on its outward journey, and was far more vulnerable than the Americans had either imagined or feared. The Americans had reasoned that by flying at heights of five or six miles the worst of the flak could be avoided. This was more or less correct, but did have the drawback that the target was often covered by clouds. The

Americans also reasoned that by flying in tight formation the massive array of 0.5in machine guns could beat off enemy fighters. This was to prove manifestly false. Losses were inflicted on German fighters, but never to the extent claimed and never on the scale necessary to wrest air superiority from the Germans. The Fortress, as any bomber, had to be provided with escorts, fighters that were prepared to fight for and secure air superiority over the enemy homeland if bombing was to prove effective. This was the fatal mistake that the USAAF made in the early years of the war; it assumed that the Fortress could command the skies through which it flew.

Moreover, certain matters directly relating to the Fortress and its performance must be made clear if one is to make any serious assessment of the B-17 and its wartime activities. It may seem incredible in the light of the fact that American industry produced over 98,000 aircraft for the USAAF – of which over 12,000 were Fortresses, over 15,000 were Mustangs and over 19,000 were Liberators – but for most of the war the American air forces operating in Europe were acutely short of aircraft. It was only in the spring and summer of 1944 that the strategic forces, the 8th and 15th Air Forces, grew into their strength, and even after that time much of their activities had to be directed toward tactical objectives. For most of the war American strategic bomber strength was very marginal to requirements. It was only in 1944, after massive reinforcement and a drastic reduction of losses as a result of the Mustang's successful fight for air superiority over Germany, that the Americans possessed the strength to mount a prolonged bombing campaign.

The lack of numerical strength was compounded by the relative lightness of the payload of the Flying Fortress. It was a sad fact of life that as good as the Fortress was as an aircraft and as a bomber, she lacked a commensurate punch for her size and crew requirements that mass attacks could not always make good. However, one must balance the scales somewhat with the observation that without her the Americans could not have mounted a strategic air offensive in the first place. The Fortress played a vital role, but in the end not quite in the manner intended.

The initial wartime agreement between the British and Americans (14 January 1942) envisaged the rapid build-up of the USAAF in Britain. On 27 January Major General Carl Spaatz was appointed to command the 8th Air Force, the unit earmarked to carry out the strategic bombing of Germany from Britain. Less than a month later, on 20 February, the commander of the 8th Air Force's Bomber Command, Brigadier General Ira C Eaker, arrived in Britain. The American objective was to concentrate in Britain a force of sixty combat groups, totalling 3500 aircraft, by the spring of 1943. Of this total 33 were to be Bombardment Groups, of which seventeen were to be heavy, ten medium and six light. By definition at this time the majority of the heavy Groups were to consist of Flying Fortresses.

A series of events was to conspire to frustrate American intentions. The Pacific situation deteriorated with such rapidity in 1942 that, despite the 'Germany first' policy, resources had to be sent first to the Pacific in order to stabilize the situation there. It was only after the Japanese had been checked that the USAAF could really begin to concentrate upon Europe, but North Africa siphoned off much strength that should have gone to Britain. The critical, though passing, danger to the British position in the Middle East in 1942 resulted in the deployment of initial USAAF strength to Egypt – from where the Americans launched their first daylight precision raid of the war against the Ploesti oil fields in Rumania. This commitment was extended by the demands of the

Torch landings in North Africa in October 1942. The AAF had to commit substantial forces to give tactical support to the land armies during this crucial phase of operations. The Mediterranean ulcer was to sap any concentration on British soil throughout the whole of 1943 because the bombers, once in the Mediterranean Theater of Operations, were naturally retained there to meet the Army's demands for support in the invasions of Sicily, Salerno and Anzio. In large measure the success of these invasions can be traced to the paralysis of German communications by the bombers. Although used tactically for much of the time, the strategic bombing campaign was to benefit in the long term by the involvement of the bombers in the MTO. Once the Italian campaign settled down to a long slogging match across the various mountain valleys, the US 15th Air Force was ideally placed to wage a bombing offensive against southern Germany (inclusive of Austria) and the Balkans. Not only was shuttle bombing carried out between the MTO and Britain, but also between Italy and southern Russia, and the latter was not really very successful. The Soviet authorities seemed indifferent to the needs and demands inherent in co-operation if such operations were to be of value, and in one brilliant opportunist attack the Luftwaffe caught and destroyed 41 Flying Fortresses on the ground, damaging still more. Nevertheless, these were minor affairs, and despite many reverses and difficulties the 15th Air Force played an increasingly significant role in the strategic bombing of Germany from 1944 onward.

The Americans' main effort was to be made where they encountered the greatest difficulties – with the 8th Air Force in Britain. The most serious of all its problems involved the physical movement of personnel and equipment to Britain and the construction of adequate facilities in UK. Airfields had to be built on a massive scale and each airfield was a major undertaking in its own right. There was no question of using grass runways for heavily loaded bombers. Airfields, therefore, had to have three concrete runways and perimeter track with dispersal points. Concrete requirements for a single airfield represented a sixty-mile road, eighteen feet wide.

The first American-built airfield took ten months to complete, required 1,500,000 man-days and cost $5 million. Given just this single consideration it is not surprising that by the end of 1942 only nine of the heavy Groups assigned to the 8th should have entered service; that one group was one complete squadron understrength and that another Group, the 93rd, should have been temporarily in North Africa. Two other groups, the 97th and 301st, were also detached from the 8th Air Force by the end of 1942. Thus only six groups were in the UK after one year of war, and with a group theoretically carrying four squadrons each of twelve aircraft, the extent of American weakness can be appreciated. To train air and ground crews, to move them to their ports of embarkation, to transport the ground elements across the Atlantic in the fast monster liners and then to settle into hastily-built bases in an alien land was a mammoth task. The sheer logistics of such a move were immense, and it must be recalled that this was just the start. The Americans had to sustain themselves; every item of military equipment had to be shipped across the Atlantic at the height of the German submarine offensive. All nonmilitary essentials similarly had to be ferried across the ocean because British resources were inadequate to fill American needs. To gauge the depth of the American difficulty it is worth noting that for them to mount a 500-bomber raid a pool of at least 1250 aircraft had to be available to allow for maintenance and repair of battle damage. To put 500 bombers into the air demanded a back-up of 75,000 officers and men, 300 tons of operational equipment, plus fuel and bombs, and a standing reserve of 8500 tons of spare parts. Given the enormity of the overheads involved, the relative slowness of the American build-up of strategic bombers in Britain can be understood. The development of the strength of the heavy bomber element within the 8th Air Force can best be represented by the chart in the Appendix.

Below: **Return to the scene of a defeat. Flying Fortresses of the 8th AF attacking ball-bearing plants, railroad yards, warehouses and machine shops at Schweinfurt on 13 April 1944.**

OPERATIONS AND TAC

With the first B-17 flying into Polebrook on 6 July 1942, the 8th Air Force was able to launch its first all-American bombing operation on 17 August when twelve B-17Fs of 97th BG, under the command of Colonel Frank A Armstrong, Jr, raided the marshalling yards at Rouen. Eaker also flew on the raid which was aided by a diversionary sortie of six Fortresses designed to draw German defenses away from Rouen. The deception was successful and all Armstrong's aircraft returned safely, having inflicted damage on the objective.

For the remainder of the year the 8th Air Force continued to mount operations ever deeper into German-occupied territory. It was not until 27 January 1943, when again under Armstrong (by then commander of the 306th), that American bombers first flew against the Reich itself. The first German city to be attacked by Fortresses was the port of Wilhelmshaven, and the Americans lost three bombers. Up until that time American losses had been small with 32 aircraft (or two percent) being lost between Rouen and the end of the year. However, there were two catches in this situation. Firstly, the Americans were working on a shoestring in terms of aircraft and air crews. With North Africa taking aircraft away from Britain, the losses were sufficiently heavy – the size of an understrength 1942 group – to cause operations to be suspended in late 1942 on two separate occasions. Secondly, the

initial raids were really only the most shallow of penetrations of enemy airspace, and the Americans were not slow to read the danger signs. Though numerical losses had been light, no single raid had carried either weight or depth. German reaction time, despite the radar warnings of aircraft forming up over southern England, was short, and the bombers usually had escort cover as they crossed the dangerous coast. The Americans, who were naturally shaken by their first losses, recognized the perils they faced if they were to conduct strategic operations that involved deep penetrations of German airspace. Such operations necessarily involved many hours of flight over the main centers of enemy strength without the benefit of fighter cover. The optimists remained unshaken, but the first contact with the enemy convinced everyone that the tactical doctrine of the bombers had to be recast in order to improve the survival chances of the bombers and to enhance their prospects of inflicting serious damage on objectives.

Throughout the war the Americans were forced to alter

Right: Bombing through cloud: the contrails, visible 50 miles away, were frozen icicles that formed some 30ft astern of the exhausts.
Below right: A B-17 is lost with its crew over Berlin.
Below: The Box Formation with B-17s in Vees and stacked to give mutual support.

ICS

Above: **The 8th Air Force in action. Fortresses, with contrails streaming, over Germany on their way to attack the port of Bremen, 20 December 1943.**

constantly their tactical formations in order to keep abreast of the state of the air battle. The tactical deployment at any one time had to be a compromise between various conflicting considerations – the ease and safety of flying individual aircraft, the need to concentrate defensive firepower and the desire to achieve the most accurate bombing possible. There was never a 'final answer' to the tactical problem posed but throughout the war the Americans showed considerable flexibility, ingenuity and enterprise in adapting tactics to meet prevailing conditions. But the fact remained that losses were not curbed; rather they increased with alarming rapidity, and bombing accuracy was never achieved until conditions of overwhelming air superiority had been achieved. This, of course was not achieved by the bombers but by the fighter escorts in the course of late 1943 and early 1944.

The pioneer of many of the tactical changes incorporated by the 8th Air Force was the first commander of the 305th BG, Colonel Curtis LeMay. To assert that he was actually liked by his men is to misunderstand the situation. He was respected and feared and his crews were devoted to him, but he was never liked and he won regard through his example, bravery and sheer ability. He was dubbed 'Iron-Ass,' by his men and went on to command the whole of the bomber division and then an entire Air Force in the latter stages of the Pacific War. It was under LeMay's constant probing that changes were made and improvements worked into American bombing technique.

When the 8th Air Force entered the fray its basic formation was a six-bomber squadron. Squadrons had a nominal strength of twelve, but operationally to have six available was

normal. The six aircraft flew in two Vees, staggered both in height and depth. The leading aircraft in the center of the two inverted Vees were below and the two outer aircraft above the leaders. The height variation between the aircraft was about 150ft. The two flank squadrons were four miles apart and were 1½ miles behind and about 1000ft below the lead squadron. The rear was brought up by a fourth squadron, 1½ miles and 2000ft above the echeloned squadrons. This squadron, though above the leader, was directly in its wake.

The Vee formation had much to recommend it. It was very easy to form up. Some of the later arrangements could take more than an hour to assemble – thus cutting down range – but this one was very simple. It was also relatively easy to fly in this formation because it was not particularly demanding on attention; aircraft were spaced on a minimal lateral distance of about seventy yards. The weakness of the formation very quickly became obvious. The six-bomber formation lacked the defensive firepower needed to deter German fighters while the staggering of 24 aircraft over so much sky left them all vulnerable and unable to give one another mutual support.

The answer was to bring units closer together and in September 1942 the Americans began to experiment with a two squadron formation, both squadrons carrying nine aircraft. Squadrons incorporated three Vees, each of three bombers, with the lead squadron some 500ft below the trailing squadron which was echeloned toward the sun. All aircraft in a squadron flew at the same altitude, there being no staggering of heights within individual squadrons. This arrangement, again, had its strengths and weaknesses. Though naturally the frontage was widened and firepower was more concentrated, but only at the cost of imposing a rather inflexible linear deployment on the whole formation that made it difficult for the outer aircraft to respond to a turn. There was a tendency for the outer aircraft to lose touch and straggle, thereby falling easy victims to lurking fighters. In addition, the linear same-altitude deployment did rob the new formation of one of the advantages of staggered formation. Though Veed, the linear deployment closed down many arcs of fire and actually reduced the mutual support the bombers could afford one another.

As a result of this consideration even before the year turned the Americans again recast their tactical doctrine – under LeMay's promptings. This time they produced an eighteen-aircraft formation, stacked toward the sun, with the lead aircraft in the center. This was a considerable improvement because it allowed all the B-17s to unmask their fields of fire. The staggering and stacking of bombers, however, had certain drawbacks. These mainly arose because the Americans used successive formations in waves. Individually echeloned $1\frac{1}{2}$ miles apart, these groups incorporated the same 900ft height-differential within the lead group, but at ever-rising altitudes. In a four formation grouping this meant that the lowest aircraft in the lead formation was 4000ft lower than the trailing aircraft in the high formation. This 'Javelin' therefore encountered the difficulty of speed-differential caused by altitude-variation within and between formations. The $1\frac{1}{2}$ miles between formations, conceived in order to deny the German fighters the chance to take the optimum line of attack from dead ahead, tended to widen, thus defeating the whole purpose of the arrangement. With the higher aircraft prone to straggling, it quickly became obvious that the Javelin had to be abandoned and that a greater concentration of aircraft and firepower had to be achieved. The main problems in attempting this, however, were that tighter formation-flying imposed additional stress on crews, threatened to resurrect the old problem of masked fields of fire and increased the very real danger of bombers unloading their payloads on their low-altitude colleagues. A partial answer was provided with the 'Wedge,' introduced in February 1943. This kept the basic group formation, with the same distance between formations as with the Javelin, but instead of formations being stacked at progressively higher altitudes behind the leader, the trailing formations were deployed in echelon above and in echelon below the leader. This cut down straggling because of speed/altitude variations, but of course it could not eliminate it.

Below: **The 15th Air Force in action. One of the very first losses suffered by the 483rd BG in April 1944 over Nis, Yugoslavia. No crewmen survived.**

Above: **A B-17, years after the war. The crews personalized their planes, painting on names, emblems and also the number of aircraft downed.**

The problem of the Wedge was that it was inadequate to meet the challenge of the Luftwaffe, then being redeployed to the west and being concentrated in order to defend German cities. With Allied fighters unable to reach Germany the Americans had to devise a 54-bomber combat wing in March 1943 in order to try to hold off the German fighters. The Combat Wing kept the eighteen-strong formation, three formations being concentrated in a very compact unit. The wing was almost an extended skirmishing line because it envisaged one formation in the center leading and two formations slightly but clearly trailing, one above and one below the leader. This meant that the wing was concentrated within a frontage of $1\frac{1}{4}$ miles with an altitude variation of little more than $\frac{1}{2}$ mile. Critically, however, the distance between lead and trail aircraft was cut to a mere 600 yards. Here, indeed, was massive concentration of defensive firepower. By drawing in squadrons and formations into one small compact whole, the Wing could be sealed off hermetically by the firepower of over 550 machine guns. Wings were supposed to fly at six-mile intervals, but in fact this organization barely flew at all.

In April 'The Tucked-in Combat Wing' was introduced. The extent of the tuck-in can be gauged by the fact that the new formation occupied 26.5 percent of the airspace filled by the original (950 yards × 425 yards × 2900ft compared to 2340 yards × 600 yards × 2900ft). This phenomenal concentration was made possible by bringing in the trailing high and low formations almost to the point where they overlapped the leader. Within formations the three-aircraft Vees were stacked in one direction; the elements and squadrons were stacked in the opposite direction. It was by such measures that an incredible degree of compression was achieved, and it was with this bristling formation that the bombers of the 8th Air Force, spearheaded by the B-17Fs and B-17Gs, embarked upon their deep-penetration raids over Germany.

This, then, was the formation used by the 8th for most of 1943 in its attempt to make the strategic bombing philosophy work. By using such a grouping of aircraft the 8th anticipated the bombers being able to fight their way to their objectives and at the same time meet the challenge of the Luftwaffe. This attempt failed, at a devastating cost. American bomber losses in 1943 reached awesome proportions. Subsequently such losses were to be sustained only by the 492nd BG which in a three-month tour in 1944 lost what was effectively the whole of its initial establishment. Such losses in 1944 were uncommon; in 1943 they were the general rule. The Bremen raid of 17 April resulted in the destruction of or severe damage to sixty of the 115 bombers thrown against the city – over Kiel on 13 June 22 bombers were lost out of sixty. Nine days later

Top Left: A Fortress goes down over Delmenhorst.
Top Right: A Fortress on Purple Heart Corner passes a stricken
colleague over Stuttgart, 6 September 1943.
Main picture: B-17Fs in the foreground; in the distance successive
units in a Combat Wing. The contrails show where previous wings
have flown. In the center is a dangerously vulnerable straggler.

Above: **LeMay's concept of 'pattern bombing' by staggered Vees. In this photograph six of the eight B-17s can be seen delivering their bomb loads.**

over Huls only sixteen bombers were lost out of 363, but no less than 170 of the survivors incurred various degrees of damage. In 'Blitz-Week' (24–30 July) the Americans lost or had to write off 100 aircraft. Ninety complete crews were lost. This represented the loss of two complete groups at a time when only fifteen had been brought up to full battle-worthiness. On the Rouen anniversary the Americans attacked Schweinfurt and Regensburg, deep in southern Germany. Of the 363 Fortresses committed sixty were destroyed – and many others written off – in the most costly raid of the war to date for the 8th. Losses were almost as heavy over Stuttgart on 6 September when fifty bombers were lost out of 388, hardly any of which found Stuttgart at all. An attempt to renew the assault on Schweinfurt in October cost the Americans 77 aircraft lost and a further 133 damaged out of a total 291 Fortresses dispatched on the mission.

By this time losses were running at nearly ten percent per mission and it was not uncommon for squadrons flying 'Purple Heart Corner' – the lowest and most exposed position in the Wing – to suffer not decimation but annihilation. The total loss of squadrons flying this vulnerable station was not unknown, and squadrons had to be rotated through this position because there was an understandable reluctance to volunteer for this station. By mid and late 1943 many groups were in a state of extremely bad demoralization as a result of their losses. Indeed, after the second Schweinfurt bombing operations had to be temporarily halted. With losses three times heavier than could be tolerated there had to be a respite. That respite, however, was tacit recognition that the bomber, despite the bravery of its crew, could not do all that was being asked of it.

Certainly the bombers had often achieved considerable successes. Many targets were badly damaged and even crippled by attacks that owed much of their effectiveness to LeMay's insistence that in formation all bombers had to bomb together. This he had advocated almost at the outset of operations, being convinced that 'pattern bombing' would be far more effective than individual bombing runs. When it came to the 1943 massed formations individual bombing runs, with aircraft jockeying for position, was out of the question. But in late 1942 LeMay and the 305th were encouraged to coordinate bombing by making all bombers drop on the signal of the leader. LeMay reasoned that while there was the possibility of all bombs being wasted as a result of error on the part of the lead bombardier, the probability was that more bombs would straddle and saturate the objective if they were dropped on the orders of the best, most highly trained and battle-experienced crew available. In this way even the weakest crew could be carried effectively. LeMay's concepts became standard operational procedure in the 8th, but that did not alter the fact that by late 1943 losses were too heavy to justify the results obtained. In 1943 the German fighters, warned by radar and deployed in depth across their homeland, could strike the heavily loaded bombers out of the skies faster than crews could be replaced.

This crisis for the American strategic offensive was overcome rapidly and in dramatic fashion in the same way fortune changed sides between March and May 1943 in the Battle of the Atlantic. In October 1943 the Fortresses (and Liberators) found they could not withstand concentrated attacks by the main-line German fighters, the FW190 and the Me109G. Soon after the tide turned for the Americans. The combination of three fighters – a much improved P-47 Thunderbolt, the P-38 twin-boomed Lightning and the P-51 Mustang – began to drive the Luftwaffe out of the skies. The most important of these aircraft was the Mustang, a fighter whose range allowed it to operate east of the Oder-Neisse. With a range of 1500 miles and a top speed of 440mph, it could outpace both the FW190 and Me109G with ease, and it could out-dive and out-turn both German aircraft. Only in rate of roll could the German aircraft compete on anything like equal terms. In the P-51 the Americans had a fighter of superb quality, and Spaatz and his fighter commander, Kepner, knew how to use it. With the strategic bombing campaign having failed, Spaatz was determined to keep the bombers in the air to force the Germans to give battle to the Mustang on unequal terms. Rather than being the means of winning air superiority through bombing, the bombers were made the means by which an air supremacy battle could be provoked and won. Kepner used his fighters not simply as escorts but as fighting patrols to seek out enemy fighters throughout the length of Germany. This did not mean that bomber losses dropped immediately. As the battle for supremacy intensified bomber losses were heavy. Over Berlin on 6 March 1944, 72 bombers were lost and 102 more received serious damage out of a total number of 730. The 350th BS lost ten of its number in this raid.

The emergence of the Mustang necessitated another tactical change for the bombers. Formations were reduced to three squadrons of twelve aircraft, with the lead squadron in the center. The lead squadron, or individual aircraft in it, were given the relatively few air-to-ground radars available in early 1944 (H2S to the British, known as H2X to the Americans). The trail squadrons formed up above and below. Cut in strength by a third, this formation occupied seventeen percent more airspace than the previous system, but was easier for the bombers to fly and the Mustangs to escort. This formation proved very effective for the best part of a year. Occasionally major efforts by the Luftwaffe, including the first use of jet attacks, were costly, but with the ebbing strength of the Luftwaffe the bombers' main threat came from ever more powerful flak defenses in the last eighteen months of the war. The problem for the bombers was simple. The Germans could deduce the bombers' probable line of approach to their objective and concentrate on that line a massive volume of fire through which the bombers had to fly in order to reach the target. To improve their chances of survival, in 1945 the Americans opened up their formations to try to confuse the German flak gunners. The bombers were deployed over a greater depth of sky (1150ft) than ever before with four nine-strong squadrons in formation. One high and one low squadron flanked the leader who was trailed by a still lower rear squadron. This formation occupied 43 percent more airspace than its predecessor, making it harder for the flak to assess altitude correctly and to shift fire with rapidity and accuracy. It was this tactical formation that saw out the end of the war.

Below: **Major General William Kepner (left) with Lieutenant General Carl Spaatz.**

Such were the tactics employed by the bombers of the 8th Air Force. The chart on page 61 clearly shows the buildup of the 8th in the course of the war. Eaker, in his earliest demands, assessed the heavy bomber needs to be 944 by 1 July 1943, 1192 by 1 October and 2702 by 1 April 1944. In fact these target figures were very nearly met at every stage, but the chart shows clearly that of the 42 groups that at various times served with the 8th (the 482nd being discounted), no less than nineteen entered combat after 30 November 1944. This was when only 21 of the once 23 heavy groups remained with the 8th Air Force. In the early months of 1944 the strength of the 8th almost doubled. The sad fact of this from the B-17s viewpoint was that whereas only four groups were equipped with B-17s, those that remained had B-24s. In the autumn, however, five groups, the 34th, 486th, 487th, 490th and 493rd converted to B-17Gs, and 72 percent of these groups' missions were flown in the Fortress. It was as a result of the massive build-up of B-24s in early 1944 that there was an almost equal balance between B-17s and B-24s in the 8th in June 1944. In that month 49.77 percent of the first line heavy bombers were B-24s; in July 48.70 percent. Both before and after that time, however, the overwhelming balance was in favor of the B-17. The B-24 build-up was mainly directed toward the invasion.

The total number of American strategic bombers available to the Supreme Allied Commander (General Dwight D Eisenhower) on any day in September was 4202. This is the strength on which the Supreme Commander could call. In fact the total number of heavy bombers within the 8th and 15th was at least 25 percent more than his paper allocation, but the extra numbers were not first-line aircraft and includes replacement, training and assorted aircraft. The total available with RAF Bomber Command was 6073. Of this final total 76 percent were operational at any one time.

Excluding the RAF and the US 15th Air Force, certain calculations may be made regarding the B-17 and the 8th Air Force. In the whole of the war the 8th flew 10,802 missions of which 6945 (64.29 percent) were flown by B-17s. Liberators flew a total of 3706 missions (34.31 percent). From the chart it can be seen that 4255 heavy bombers were listed as Missing in Action, and an unknown number were written off. Roger Freeman in *The US Strategic Bomber* (MacDonald and Jane's, London, 1975) gives the losses of the 8th as 5548 heavy bombers from all causes during combat. Of this total German aircraft are credited with 44.20 percent and flak with 43.96 percent. There seems to be no complete total of heavy bombers lost outside of combat. With incomplete data drawn from just 27 groups there were at least 864 bombers classified as 'Other Operational Losses.' Of these totals it would seem that at least 75 percent of the losses were sustained by the Fortresses because losses equipped only with the B-24 totalled 944, while 290 aircraft were lost from the five 'mixed' groups. What this meant in human or in Group terms can be seen by a reference to the career of the 388th, the Group selected for the Castor experiments. Its total operational losses were 179 aircraft with an additional 34 written off as a result of accidents and other causes. Only 270 aircraft served with the Group, which means that in addition to losing between four and five times its original strength, the group lost 78.89 percent of its total effective strength in the course of its operations. One hundred and thirty five of its 450 crews were listed as Missing in Action. In two years of combat some ground crews serviced as many as eight different aircraft, seventy airmen having passed by in that time. Only two aircraft of the original batch were still in service at the end of the war, and not that many more of the original crewmen. Such was the price of victory.

APPENDICES

1. Deployment of B-17 Flying Fortresses, other than those with 8th Air Force

Metropolitan Homeland, USA

Number of Groups: 21.
 (Bombardment: 18. Search Attack: 1. Reconnaissance: 1.
 Bombardment/Search Attack: 1.)
Bombardment Groups (with squadrons):

6th (3/25/74/395/397)	346th (502/503/504/505)
29th (6/29/52)	383rd (540/541/542/543)
34th (4/7/18/391)	393rd (580/581/582/583)
39th (6/61/62)	395th (588/589/590/591)
40th (29/44/45/74)	396th (592/593/594/595)
88th (316/317/318/399)	444th (676/677/678/679)
304th (361/362/363/421)	469th (796/797/798/799)
331st (461/462/463/464)	504th (393/398/421/507)
333rd (466/467/468/469)	505th (482/483/484/485)

Nominal squadron strength: 71
Actual squadron strength: 70 (29th BS in two Groups)

Reconnaissance Group: 9th No squadrons permanently attached.
Search-Attack Group: 1st Three squadrons attached: 2nd, 3rd and
 4th.
Dual-Role Group: 9th Four squadrons attached: 1st, 5th, 99th and
 430th.

Pacific Theater of Operations

Number of Groups: 5.
 (Bombardment: 4. Reconnaissance: 1.)
Bombardment Groups (with squadrons):

4th (23/31/72/394)	19th (14/28/30/40/93)
11th (26/42/98/431)	43rd (63/64/65/403)

Nominal squadron strength: 17.
Reconnaissance Group: 11th. Three squadrons attached: 1st, 3rd
 and 19th.

PTO/China-Burma-India Theater

Total strength was the 7th Bombardment Group with four
squadrons, the 9th, 11th, 22nd and 88th attached.

The MTO/ETO

In the course of the war various US Air Forces served in the
Mediterranean area, with groups and squadrons being 'borrowed'
almost as standard practice between forces. This makes giving an
account of units in the area extremely complicated, but it is
probably easiest to account for B-17 participation in the MTO/ETO
with reference to the 15th Air Force.

Formed from various forces in the Mediterranean, the 15th
operated a total of 21 Bombardment Groups. Of this total six were
equipped with B-17s. These were the

2nd (20/49/96/429) Entered service 28 April 1943 with 2nd
 Air Force.
97th (340/341/342/414) Entered service 17 August 1942 with 8th
 Air Force.
99th (346/347/348/416) Entered service 31 March 1943.
301st (32/352/353/419) Entered service 5 September 1942 with
 8th Air Force.
463rd (772/773/774/775) Entered service 16 March 1944.
483rd (815/816/817/818) Entered service 12 April 1944.

All these groups were allocated to the 5th Bombardment Wing,
one of six operated by 15th Air Force.

Until the end of 1943 there were more B-17s than B-24s with the
15th, but thereafter the massive build-up of B-24 strength clearly
relegated the B-17 to second place. By June 1944 less than one in
four heavy bombers was a B-17, though this imbalance was
'corrected' slightly before the end of the war as a result of the
decline in overall numbers of Liberators on station and the
expansion of the numbers of Fortresses. By May 1945 B-17s formed
nearly forty percent of the total first line bomber strength
available to the 15th Air Force.

Total losses among the Bombardment Groups is given by
Freeman as 2519. With no breakdown available one can make no
comment other than that the vast majority of these losses must
have been sustained by the B-24s.

In addition to the Bombardment Groups two B-17 equipped
Reconnaissance Groups served in the Mediterranean. These were:
 5th (21/22/23/24) and 68th (16/111/122/125/127/154).
The 3rd Photographic Group, containing one squadron with B-17s,
also served in the Mediterranean.

Note:
One Bombardment Group, the 34th, appears in two lists: the
Metropolitan Homeland and the 8th Air Force. For most of the war
it was in the USA where it served as the training cadre for the 8th
Air Force. It was activated for war in early 1944.

Below: One of the very last B-17s, one of batch B-17G-100-VE. Too
late to see service, she was used in radio-controlled flight tests and
at Bikini.

2. Nominal Role of the Bombardment Groups that served with the 8th Air Force in Britain

Group:	sqn:	sqn:	sqn:	sqn:	ttl;	.ac.	.ac.	1942 JJASOND: 1943 JFMAMJJASOND: 1944 JFMAMJJASOND: 1945 JFMA	Missions	Sorties	Payload in tons	MIA	OOL
34th	4	7	18	391	4	G	24	M———	108/170	5,713	13,425	34	39
44th					4		24	N———	343	8,009	18,980	153	39
91st	322	323	324	401	4	F	G	N———	340/340	9,591	22,142	197	?
92nd	325	326	327	407	4	F	G	S———	308/308	8,633	20,829	154	?
93rd					4		24	O———	396	8,169	19,004	100	40
94th	331	332	333	410	4	F	G	M———	324/324	8,884	18,925	153	27
95th	334	335	336	412	4	F	G	M———	320/320	8,903	19,769	157	39
96th	337	338	339	413	4	F	G	M———	321/321	8,924	19,277	189	50
97th	340	341	342	414	4	E	F	A–O	14/ 14	247	395	4	?
100th	349	350	351	418	4	F	G	J———	306/306	8,630	19,257	177	52
301st	32	352	353	419	4	F		S –N	8/ 8	104	186	1	?
303rd	358	359	360	427	4	F	G	N———	364/364	10,721	24,918	165	?
305th	364	365	366	422	4	F	G	N———	337/337	9,231	22,363	154	?
306th	367	368	369	423	4	F	G	O———	342/342	9,614	22,575	171	?
322nd					4		26	M—O	34	?	?	12	?
323rd					4		26	J—O	33	?	?	3	?
351st	508	509	510	511	4	F	G	M———	311/311	8,600	20,357	124	?
379th	524	525	526	527	4	F	G	M———	330/330	10,492	26,460	141	?
381st	532	533	534	535	4	F	G	J———	296/296	9,035	22,160	131	?
384th	544	545	546	547	4	F	G	J———	314/314	9,348	22,415	159	?
385th	548	549	550	551	4	F	G	J———	296/296	8,264	18,494	129	40
386th					4		26	J—O	30	?	?	6	?
387th					4		26	A—O	29	?	?	2	?
388th	560	561	562	563	4	F 24	G 34	J———	306/331	8,051	18,162	142	37
389th					4		24	J———	321	7,579	17,548	116	37
390th	568	569	570	571	4	F	G	A———	300/300	8,725	19,059	144	32
392nd					4		24	S———	285	7,060	17,452	127	57
398th	600	601	602	603	4	G		M———	195/195	6,419	15,781	58	?
401st	612	613	614	615	4	G		N———	255/255	7,430	17,778	95	?
445th					4		24	D———	282	7,145	16,732	108	25
446th					4		24	D———	273	7,259	16,819	58	28
447th	708	709	710	711	4	G		D———	257/257	7,605	17,103	153	27
448th					4		24	D———	262	6,774	15,272	101	34
452nd	728	729	730	731	4	G		F———	250/250	7,279	16,467	110	48
453rd					4		24	F———	259	6,655	15,804	58	?
457th	748	749	750	751	4	G		F———	237/237	7,086	16,916	83	?
458th					4		24	F———	240	5,759	13,204	47	18
466th					4		24	M———	232	5,762	12,914	47	24
467th					4		24	A———	212	5,538	13,333	29	19
482nd	812	813	814		3	F/G	24	S———	?	?	?	7	? *
486th	832	833	834	835	4	G	24	M———	142/188	6,173	14,517	33	24
487th	836	837	838	839	4	G	24	M———	139/185	6,021	14,041	33	24
489th					4		24	M—N	106	2,998	6,951	29	12
490th	848	849	850	851	4	G	24	M———	118/158	5,060	12,407	22	32
491st					4		24	J———	187	5,005	12,304	47	23
492nd					4		24	M—A	64	1,513	3,757	51	6
493rd	860	861	862	863	4	G	24	J———	110/157	4,871	12,188	41	31

Key:

- sqn squadron number
- ttl total squadrons in group
- ac type of aircraft used: letters refer to Mark of B-17 and numbers to other types of bomber
- MIA aircraft missing in action
- OOL other operational losses
- ? Information unavailable

Letters in date list give month of first operational mission by group or part of group and, where appropriate, when left 8AF

Missions: first figure is B-17 total
second figure total all aircraft

*Unit raised in UK. Used in radio, radar and pathfinder tasks.

Others:

5th Emergency Rescue Squadron: used B-17Gs after Mar 45.

15th Photographic Squadron: One of five squadrons; only one to use B-17F. Part of 3rd PG. Assigned to but not active with 8AF.

422nd BS (renumbered 858th then 406th) Night Leaflet Squadron. B-17F/G from Sep 43 until Aug 44.

652nd BS One of four squadron, part of 25th BG (Recce). Only squadron with B-17Gs; after Nov 44.

803rd BS (renumbered 36th) Formed Jan 44 as ECM unit. Used B-17F/G after Jun 44.

3. Specifications of the B-17 Flying Fortress

Model	299	Y1B-17	Y1B-17A	B-17B	B-17C	B-17D	B17E	B-17F
Engine	R-1690-E	R-1820-39	R-1820-51	R-1820-51	R-1820-65	R-1820-65	R-1820-65	R-1820-97
Orthodox hp	750	930	1,000	1,000	1,200	1,200	1,200	1,200
Span	103ft 9in	103ft 9in	103ft 9in	103ft 9in	103ft 9in	103ft 9in	103ft 9in	103ft 9in
Length	61ft 10in	68ft 4in	68ft 4in	67ft 11in	67ft 11in	67ft 11in	73ft 10in	74ft 9in
Empty Weight	21,657lb	24,460lb	31,160lb	27,650lb	30,600lb	30,960lb	32,250lb	34,000lb
Maximum Weight	43,000lb	43,650lb	45,650lb	48,000lb	49,650lb	49,650lb	54,000lb	65,500lb
Maximum Speed	236mph	256mph	295mph	292mph	323mph*	318mph	317mph	299mph
Service Ceiling	24,600ft	30,000ft	38,000ft	38,000ft	37,000ft	37,000ft	36,500ft	37,500ft
Rate of climb	6mins to 10,000ft	6mins 30sec to 10,000ft	7mins 48sec to 10,000ft	7mins to 10,000ft	7mins 30sec to 10,000ft	7mins 12sec to 10,000ft	7mins 6sec to 10,000ft	25mins 42sec to 20,000ft
Normal Range	2,400 miles	2,400 miles	2,400 miles	2,400 miles	2,000 miles	2,000 miles	2,000 miles	1,300 or 2,200 miles
Maximum Range	3,000 miles	3,400 miles	3,600 miles	3,600 miles	3,400 miles	3,400 miles	3,200 miles	2,680 or 3,800 miles
Normal bomb load	4,000lb	4,000lb	4,000lb	4,000lb	4,000lb	4,000lb	4,000lb	4,000lb
Normal maximum bomb load	4,000lb	8,000lb	8,000lb	8,000lb	4,000lb	4,000lb	4,000lb	13,600lb
Crew members	6	6	6	6	6	6	10	10
Defensive Firepower	Five .3	One .3 Six .5	One .3 Six .5	One .3 Six .5	One .3 Six .5	One .3 Six .5	One .3 Eight .5	Eleven .5

*The speed given for the B-17C takes no account of the speed of 353mph achieved by a B-17C of the Royal Air Force. All characteristics listed are liable to dispute because there are as many 'maximum speeds' as there are sources. Much depends on the state of an aircraft, climatic conditions etc, in any giving of weights, speeds etc. The list given is an attempt to collate various information, but the basis for this material is Roger A Freeman's *American Bombers of World War Two*.

4. Construction of B-17s

Prototypes and early Marks

229	1	No military serial number
		Registration number NX-13372
Y1B-17	13	36-149ff
Y1B-17A	1	37-369
B-17B	39	38-211 to 38-223
		38-258 to 38-270
		38-583 to 38-584
		38-610
		39-1 to 39-10
B-17C	38	40-2042 to 40-2079
B-17D	42	40-3059 to 40-3100
B-17E	512	41-2393 to 41-2669
		41-9011 to 41-9245

In the subsequent lists, the construction per company (Boeing, Douglas and Vega) is shown with Batch Number, full designation and military serial numbers. All aircraft in a given batch are numbered consecutively unless otherwise stated.

B-17F

B-17F- 1-BO	50	41-24340ff	B-17F- 1-DL	3	42-	2964ff
B-17F- 5-BO	50	41-24390ff	B-17F- 5-DL	12	42-	2967ff
B-17F- 10-BO	50	41-24440ff	B-17F- 10-DL	25	42-	2979ff
B-17F- 15-BO	14	41-24490ff	B-17F- 15-DL	35	42-	3004ff
B-17F- 20-BO	36	41-24504ff	B-17F- 20-DL	35	42-	3039ff
B-17F- 25-BO	45	41-24540ff	B-17F- 25-DL	75	42-	3074ff
B-17F- 27-BO	55	41-24585ff	B-17F- 30-DL	40	42-	3149ff
B-17F- 30-BO	29	42- 5050ff	B-17F- 35-DL	40	42-	3189ff
B-17F- 35-BO	71	42- 5079ff	B-17F- 40-DL	55	42-	3229ff
B-17F- 40-BO	100	42- 5150ff	B-17F- 45-DL	55	42-	3284ff
B-17F- 45-BO	100	42- 5250ff	B-17F- 50-DL	55	42-	3339ff
B-17F- 50-BO	135	42- 5350ff	B-17F- 55-DL	29	42-	3394ff
B-17F- 55-BO	65	42-29467ff	B-17F- 60-DL	26	42-	3423ff
B-17F- 60-BO	100	42-29532ff	B-17F- 65-DL	34	42-	3449ff
B-17F- 65-BO	100	42-29632ff	B-17F- 70-DL	21	42-	3483ff
B-17F- 70-BO	100	42-29732ff	B-17F- 75-DL	59	42-	3504ff
B-17F- 75-BO	100	42-29832ff	B-17F- 80-DL	6	42-37714ff	
B-17F- 80-BO	100	42-29932ff	B-17F- 1-VE	5	42-	5705ff
B-17F- 85-BO	100	42-30032ff	B-17F- 5-VE	15	42-	5710ff
B-17F- 90-BO	100	42-30132ff	B-17F- 10-VE	20	42-	5725ff
B-17F- 95-BO	100	42-30232ff	B-17F- 15-VE	20	42-	5745ff
B-17F-100-BO	100	42-30332ff	B-17F- 20-VE	40	42-	5765ff
B-17F-105-BO	100	42-30432ff	B-17F- 25-VE	50	42-	5805ff
B-17F-110-BO	85	42-30532ff	B-17F- 30-VE	50	42-	5855ff
B-17F-115-BO	115	42-30617ff	B-17F- 35-VE	50	42-	5905ff
B-17F-120-BO	100	42-30732ff	B-17F- 40-VE	75	42-	5955ff
B-17F-125-BO	100	42-30832ff	B-17F- 45-VE	75	42-	6030ff
B-17F-130-BO	100	42-30932ff	B-17F- 50-VE	100	42-	6105ff

Production:	Boeing	2,300
	Douglas	605
	Vega	500
		3,405

B-17G

				B-17G- 50-DL	250	44-	6251ff
				B-17G- 55-DL	125	44-	6501ff
B-17G- 1-BO	100	42- 31032ff		B-17G- 60-DL	125	44-	6626ff
B-17G- 5-BO	100	42- 31132ff		B-17G- 65-DL	125	44-	6751ff
B-17G- 10-BO	100	42- 31232ff		B-17G- 70-DL	125	44-	6876ff
B-17G- 15-BO	100	42- 31332ff		B-17G- 75-DL	125	44-	83236ff
B-17G- 20-BO	200	42- 31432ff		B-17G- 80-DL	125	44-	83361ff
B-17G- 25-BO	100	42- 31632ff		B-17G- 85-DL	100	44-	83486ff
B-17G- 30-BO	200	42- 31732ff		B-17G- 90-DL	100	44-	83586ff
B-17G- 35-BO	185	42- 31932ff		B-17G- 95-DL	200	44-	83686ff
B-17G- 40-BO	115	42- 97058ff		B-17G- 1-VE	100	42-	39758ff
B-17G- 45-BO	235	42- 97173ff		B-17G- 5-VE	100	42-	39858ff
B-17G- 50-BO	165	42-102379ff		B-17G- 10-VE	100	42-	39958ff
B-17G- 55-BO	200	42-102544ff		B-17G- 15-VE	100	42-	97436ff
B-17G- 60-BO	235	42-102744ff		B-17G- 20-VE	100	42-	97536ff
B-17G- 65-BO	165	43- 37509ff		B-17G- 25-VE	100	42-	97636ff
B-17G- 70-BO	200	43- 37674ff		B-17G- 30-VE	100	42-	97736ff
B-17G- 75-BO	200	43- 37874ff		B-17G- 35-VE	100	42-	97836ff
B-17G- 80-BO	200	43- 38074ff		B-17G- 40-VE	100	42-	97936ff
B-17G- 85-BO	200	43- 38274ff		B-17G- 45-VE	100	44-	8001ff
B-17G- 90-BO	200	43- 38474ff		B-17G- 50-VE	100	44-	8101ff
B-17G- 95-BO	200	43- 38674ff		B-17G- 55-VE	100	44-	8201ff
B-17G-100-BO	200	43- 38874ff		B-17G- 60-VE	100	44-	8301ff
B-17G-105-BO	200	43- 39074ff		B-17G- 65-VE	100	44-	8401ff
B-17G-110-BO	200	43- 39274ff		B-17G- 70-VE	100	44-	8501ff
B-17G- 5-DL	1	42- 3563		B-17G- 75-VE	100	44-	8601ff
B-17G- 10-DL	84	see note		B-17G- 80-VE	100	44-	8701ff
B-17G- 15-DL	90	42- 37804ff		B-17G- 85-VE	100	44-	8801ff
B-17G- 20-DL	95	42- 37894ff		B-17G- 90-VE	100	44-	8901ff
B-17G- 25-DL	95	42- 37989ff		B-17G- 95-VE	100	44-	85492ff
B-17G- 30-DL	130	42- 38084ff		B-17G-100-VE	100	44-	85592ff
B-17G- 35-DL	250	42-106984ff		B-17G-105-VE	100	44-	85692ff
B-17G- 40-DL	125	44- 6001ff		B-17G-110-VE	50	44-	85792ff
B-17G- 45-DL	125	44- 6126ff					

Production:	Boeing	4,035
	Douglas	2,395
	Vega	2,250
		8,680

Note: The 84 production models of B-17G- 10-DL given serial numbers 42-37716 and 42-37721ff.

Summary of Construction

Model	Orders	Boeing	Douglas	Vega
229	1	1		
Y1B-17	1	13		
Y1B-17A	1	1		
B-17B	1	39		
B-17C	1	38		
B-17D	1	42		
B-17E	1	512		
B-17F	56	2,300	605	500
B-17G	65	4,035	2,395	2,250
		6,981	3,000	2,750
		(54.83%)	(23.56%)	(21.60%)

Total production: 12,761.

Left: A B-17E in service with RAF Coastal Command, 1945. Many later B-17s with the RAF were used in airborne radar navigation and ECM roles.

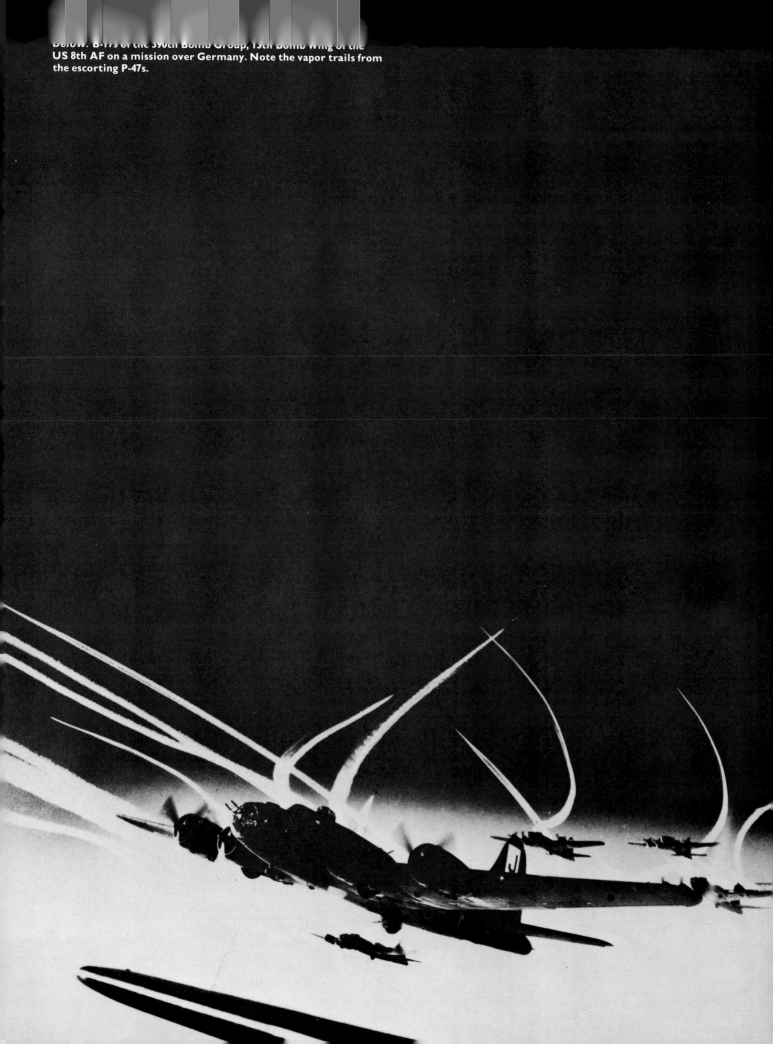

Below: B-17s of the 390th Bomb Group, 13th Bomb Wing of the US 8th AF on a mission over Germany. Note the vapor trails from the escorting P-47s.

P-51
MUSTANG

P-51
MUSTANG

William Newby Grant

Below: **Prototype Cavalier Mustang II – a postwar COIN development.**

INTRODUCTION

The North American P-51 Mustang fighter which flew with the United States Army Air Force and the Royal Air Force during World War II epitomizes American drive and initiative in its conception and design, while its performance was greatly enhanced in later models by the fitting of the British Rolls-Royce Merlin engine. Its story is one of success; from unpromising beginnings, the Mustang went on to become the high-altitude long-range escort fighter *par excellence* once the Merlin was installed. Before this it mainly flew low-level reconnaissance missions for which it proved eminently suitable. However with long-range tanks, the Merlin Mustangs could reach beyond Berlin and range over Europe as far as Austria and Czechoslovakia from the United Kingdom.

During the war it was employed as a fighter, fighter-bomber, dive bomber and reconnaissance aircraft. The basic design was so sound that the only modifications, apart from the engine, were concerned with increasing its armament, its range, and its pilot's all-round vision.

From airfields and landing grounds along the east coast of Britain, in Italy, France, Burma, China and the Pacific, the P-51 carried the war to the enemy and from 1944 played a large part in dominating the skies over Germany. Between 1 July

P-51D of the 376th Fighter Squadron, 361st Fighter Group based at Little Walden wearing invasion stripes.

1940 and 31 August 1945 a total of 14,501 P-51s of all Marks were produced, and the original stipulated cost per machine of $50,000 was only exceeded by $500. By way of comparison a Republic P-47 Thunderbolt cost $83,000 and a Boeing B-17 Flying Fortress $187,742.

The P-51 was a fine airplane. Most pilots who flew the early Allison-engined aircraft preferred them to the later Merlin-powered ones which were harder to handle. The Mustang was on balance the equal of all piston-engined opponents which it encountered, and also had the pleasing lines which so often herald a machine with performance to match. It was

maneuverable, carried a respectable armament and because of its weight was fast in the dive. While the P-51 must be placed in context with all the other participants of the war in the air, it is fair to say that it made an inestimable contribution to ultimate Allied victory. The narrative which follows unfolds its development and traces its participation in the battles of World War II and Korea, where the Mustang also played an important part, as well as touching on the more peaceful but no less hectic uses to which it was put in peacetime.

William Newby Grant

CONCEPTION AND EA

When the British Purchasing Commission led by Sir Henry Self was sent to the United States in 1938 with the aim of acquiring American-built military aircraft which the Government realized would soon be needed, it visited a number of major aircraft manufacturing companies. At the time America was pursuing a policy of strict neutrality but nevertheless, during the years of depression in the 1930s, its aircraft manufacturers were delighted to receive orders to build warplanes of various types. Providing the purchasing power was not actually at war this was acceptable to Congress. The Royal Air Force promptly benefited from the purchase of the Lockheed Hudson – based on the Company's Model 14 Electra airliner – and the AT–6 Harvard which was manufactured by North American Aviation Inc.

North American Aviation typified American drive, energy and enthusiasm and, as a result of the Harvard contract, took its place among the front rank American aviation companies. It had arrived on the scene comparatively late in 1928, and since 1934 had devoted its attention to building military airplanes. It was a California-based company, located at the Los Angeles Municipal Airport (or Mines Field) at Inglewood.

In 1939 the United States placed an embargo on the export

of military equipment, but an act passed by Congress permitted the shipment of this in the purchasing power's own merchant vessels. As a result the British and the French, who were equally interested in ordering military aircraft for the Armée de l'Air, were still able to acquire them. The decision to allow the exporting to continue reflects the fundamental American good will toward the two nations. It also made sound business sense, enabling the American aircraft industry to gear itself up to mass-production methods. This was of considerable importance to the United States after the Japanese attack on Pearl Harbor brought her into the war in December 1941.

The president of North American Aviation was James H Kindelberger. 'Dutch' Kindelberger had amassed a wealth of manufacturing experience with the Glenn Martin and Douglas Companies before joining North American Aviation. He had also toured Germany and Great Britain to visit their respective aircraft factories in the late 1930s. His vice-president was John Atwood who had been chief engineer of the company, a post now filled by Raymond Rice. North American had been both efficient and punctual with its deliveries of AT-6 Harvards to Great Britain, and it was natural that the British

Below: **Curtiss P-40 Hawk. The British Purchasing Commission were so impressed by the Hawk's performance that they commissioned North American to produce an improved P-40 – the P-51.**

RLY HISTORY

Purchasing Commission should approach it with a view to producing the Curtiss P-40 Hawk (which was to become the RAF's Tomahawk 1), a type for which orders had been placed in 1940 by the British and the French. The Curtiss Hawk utilized the Allison in-line engine and proved to be a machine of versatility and strength, particularly suited to Army co-operation and low-level attack operations. However it was not supercharged, and this meant its performance at altitude was mediocre. The Purchasing Commission was well aware of its limitations, but *faute de mieux* pressed ahead with orders which amounted to a total of 1740, shared between the RAF and the Armée de l'Air.

To the board of North American Aviation it appeared that, however worthy an airplane the P-40 might be, a better machine could be designed. When the proposition to build the P-40 was put to the company in January 1940, James Kindelberger and John Atwood approached the British Purchasing Commission with the suggestion that North American design a fighter of their own. They saw Colonel William Cave and Air Commodore G B A Baker of the Commission at their New York offices and discussed the proposal. It was evidently well received since in April, Atwood was

summoned to Sir Henry Self who, after studying P-40 wind-tunnel test reports furnished by John Atwood, signed a draft contract for 320 NA-73 fighter aircraft – as the projected machine's designation was to be. The aircraft would incorporate the Allison engine of the P-40 in a revolutionary low-drag airframe capable of mass production and armed to British specifications.

Time was of the essence in the spring of 1940 and Sir Henry Self's decision was a daring one. Despite their proven efficiency in Harvard deliveries the North American Company had no experience of building fighter aircraft, so the ordering of 320 machines of a type not yet even designed was a singular act of faith.

Frantic activity now took place at the company. On 24 April 1940 the engineers at Inglewood were notified by telegram and immediately commenced drawings, for only outline sketches had been available for Sir Henry Self's perusal. Plans were made overnight by Edgar Schmued, Chief Designer of the company, in collaboration with Raymond Rice and sent direct to John Atwood in New York. There he presented them to the members of the Commission who confirmed the order for the 320 machines on 29 May 1940.

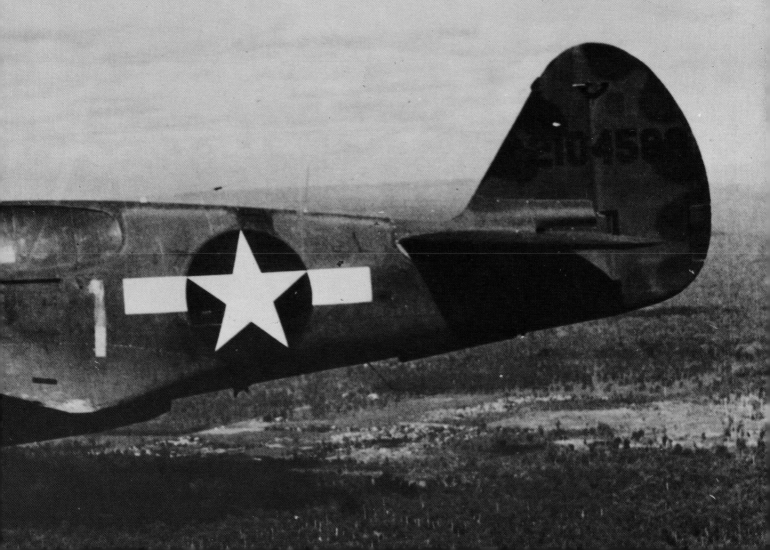

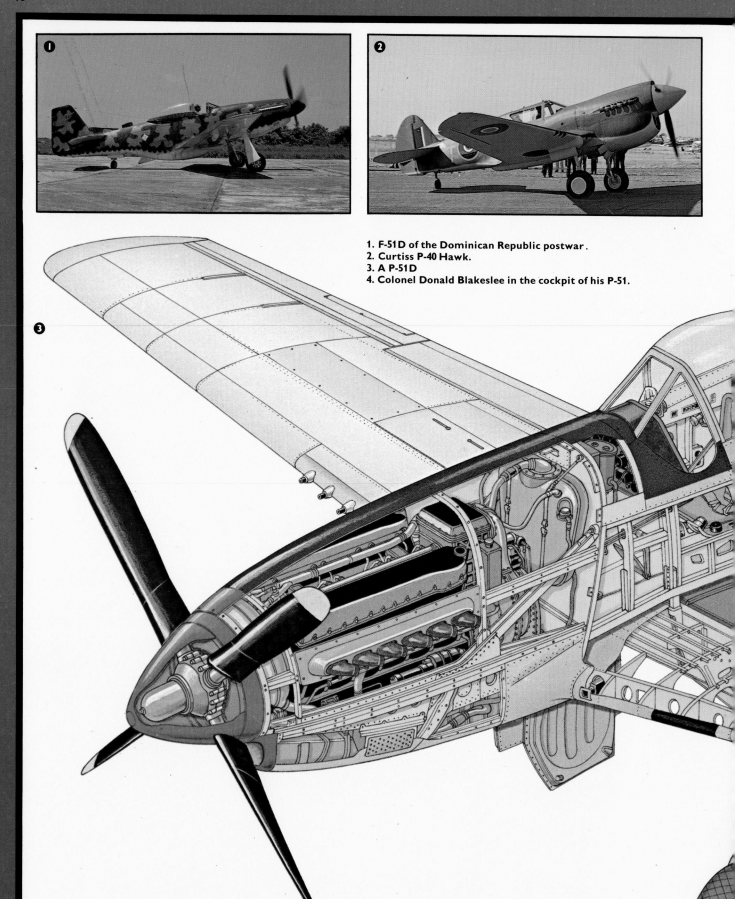

1. F-51D of the Dominican Republic postwar.
2. Curtiss P-40 Hawk.
3. A P-51D
4. Colonel Donald Blakeslee in the cockpit of his P-51.

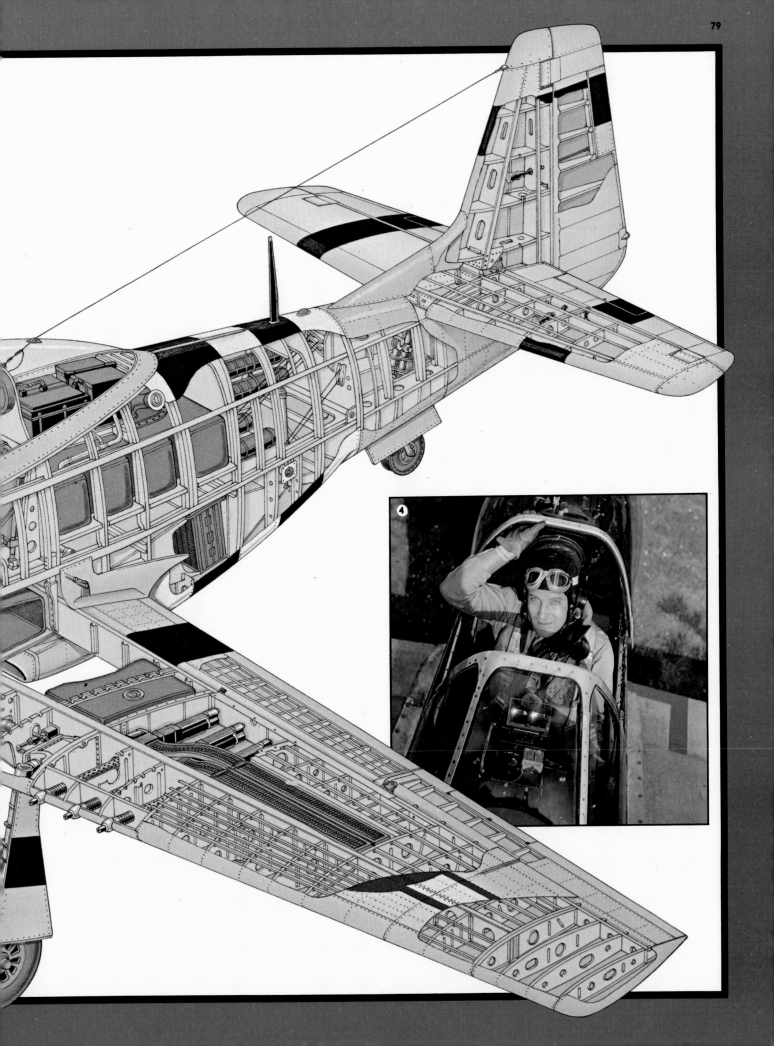

④

1. P-51D of the 504th Fighter Squadron, 339th Fighter Group based at Fowlmere, Cambridgeshire.
2. The fourth production XP-51 (serial 41-38) tested by the USAAF.
3. A P-51D, an earlier version with six .5 caliber machine guns.
4. Staff Sergeants James Lammering and Wilbur Stewart working on a P-51.
5. 108 US-gallon auxiliary fuel tank is fitted beneath a P-51.
6. Control column and cockpit detail.
7. Cockpit controls:

1 cockpit floodlight	25 oxygen economizer
2 gunsight	26 cockpit cover jettison handle
3 cockpit floodlight	27 cockpit floodlight switch
4 cockpit floodlight	28 control column
5 throttle	29 gun and bomb switches
6 compass	30 parking brake
7 clock	31 instructions for parking brake
8 suction gauge	32 engine primer
9 manifold pressure gauge	33 oxygen pressure gauge
10 remote control	34 oxygen system warning light
11 altimeter	35 bomb lever
12 directional gyro	36 undercarriage selector
13 flight indicator	37 booster pump switches
14 RPM counter	38 supercharger control
15 oxygen flow blinker indicator	39 warning light for supercharger
16 mixture lever	40 starter
17 propeller control	41 oil dilution switch
18 carburetor mixture control	42 ignition switch
19 undercarriage position indicator	43 compass light switch
20 air speed indicator	44 gunsight lamp switch
21 turn and bank indicator	45 cockpit floodlight switch
22 rate of climb indicator	46 fuel cock and tank selector
23 coolant temperature gauge	47 hydraulic pressure gauge
24 oil temperature and fuel and oil gauges	48 fairing door emergency control

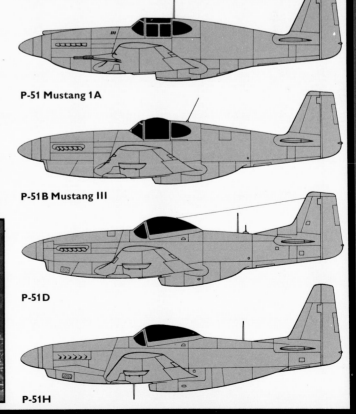

P-51 Mustang 1A

P-51B Mustang III

P-51D

P-51H

Stipulations accompanied the order, however. The NA-73 prototype was to be ready in the time it would have taken North American to tool up for P-40 production, namely 120 days, and the cost per aircraft was not to exceed $50,000. Of these the time scale was critical, and the company set to at once. The Allison V-1710 power plant was to be housed in a low-drag airframe and from the start strenuous efforts were made to reduce drag in every conceivable way. The fuselage was as thin as practicable, with the Allison mounted in a close-fitting cowling. Its radiator was installed below the fuselage slightly to the rear of the cockpit, and there was a small carburetor air intake above the nose. To reduce the unavoidable drag of the radiator duct this was aerodynamically designed, and a certain amount of additional thrust was even provided by a variable exit shutter. Such attention to detail was to be fully rewarded.

An innovation in fighter airplane design was the laminar flow airfoil section wing. This was an advanced concept only recently pioneered and designed by the National Advisory Committee for Aeronautics at North American Aviation. It consisted of a section in which the maximum chord thickness was well aft of the conventional position near the leading edge. The laminar flow was thereby maintained longer before it began to create turbulence, and by maintaining the boundary layer was instrumental in reducing drag. The original NA-73 was not intended to have this wing, and its adoption was the result of Ed Horkey and his team of aerodynamicists' studies. Initial wind-tunnel tests held at the California Institute of Technology on a one-quarter-scale wing proved disappointing, however; the wing's behavior in the stall appeared unsatisfactory, and minor alterations had little effect. This was a severe setback for the design team, but tests conducted in a larger wind-tunnel at the University of Seattle, Washington, proved that the previous results had been misleading, and that the wingtip turbulence problems previously indicated had now disappeared.

These tests also highlighted the drag induced by the unavoidably large radiator duct needed for cooling the glycol for the liquid-cooled Allison. Laminar flow problems associated with the boundary layer in front of it appeared to result in air not being reduced in velocity as it entered the radiator as planned, without which the projected ram effect to help counteract drag could not take place. The slight lowering of the front of the duct solved this problem, and the air slowed down and expanded to draw heat from the radiator before being ejected.

Everyone at North American was working to maximum capacity. Each department constantly checked findings and mockups were made of all assemblies. The NA-73 had to be suitable for mass-production methods, and so castings were employed. The 120-day deadline was achieved. Indeed the prototype NA-73X was wheeled out on 30 August 1940 with three days to spare. The machine lacked an engine, and rested upon AT-6 wheels, but at least it was an airplane of clean lines which had taken a mere 117 days from conception to birth. Allisons had suffered production delays with the 1550hp V-1710-F3R engine and it was October before engine and airframe could be married, but during this period it was apparent to the Purchasing Commission that the design was sound, and a further 300 machines were ordered.

On 26 October 1940 the prototype NA-73X, registration number NX 19998, with chief test pilot Vance Breeze at the controls lifted off Mines Field. The twenty-minute flight which

Left: **P-51B undergoing repair at Repair and Maintenance Centre, Warton, Lancs.**

followed was the realization of a highly ambitious project and a triumph for the North American company. The pilot's report was satisfactory, and the only problems which manifested themselves during the first four flights were minor overheating ones. Unfortunately the fifth flight on 20 November ended in disaster with the aircraft lying on its back beyond the airfield's perimeter. The test pilot, Paul Balfour, escaped unhurt. An error in switching fuel tanks had resulted in fuel starvation. In the inevitable forced landing which followed the machine struck soft ground and overturned.

This was naturally enough a severe blow to the company, but sufficient had already been learned about the NA-73 to realize that it was a success, and production could begin on the 620 machines which the British had ordered. At this time it acquired the name of Mustang; the British have always preferred names to designations and that of the wild horse of the southern states seemed a suitable choice, as it combined power and American ancestry.

The Mustang Mark I supplied to the Royal Air Force was provided under the terms of the Lend-Lease Bill which became law in March 1941. By that time British dollar reserves were seriously depleted and President Franklin D Roosevelt, intent on maintaining the flow of supplies to beleaguered Great Britain, had inaugurated the Bill as a gesture of solidarity as well as of unparalleled generosity. Considering Great Britain's survival 'vital to the defense of the United States' he authorized supplies to continue, and the second production Mustang, serial AG 346, was shipped to the United Kingdom in October 1941 to arrive at Liverpool on the 24th. During the Atlantic crossing the convoy with which it travelled was subjected to air attack, but it arrived safely, was assembled at Speke and test flown in November. The first Mustang produced, AG 345, remained in the United States for flight development testing.

*Below: **AG 345** – the first production Mustang for the RAF was retained for testing in the USA after its first flight which took place on 16 April 1941.*

In construction the Mustang was a low-wing cantilever monoplane whose laminar flow wing consisted of two sections bolted together at the center line of the fuselage, where the upper surface formed the cockpit floor. The wing, with five-degree dihedral, was a two-spar all-metal structure with an Alclad skin, and the spars had single-plate flanges and extruding top and bottom booms. The finish of the wing was critical to its performance, and had a direct influence upon the aircraft's speed and range. The remainder of the structure consisted of pressed ribs with flanged holes cut to lighten them and extruding lateral stringers. On each side of the center line and between the spars on each wing were self-sealing nonmetallic fuel tanks, with a total capacity of 184 US-gallons, to which access was gained by small hatch covers on the underneath of each wing. The wing's rear spar accommodated the aileron hinges and slotted flaps, which could be lowered to up to fifty degrees in five seconds to enable high rate turns to be made. The pitot head tube was fitted beneath the starboard wing, a landing light was set in its leading edge. The wing area was 233.19sq ft.

The fuselage of the Mustang was oval in shape and consisted of three sections – engine, main and tail. The engine section mounted two V-shaped cantilever engine bearers built up of plate webs, and with top and bottom extruded numbers, each of which was attached at two points to the 6mm-thick fireproof front bulkhead of the main section. The Vee 12-cylinder Allison engine was attached to these bearers, encased in the streamlined engine cowling, whose line was interrupted only by the top-mounted carburetor air intake. A twelve US-gallon oil tank was housed in the engine compartment.

The main fuselage section consisted of two beams, each side beam comprising two longerons which formed the caps, and the skin was reinforced by vertical frames forming the webs. These two longerons continued aft of the cockpit – which was set low into the fuselage to minimize drag and to which access was gained via a small door opening to port, while the canopy hinged to starboard – to a semi-monocoque structure which was reinforced by vertical frames. The rear part of the main

fuselage section extended further aft to form the detachable tail section. For the pilot's protection the front windshield was of 38mm laminated bullet-proof glass, and 8mm and 11mm armor plating was fitted behind his back. A reinforced crash arch offered protection in the event of his machine overturning, and the SCR-695 radio was mounted behind the cockpit.

The cantilever tail assembly consisted of a one-piece tailplane with detachable tips. The tailplane and fin were built up from two spars with extruded stringers and pressed ribs, and were also Alclad-covered. Trim tabs were fitted to the dynamically-balanced control surfaces, and the elevators and rudder were interchangeable.

The main landing gear was retractable, as was the steerable tail wheel. The two cantilever legs with their shock-absorbers were hinged to large forged fittings which, in turn, were bolted to reinforced ribs. When retracted inward by hydraulic pressure the undercarriage assembly lay forward of the main spar and was covered by wheel well covers, and even when the undercarriage was lowered the inner covers closed to improve the air flow. The brakes were also hydraulically operated, and the 11ft 10in wide track undercarriage endowed the aircraft with considerable stability when operating with a heavy load from rough ground.

Until now the Mustang had been designed by Americans for use by the British; initial United States Army Air Force (USAAF) interest was shown when two of the first production batch of ten machines were acquired as XP-51s and sent to the USAAF Test Center at Wright Field, Ohio. In the meantime Mustang Is began to arrive across the Atlantic in convoys and on arrival were assembled at Speke. Of the original 620 ordered, twenty were lost at sea when the merchantmen carrying them were sunk, but a steady stream arrived in 'CKD' condition – Crated Knocked Down – inside 35ft long wooden crates and covered in protective packing and grease. They were already camouflaged in the standard RAF day-fighter color scheme of dark green and dark earth upper surfaces, with sky (duck-egg blue) below, and spinners and an 18in wide fuselage band of the same color.

Above: **Franklin D Roosevelt and Winston Churchill meet at Quebec in August 1943, to discuss the second front in Europe.**

Tests were conducted as soon as possible at the Aeroplane and Armament Experimental Establishment at Boscombe Down on Salisbury Plain. These revealed that the Mustang I was a very sound machine with a useful turn of speed. It was capable of 375mph at 15,000ft, whereas the RAF's Spitfire V achieved some 340mph, but the Spitfire's rate of climb was superior at seven minutes to 20,000ft. The Mustang needed eleven minutes, mainly because of the limitations of the unsupercharged Allison engine at altitude, and partly because the Mustang, at 8600lb was some 1700lb heavier. It immediately became apparent that the V-1710 engine was the Mustang's greatest disadvantage. At 11,800ft it produced 1150hp (1470hp for War Emergency) but above this height performance tailed off considerably, maximum speed dropping to 357mph at 21,000ft, which meant that it was outclassed by both the Spitfire V and the Messerschmitt Bf 109F.

During the 1920s and 1930s the American Aviation industry had largely ignored the liquid-cooled in-line engine, choosing instead to concentrate on the development of the air-cooled radial. The latter was simpler, lighter and of known reliability, and even with the advent of modern low-wing monoplane fighters of the 1930s, designers still tended to retain the radial, despite the drag penalty incurred by the larger frontal area. The state of development of in-line engines was, therefore, not as advanced in the United States as elsewhere.

Various other drawbacks came to light, including the limitations of visibility from the cockpit, and the difficulty of fitting tall pilots into it. There was also the risk of damage from foreign objects when the slipstream from the propeller blasted loose objects into the mouth of the radiator duct when taxying over rough ground. These were, however, offset by the findings of the pilots engaged in the evaluation of the Mustang. At low altitudes it handled beautifully, was responsive, stable, maneuverable and fast in the dive. Initial skepticism from the RAF about American claims on the latter was dispelled when a speed of 500mph was attained and the Allison engine ran sweetly.

The question now arose as to how the airplane might best be employed. Its poor performance at altitude clearly indicated that it would not survive when matched against the latest Messerschmitt 109 fighters, and by the winter of 1940, with the Battle of Britain won, Fighter Command was intent on developing the Spitfire for high-altitude work. The lower the Mustang flew the happier it seemed, so the logical place for it was with Army Co-operation Command. This Command's objective was to provide close support for the Army, acquire intelligence for it by means of aerial photography and fly tactical reconnaissance missions. The Mustang was admirably suited to this work.

ALLISON-ENGINED MU

A change in philosophy took place in the Royal Air Force's Army Co-operation Command following experience gained in France in 1940. It was clear that only fast moving, highly maneuverable aircraft would stand a reasonable chance of survival in low-level photographic reconnaissance missions. The Mustang Is of Army Co-operation Squadrons were fitted with F24 cameras which were mounted behind the pilot's seat to point out to port through a clear-vision panel, and which could take films of either 125 or 250 exposures to produce prints 5in by 5in. Camera alignment was by means of a mark on the trailing edge of the port wing, and this required both nicety of judgment and a cool head when flying against defended targets. Operational height was around 900ft and Mustangs flew in pairs; the leader took the photographs while his wingman provided top cover.

The Mustang was a welcome replacement for the aircraft which it had eclipsed, the Curtiss P-40 Tomahawk which had been employed until 1942 on Army Co-operation duties. In January that year the first Mustang had been collected by the first of eighteen planned Mustang Squadrons. By April 1942 26 Squadron, based at Gatwick Airfield south of London, was equipped but not operational, as were 2, 238, 400 and 414 Squadrons of the RAF's 39 Wing. The 400 (City of Toronto) and 414 (Sarnia Imperials) Squadrons were from the Royal Canadian Air Force. The Mustang was capable of considerably more than merely taking photographs; its low-level operating

height meant that opportunity targets which presented themselves could be engaged using the aircraft's armament. This consisted of two .5in Browning machine guns with 400 rounds of ammunition, each mounted inside the Allison's engine compartment, synchronized to fire through the propeller arc and with blast tubes emerging beneath the nose. In each wing a further .5in with two .3in machine guns were housed, thus bringing the total of guns to eight. For the .5in guns a variety of ammunition was available. The M2 Ball Cartridge fired a 700 grain bullet at 2810ft per second, and Armor Piercing M2, Tracer M10, Incendiary M1 and AP/Incendiary rounds were also used. The rate of fire per barrel was 800 rounds per minute.

On 10 May 1942 the Mustang I flew its first operational sortie against the French coast in the area of Berck-sur-Mer. It was AG 418, flown by Flying Officer G Dawson of 26 Squadron based at Gatwick. This was the first of many such forays – known as Populars – during the course of which Mustangs engaged many targets of opportunity and encountered the highly accurate German light anti-aircraft defenses which were to exact such a toll of them. These defenses and the very nature of low-level high-speed flying combined to make such reconnaissance missions extremely dangerous; the first Mustang to be lost was AG 415, flown by Pilot Officer H Taylor, which crashed into the water while strafing a barge in mid-July. On 24 July a press day was held at Sawbridgeworth.

RAF Army Co-operation Command Mustang Is of 2 Squadron, Sawbridgeworth.

STANGS

Mustangs from all five Squadrons flew in support of the ill-fated amphibious assault on Dieppe on 19 August 1942. A total of 72 sorties were flown and nine aircraft were lost and two further ones were written off. The British losses were only partly offset by the destruction of one enemy aircraft – a Focke Wulf FW 190 – which fell to the guns of a 414 (Canadian) Squadron Mustang flown by Flying Officer Hollis Hills, an American volunteer flying with the RCAF. Despite the losses, Mustangs continued to harass the enemy along the Channel coast and inland areas, and maintained the task of keeping up-to-date photographic intelligence of German defenses. Other tasks allotted included flying sorties to identify shipping and intercepting low-level attacks by Focke-Wulf 190s along the British south coast. Over Europe any train spotted was attacked, as were enemy transport columns and trainer aircraft, and the constant surprise attacks in rear areas must have been most unsettling for the Germans. At the same time it provided evidence to the populations of the occupied countries that the Allies were again on the offensive.

In October 1942 a new type of operation was authorized. This was known as the Rhubarb, and made use of bad weather and low cloud to provide suitable conditions for engaging specific targets on the Continent. For these missions Army Co-operation Command Mustangs flew under the operational control of Fighter Command, and targets included enemy airdromes, transport of all types and any aircraft encountered. A long-range operation took Mustangs into German airspace for the first time on 21 October on a mission to the Dortmund–Ems canal which also incorporated shipping strikes in the Netherlands on the return flight. These Rhubarbs placed an additional strain on the pilots, who now had to contend with poor weather conditions as well as the usual hazards, demands of pilot navigation at low level and the transcription of intelligence data onto special knee pads.

At this time Mustangs carried, in addition to the Sky identification bands around their rear fuselages and spinners, a narrow yellow band painted just inboard of the roundels on the wings. These were introduced to help prevent misidentification of the aircraft by friendly air and ground forces, and were conceived after several Mustangs had been shot down by Allied fighters whose pilots had mistaken the then unfamiliar shape for that of the German Messerschmitt Bf 109 – an understandable mistake since the 109E had square wing tips too. The general outline was also similar, and in any case in air fighting the pilot had to decide whether to open or hold fire in a matter of seconds. The bands tended to compromise the green and gray camouflage pattern and, with the improvements in recognition, were removed before long. The early color scheme had been changed in August 1941 to dark green and ocean gray upper and sea-gray medium lower surfaces. This color scheme was more suited to the cross-Channel operations in which the aircraft were increasingly taking part. At the same time new roundels were introduced and the white part of the fin flash was considerably reduced.

The radius of action of 300 miles was unique for a single-engined fighter and resulted from its clean lines and laminar flow wing. This radius included a generous margin for safety's sake, and took into account transit and operational heights and speeds. It was twice that of Hurricanes and Spitfires and, in an attempt to show the high standard a Mustang was capable of achieving, an enterprising Flight Lieutenant named J Lewkowicz of 309 Czerwienskiej (Polish) Squadron made an unauthorized flight from his base at Dalcross near Inverness in Scotland to Stavanger in Norway and back again on 27 September. Over Stavanger he indulged in a little strafing, and his feat of calculated risk and first-class navigation brought him a

commendation as well as the inevitable reprimand. It had proved that the Mustang could penetrate to far greater distances than had previously been considered possible.

In 1943 the first Ranger missions were undertaken. These were flown by small free-lance groups of Mustangs at low level and at 300mph over occupied Europe and over the Bay of Biscay by 414 (Canadian) Squadron. Losses continued to mount, and not all were attributable to enemy action; a flight of four Mustangs from 2 Squadron lost three airplanes when they encountered sea fog while crossing the English coast in Dorset in May and hit high ground. By this time additional Squadrons had been formed or re-equipped with Mustangs, and the RAF now had at its disposal, in addition to the original five, 4, 13, 16, 63, 116, 168, 225, 239, 241, 268, 309 (Polish), 430 (Canadian) and 613 Squadrons. Among them all, 400 (Canadian) Squadron had enjoyed particular success with the large-scale destruction of enemy trains, and one pilot, Flight Lieutenant D Grant, had claimed thirty. Many enemy aircraft had been shot down by day and by night and worthwhile targets had been regularly attacked.

Squadrons were rotated and when not flying on operations provided the air element for Army exercises. Mustang Squadrons – some now equipped with the Mustang Mark IA with four 20mm cannons in place of the eight machine guns – were attached to individual Army formations and helped to train their troops for the invasion. Army Co-operation Command was incorporated into the Second Tactical Air Force in June 1943. Its Mustangs had done excellent work, and a year previously the *Aeroplane* journal provided the following comment on the type: 'Pilots who fly the Mustang praise it so lavishly that they exhaust their superlatives before they have finished their eulogies.'

While the Mustang was winning its spurs in the skies over Europe, the United States had ordered 150 Mustang IAs with their quadruple 20mm M-2 cannons as P-51-NAs in September 1941, and had, of course, taken delivery of the two original RAF production batch. American interest in the field of air support to ground forces for reconnaissance had been heightened following a study of British experience, and when America entered the war on 7 December 1941 after the Japanese attack on Pearl Harbor, attention was directed toward the two rather neglected XP-51s which had been languishing at Wright Field. Fifty-five of the Mustang IAs ordered for the RAF were repossessed and fitted with two K.24 (American-built British F.24) cameras. These were given the designation F-6A and were originally intended to bear the name Apache; however, the name adopted for the RAF machine stuck. The first F-6As flew tactical reconnaissance missions with two Observation Squadrons (111th and 164th) of the 68th Observation Group in North Africa in March 1943. On their tailplanes they carried the Stars and Stripes.

The P-51A was a fighter version ordered for the United States Army Air Force. In place of the cannon they mounted four .5in Brownings in their wings, and 358 were ordered. The P-51A dispensed with the nose armament and was powered by an Allison V-1780-81 engine which provided 1200hp on takeoff and full power at 20,000ft, a considerable advance upon the original P-51. Pylons were provided for underwing stores, which could be either two 500lb bombs or 75 or 150 US-gallon drop tanks. The RAF received fifty examples of the P-51A as the Mustang Mark II; the only Allison-engined Mustangs used by the Americans in the United Kingdom were P-51As converted to F-6A status and flown by the 107th Tactical Reconnaissance Group in October 1943.

The spring of 1942 had seen another development of the Mustang, the A-36A dive bomber. Studies of other air forces

Above: **In its element – an RAF Mustang flies low and fast. The Mustangs' tactics over Occupied Europe were to fly just above the ground and treetops.**

had indicated that fighter aircraft could be employed in this role, and the Mustang's high speed in the dive was put to good use. The first A-36A flew in September 1942 and incorporated various modifications necessary to strengthen the machine. Hydraulically-operated air brakes which opened above and below the wing slowed the rate of descent in a high-angle dive to some 300mph, and bomb shackles were fitted to a heavier than standard wing. Each wing also housed two .5in machine guns and the ventral radiator air duct was modified. An order for 500 A-36s was placed and the first saw action over Pan-

telleria in June 1943 with the 27th Bomb Group. In Sicily this was joined by the 86th Bomb Group and targets on the island and on the Italian mainland continued to be attacked in support of ground forces from September. The same month saw the title changed to Fighter Bomber Groups and the reduction of one of the four Squadrons in each. Losses had been moving toward unacceptable levels, however; the A-36A was vulnerable in its low-level pull out, and aircraft were known to disintegrate when the unequal extension of the air brakes led to their being over-stressed. Eventually the A-36s were replaced by P-47 Thunderbolts in early 1944, but not before the 27th FB Group won a Distinguished Unit Citation for its operations during the Salerno landings on 10 September 1943.

A-36s flew aerial resupply missions to American ground forces in Italy and some served with the 111th Tactical Reconnaissance Squadron. The name Invader was bestowed upon the aircraft briefly in 1943, but was subsequently allocated to the Douglas A-26 bomber. The RAF received a single A-36A which became EW 998 and on which bombing trials were carried out.

At this stage it is worth comparing the Allison-engined Mustang with an enemy fighter with which it frequently came into contact, the Focke-Wulf FW 190. During the war comparative trials were held both in Great Britain and the United States to evaluate captured enemy machines with the aim of subsequently exploiting any weaknesses. The results of these trials serve only as a guide, for there was a natural enough prejudice toward and preference for one's own machines, and a skilled pilot in an inferior aircraft would probably be able to defeat a less experienced one in a better machine. In a trials report of August 1942 a captured Focke-Wulf 190A-3 was flown against a Mustang IA of the RAF.

Up to 23,000ft, speeds showed little difference except in the band between 10,000ft and 15,000ft, at which height the Mustang was 10-15mph faster. In both standard and zoom climbs the FW 190 was superior, while in a dive there was little to choose. In terms of maneuverability the FW 190 was superior except in radius of turn, and the Mustang was slower to accelerate. If attacked, the FW 190's best option was to climb, since, unlike the Spitfire with its gravity-fed carburetor which cut off fuel under conditions of negative G, the Mustang could dive in pursuit without having to roll inverted and pull back on the stick. To evade the FW 190, a Mustang's pilot's best bet was to execute a sharp turn, since diving would not help. The trial found that the optimum height for the Mustang IA was between 5000ft and 15,000ft. To some extent the report was outdated at the time it appeared because the FW 190A-4 with its water-methanol injection improved its speed, but P-51 development was not static, and the Merlin-engined P-51B was on its way.

Above left: **Training for war – fighter-bomber releasing its bombs at the AAF Tactical Center, Orlando, Florida.**
Left: **Tactical reconnaissance operations: presortie briefing, England, 5 April 1943.**

MERLIN-ENGINED MUS

The Allison Mustangs had proved beyond doubt that the basic design of the airplane was sound, but the limitations of its engine above 25,000ft were succinctly summarized in the RAF opinion that it was 'a bloody good airplane, only it needs a bit more poke.' Consideration had been given to this problem on both sides of the Atlantic, and in England a test pilot named Ronald Harker flew a Mustang I in April 1942 as part of his job of evaluating Allied and enemy types, at the Air Fighting Development Unit at Duxford in Cambridgeshire. Impressed by its handling, he suggested to Rolls-Royce's Chief Aerodynamic Engineer at Hucknall, W Challier, that the Mustang's performance would be considerably enhanced if a Rolls-Royce Merlin 61 with two-speed two-stage supercharger were fitted. This engine had powered a prototype Spitfire IX in which it had produced 417mph at 28,000ft, and both men realized that the combination of this sort of performance with the aerodynamically efficient airframe of the Mustang would revolutionize its potential. Challier estimated that the combination would result in 441mph at 25,600ft. The American Assistant Air Attaché in London, Lieutenant Colonel Thomas Hitchcock, was greatly excited by the prospect, and via his Ambassador arranged to provide the USAAF's General Henry H 'Hap' Arnold with details, and the recommendations of senior RAF officers, including Air Chief Marshal Sir Trafford Leigh-Mallory. Colonel Hitchcock – who, ironically, was to lose his life while flying a Mustang which disintegrated near Salisbury in April 1944 – was convinced the conversion would work, but General Arnold reserved judgment until practical experience had been gained. After all, the USAAF had the

P-38 Lightning and the P-47 Thunderbolt in service and, by this stage in 1942 their limitations had not yet been discovered.

Rolls-Royce began to effect the necessary conversion of four Mustangs designated Mustang Xs at Hucknall in June 1942. These aircraft were directed there from Speke and bore the serials AM 203, AM 208, AL 963 and AL 975. This last was the first conversion and, in place of the proposed Merlin 61, a special Merlin 65 with a two-stage supercharger and Bendix-Stromberg fuel injection was fitted. On 13 October 1942 AL 975G took to the air with Rolls-Royce's Chief Test Pilot Ronald Shepherd at the controls.

The Merlin had been neatly installed in the sleek nose of the Mustang on a new engine mounting. Visually the Merlin Mustang differed from its Allison-engined predecessor by the removal of the latter's carburetor air intake above the nose, and its incorporation with the intake scoop for the supercharger intercooler now located below the nose just aft of the spinner. The propeller on AL 975G was a 10ft 9in diameter four-bladed Rotol, although other conversions were tested with a specially designed 11ft 4in propeller. All four machines were to embody a number of modifications in the quest for optimum performance, including a series of alterations to the intercooler air exit on the fuselage sides between exhaust stubs and cockpit. Speed gradually improved, with 413mph in the full supercharger model being attained in November, and 390mph with medium supercharger. Various minor problems such as undercarriage doors opening in flight were rectified. Most striking to the test pilots was the difference the more powerful engine made to the airplane. To those accustomed

Right: The clean lines of a Packard Merlin-engined P-51.
Above right: The neat installation of the Packard-built Rolls-Royce Merlin.

TANGS

to the docile handling characteristic of the Allison Mustang, its successor proved a very different proposition. It was more vicious in the stall, less directionally stable – although the fitting of a dorsal strake in front of the fin improved this – and much noisier. By early 1943 the performance was such that it took the Merlin-engined Mustang just over six minutes to climb to 20,000ft as opposed to just over nine in the Mustang I.

The second Mustang to be converted was AM 208, and in this aircraft a speed of 433mph was reached at 22,000ft using full supercharger with 18lb per square-inch boost. The AM 203, the third conversion, carried the larger propeller; trials were carried out on this model to determine how new paint finishes affected performance. In February 1943 it was loaned to the USAAF for evaluation. The AL 963 was used for stability and carburation trials, and a special Merlin 65 with maximum boost pressure of 25lb per square inch and finally a Merlin 66 with a new intercooler was fitted. The AM 121, the first Mustang destined for conversion, had been retained for calibration trials but in turn was also fitted with a Merlin. It was extensively tested by the USAAF at Bovingdon, where it flew in the olive drab color scheme and American markings. Rolls-Royce also later studied the feasibility of fitting a Griffon 61 engine, but this venture never proceeded beyond the design stage.

In the United States development was proceeding, too, with the redesign of the P-51 to accommodate the Packard-built Merlin XX engine, the V-1650-3, which corresponded to the Merlin 61. The first two American conversions bearing the serial numbers 41-37352 and 41-37421 were carried out on two Mustang 1As, built for the RAF, and received the designation XP-51B. The first was flown on 30 November 1942 by test pilot Robert Chilton, and suffered overheating problems. These delayed the next flight until late December but General Arnold, now satisfied with the data supplied to him on British experiences with the Mustang X, recommended that large numbers be built, and the first P-51B production aircraft were delivered in June 1943. By careful design both intercooler radiator and main coolant radiator were incorporated into the same scoop, while beneath the nose only a small aperture was needed for the carburetor air intake. The improvement in performance over the P-51A Allison-engined Mustang was dramatic, and a top speed of 453mph at 28,800ft was attained using 1298hp War Emergency boost and a Hamilton Standard four-bladed constant speed propeller of 11ft 2in diameter with paddle blades. Armament consisted of four or six .5in Brownings with a total of 1260 rounds. The wing shackles could accept two 1000lb bombs or drop tanks of 75 or 150 US-gallon capacity. The P-51B weighed 6840lb empty and, in comparison with the P-51A, developed 1400hp for takeoff, 1530hp at 15,750ft, and 1300hp at 26,500ft, thus improving the P-51A's horsepower at optimum height by some 300.

The P-51B-NA was manufactured from June 1943 by North American Aviation at their Inglewood plant in Los Angeles, where a total of 1988 was eventually produced. The P-51C-NT was built at Dallas in Texas in a second North American factory which began production in August 1943, and where 1750 were built. There was no difference between the aircraft, and the designation merely indicated from which factory they had come. The RAF received 274 P-51Bs and 636 P-51Cs as Mustang Mark IIIs, and the Americans converted a total of 91 into F-6C reconnaissance aircraft. It was in the P-51B and P-51C that the Fighter Commands of the United States Army Air Forces were to go to war in Europe.

Right: **P-51s nearing completion on the Dallas production line, where a total of 1750 P-51Cs were built.**

USAAF OPERATIONS I

On 20 February 1942 General Henry Arnold, Commanding General of the USAAF, sent Brigadier General Ira C Eaker to the United Kingdom to establish the Headquarters of the United States 8th Air Force. In June its Commander, Major General Carl A Spaatz, arrived with a group of Staff Officers at RAF Hendon, and established his Fighter Headquarters on 18 June at Bushey Park a few miles beyond the suburbs of London, close to RAF Fighter Command's HQ at Bentley Priory. Brigadier General Eaker's aim was to launch a strategic air offensive against Germany using the Boeing B-17 Flying Fortress as his principal weapon. The Fortress had a heavy defensive armament, and initially the theoreticians were of the opinion that box formations could lay down such a heavy defensive fire with the interlocking arcs of their .5in machine guns that they would be immune to fighter attack. At this stage the fighter element of the 8th AF was regarded as a purely tactical arm, and thus the first P-51Bs were assigned to the US 9th Air Force, formed in October 1942 for tactical operations – at first with the Middle East Air Force – in support of the forthcoming invasion of Europe under the command of Major General Lewis H Brereton. The 9th AF's 100th Fighter Wing consisted of three Fighter Groups, the 354th (with 353, 355 and 356th Fighter Squadrons), the 357th (with 362, 363 and 364th Fighter Squadrons), and the 363rd (with 380, 381 and 382nd Fighter Squadrons) and moved to the United Kingdom in September 1943. Each Squadron consisted of sixteen aircraft.

All this was in the future. Air Chief Marshal Arthur Harris of Bomber Command and General Spaatz shared the belief that the war with Germany could be won by strategic bombing. While the two bomber forces shared the common aim of destroying Germany's aircraft-manufacturing and oil-production industries, their operations were conducted independently. From the outset the US 8th AF employed day-bombing techniques while the RAF's Bomber Command operated at night.

General Arnold suggested the establishment of five Pursuit – or Fighter – Groups, two of which would be reserved for UK defense while the other three conducted offensive air operations against the Germans. The first Fighter Group which arrived in June 1942 was equipped with Spitfire Vs, the type which had also been flown by the three Eagle Squadrons (71, 122 and 133) of American volunteers serving with the Royal Air Force. Meanwhile the B-17 Bombardment Groups had been formed and began to launch their first unescorted raids against targets in France. The first was an attack on Rouen on 17 August 1942 when twelve B-17s of 97th Bombardment Group accompanied by General Eaker encountered little resistance. The confidence which these early raids built up was soon to be dispelled.

In September 1942 the Eagle Squadrons were transferred to 8th AF Command, but most pilots were reassigned to the

Right: **Escort for the heavy bombers – a Packard Merlin P-51 in olive drab livery.**
Inset: **Brigadier General Ira C Eaker commander of the 8th AF's bomber command, was later to become C in C of the Mediterranean Air Command.**

EUROPE

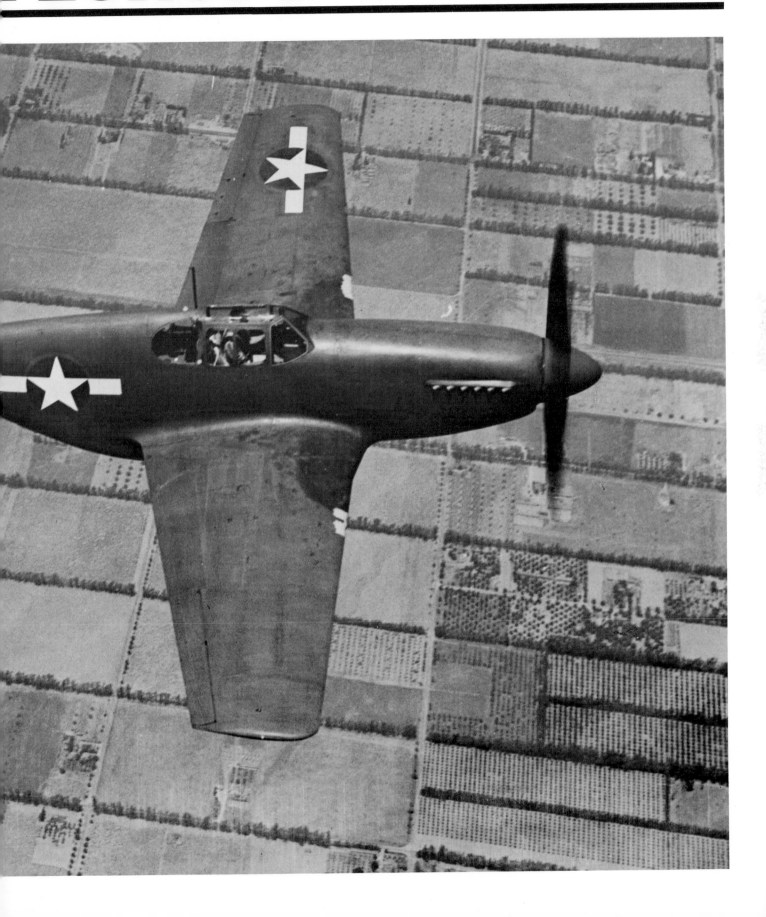

96

Above: **A 9th Air Force P-51B of the 355th Fighter Squadron, 354th Fighter Group.**
Below: **P-51B** – the radio and gunsight are visible.

12th Air Force in North Africa to fly P-38 Lightnings. In December 1942 8th AF Fighter Command began to receive the Republic P-47 Thunderbolt fighters which equipped the 4th, 56th and 78th Fighter Groups for escort duty with the bomber formations. However their maximum range on internal tanks was a mere 175 miles and this meant that, beyond a given point, the bombers flew on unescorted and faced the German fighters alone. In order to increase this range 200 US-gallon ventral drop tanks were fitted, but these proved unsatisfactory since they leaked and because of pressurization problems did not deliver fuel at heights of over 23,000ft. The first raid on Germany accompanied by P-47s was on 17 April 1943 when Bremen was attacked and sixteen B-17s were lost.

During the spring and summer of 1943 the 8th Air Force doggedly continued to send its bombers against Germany and suffered terrible losses as a result, culminating in the second raid on the German ball-bearing factories at Schweinfurt on 27 September 1943 when, of 291 B-17s dispatched, sixty were shot down, seventeen were severely damaged and 121 more were slightly damaged. During a previous raid on the same target in mid-August 36 aircraft had been lost out of a force of 230 on the same day as 24 were shot down during a simultaneous attack on the Messerschmitt factory at Regensburg.

These losses simply could not be sustained. The P-47 fighter escorts had sufficient range to escort the bombers only as far as Aachen on the second Schweinfurt raid, and 8th AF demands for P-51s with their vastly superior range were only met when the first P-51 Group arrived in the November of 1943. From then on the P-47 and P-51 were increasingly to exchange their roles. The P-51 began to operate as an escort at higher altitudes and the P-47 began to operate at a low level.

The 354th Fighter Group had been raised in the United States, trained on P-39 Airacobras, and arrived at Greenham Common airdrome near Newbury in Berkshire on 3 November 1943. This Pioneer Mustang Group was assigned not to the 8th but to the 9th Air Force, but Major General William Kepner of the former swiftly 'borrowed' them for escort duties. On 11 November the first P-51Bs arrived, much to the surprise of the pilots who had been expecting P-47 Thunderbolts. The 354th FG moved to Boxted near Colchester on the Essex coast to gain experience of the type under the command of Lieutenant Colonel Kenneth R Martin. Pilots checked out there on P-51As borrowed from the 10th and 67th Reconnaissance Groups of the 9th AF, and were reinforced by ex-Eagle Squadron members. No longer would the bombers have to fly alone, and the P-51 began to assume a strategic role.

The 354th FG consisted of three Fighter Squadrons, the 353rd, 355th and 356th, and flew its first operational mission on 1 December 1943, the date by which Colonel Martin had stated the Group would be operational. It was led by Major Donald J M Blakeslee, a highly experienced ex-Eagle Squadron pilot who had been sent to Boxted to fly the Mustang in November. Twenty-four P-51Bs took off from this airfield to carry out an offensive sweep over the Belgian and French coasts. The Group's first escort mission was to Amiens on 5 December, this was followed by raids on Emden and Kiel during which 75 US-gallon drop tanks provided a range of 500 miles. The first enemy aircraft to fall to the Group, a

Above: **P-51D from the 343rd Fighter Squadron, 55th Fighter Group, Wormingford, UK.**
Below: **The prototype P-51D.**

Messerschmitt Bf 110, was shot down by Lieutenant Charles Gumm of 355th FS during a raid on Bremen on 16 December, but on the same day the Commanding Officer of the 353rd FS, Major Owen M Seamen, went down into the icy gray waters of the North Sea after suffering engine failure.

By the New Year eight enemy aircraft had been claimed and eight P-51s had been lost, mainly because of mechanical failures. These were mostly problems associated with high-altitude flying, where windshields became covered in frost in the rarefied air six miles above the earth due to inadequate heating. The Packard-built Merlins suffered coolant leaks, and spark plugs became fouled. This problem was solved by the fitting of British-made ones. Guns iced up but a design weakness also manifested itself. When reports of the .5in Brownings' failure to fire were analyzed, it became clear that, when the aircraft was banked in a tight turn, the G forces applied to the belt feed mechanism retarded the ammunition belt and caused difficulties in feeding. Utilizing the recoil energy of the gun, the belt pull was increased to 70lb or to 80lb when an electric motor was used. This led to an improvement, but the configuration of the gun bays still meant that the Brownings had to be canted. A total of 1260 rounds were carried, and in October a new cartridge combining AP, Incendiary and Tracer was introduced.

In a Christmas message to the 8th and 15th Air Forces on 27 December, General Arnold stated 'Destroy the Enemy Air Force wherever you find them, in the air, on the ground and in the factories.' While their task of escorting bombers improved the crews' morale and chances of survival, the P-51 pilots were under considerable strain. Whereas the B-17s had two pilots and a crew, the P-51 pilot sat alone in his pressurized cockpit watching, navigating, scanning his instruments and oxygen supply, with the prospect of two flights over the North Sea in his single-engined machine with possible battle damage on the return one. To add to his difficulties the old problems of misidentification began to recur. On occasions Mustangs were attacked by Thunderbolts.

When he did engage the two most frequently-encountered German fighters, the P-51B pilot did have the advantage of the results of comparative trials carried out in the United Kingdom between his machine and the Messerschmitt Bf 109G-2 and the Focke-Wulf FW 190. These indicated that the P-51B was 50mph faster at all heights up to 28,000ft, beyond that 70mph faster than the FW 190, and between 30mph and 50mph faster than the Me 109. Rates of climbs were similar for all three aircraft, but the Mustang could outdive both German machines. Its radius of turn was marginally better than the Focke-Wulf's and much better than the Messerschmitt's, but while the former's rate of roll was superior, the latter's was inferior because its wing slots had the disconcerting habit of opening. Nevertheless several German fighter pilots maintain that both the German machines' rates of turn were superior and one, Erich Hartmann, who amassed a total of 352 Allied aircraft shot down in 1400 missions, maintains that he could outpace P-51s in the 109, and also obtain an indicated air speed of 480mph at 12,000ft.

With drop tanks fitted the speed at all heights was reduced by some 40–50mph because of additional weight and drag factors, but aerobatics were still possible and, provided the Mustang could convert height into speed, it could still be used offensively. At this stage the P-51B had a range of 1080 miles using its 170 US-gallon internal tanks, and a maximum range of 2600 miles when carrying two 150 US-gallon drop tanks. With 75 US-gallon ones fitted to the wing shackles, the range became 1800 miles, and with an additional self-sealing 85 US-gallon internal fuel tank mounted in the fuselage behind the pilot, the range became 1350 miles at 10,000ft on internal tanks. Consumption was calculated to be 8.85 air miles per gallon. A most important development at this time was the expendable lightweight 108 US-gallon drop tank built by the British firm of Bowaters from compressed paper, plastic and glue. Its life was limited but long enough for the four hours maximum required, and it could be converted into a weapon; unexpended fuel in the tanks could be ignited by incendiary

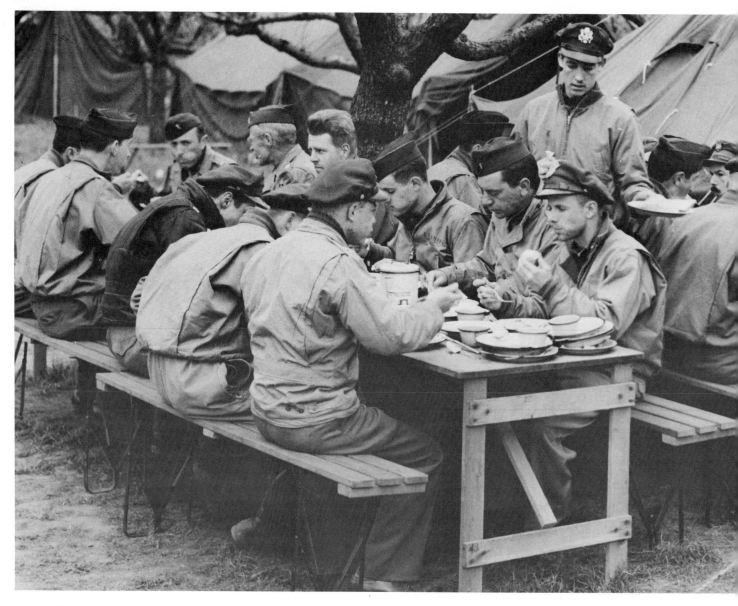

Above: **9th Air Force pilots 'chow up' at an advanced landing ground after returning from a bombing mission on Le Bourget, an airport in northern France.**

bullets if the tanks were dropped on enemy targets. Engine life of the Merlin was reckoned to be 200 hours.

By way of comparison the P-47 – designed as a bomber escort – originally carried a total of 305 US-gallons internally, which provided 605 miles at cruising speed. The P-47D with its 150 US-gallon ventral tank provided 850 miles. The -25RE could carry 780 US-gallons which, from March 1944 enabled the aircraft to reach Berlin. The P-47, incidentally, doubled the P-51B's armament.

In January 1944 the 354th Pioneer Mustang Group, still under the operational control of the 9th Air Force, was reinforced by two additional P-51 Groups. The 8th Air Force only gained its own P-51s when it exchanged its 358th (P-47) Fighter Group with the 9th Air Force's 357th (P-51) Fighter Group.

This second Mustang Group began operations from Leiston airfield - also known as Saxmundham – just inland from the Suffolk coast on 11 February 1944 under the command of Lieutenant Colonel James Howard. A former Commanding Officer of the 354th FG, Howard had been awarded the Congressional Medal of Honor on 11 January for attacking, single-handed, a large formation of Messerschmitt 110s which were

attacking a B-17 Group he was escorting over Halberstadt. Flying P-51B 43-6315 he disrupted the attack and claimed six probables. The same Fighter Group was to provide the 9th AF's top-scoring fighter pilot, Lieutenant Glenn Eagleston, with 18.5 victories, and the 353rd FS's Captain Don M Beerbower shot down 15.5.

The third Mustang Group, the 363rd, was established at Rivenhall in Essex and became operational on 22 February. Three days later the 4th Fighter Group, commanded by Lieutenant Colonel Donald Blakeslee, converted to the P-51 at Debden, and so in the spring of 1944 several hundred Mustangs regularly ranged over the skies of Germany. The 4th Fighter Group provided some of the most successful American fighter pilots of the war, including Captain Don S Gentile, an ex-133 Eagle Squadron member now flying with the 336th Fighter Squadron. Flying P-51B 43-6913 *Shangri-La* and forming a lethal partnership with his wingman, Captain John T Godfrey, Gentile shot down 21.8 enemy aircraft confirmed and his partner eighteen.

The 4th Fighter Group with its component 334, 335 and 336th Fighter Squadrons flew its first mission while the pilots had less than one hour logged on the type. The 336th FS became dispersed on the first planned raid over Berlin on 3 March 1944 because of bad weather, but Blakeslee's P-51s escorted American bombers over the German capital on the

destroyed while ground strafing was made at this time. Such was the attrition for the German Jagdverbände that by the end of April the 4th FG had amassed 500 victories. On 13 April Don Gentile had contrived to hit the ground while beating up his base at Debden prior to returning to the United States having completed his tour. The tempo increased with the build up to D-Day on 6 June 1944, and over a thousand American fighters were in the air over occupied Europe on a single day late in May.

To follow the fortunes of the 354th Pioneer Mustang Group, on 1 March Lieutenant Gumm suffered engine failure on take off from Boxted in 43-12410 and was killed in the ensuing forced landing. On 17 April the Group moved to a new base at Lashenden in Kent under the command of Lieutenant Colonel George R Bickell, and was awarded a Distinguished Unit Citation. Following the invasion, it flew to France and in July the Supreme Allied Commander, General Dwight D Eisenhower, flew over the battlefield in a Squadron two-seater conversion 43-6877. Shortly after receiving a second Distinguished Unit Citation for destroying 51 enemy aircraft on 25 August, the 354th was ordered to convert on to P-47s. It voiced its displeasure so strongly that in February 1945 it received P-51s back. When the war ended the 354th was the highest scoring USAAF Fighter Group with 701 aerial and 255 ground victories.

The Royal Air Force had, meanwhile, received P-51Bs as the Mustang III, and one Wing operated them from Gravesend in Kent. This was 122 Wing, and consisted of three Squadrons, 19, 65 and 122. Partly because tall pilots found themselves cramped beneath their canopies and partly to improve rearward vision, a bulged canopy similar to the Spitfire's was designed by R Malcolm, and fitted at the A and AEE Boscombe Down. This became known as the Malcolm hood and alleviated the problem which was only solved by the introduction of the full blister canopy on the P-51D. In February 1944 the RAF received its first Malcolm-hooded Mustangs, and the USAAF began a program of modification for its P-51Bs and Cs.

A new Mark of P-51 arrived in the United Kingdom at the time of the invasion, the P-51D. The first Inglewood-built models began to leave the production lines in February 1944 and Dallas-made ones in July. In addition to the blister canopy with its five-ply armored Lucite front panel, other modifications included the lowering of the fuselage top necessitated by the new canopy. This naturally resulted in a reduction of fuselage side area, and a strake was fitted in front of the fin to later P-51Ds – and retro-fitted to many earlier ones – to compensate and improve directional control. The P-51D also had an improved armament fit of six .5in Browning MG-53-2 machine guns; the inner guns carried 400 rounds and the center and outer ones 270 each, giving a total of 1800 rounds. All six barrels produced a total of eighty rounds a second. The prime task of the P-51s was still escorting the bombers, but the available firepower was put to good use over the Continent whenever the circumstances allowed.

The K-14 gyroscopic gun sight developed from the RAF's Gyro Gunsight Mk IID was first fitted to Colonel Donald Graham's brand new P-51D 41-3388 'Bodacious' of the 357th FG. Shortly afterward it began to replace the N-9 sight and, once mastered, provided more accurate deflection shooting. The P-51D carried the 85 US-gallon tank in its fuselage as a standard fitting. Its wings were strengthened to accept two 1000lb bombs or a combination of 500lb ones and drop tanks, or 5in High Velocity Aircraft Rockets, for which projector mountings were fitted to the last 1100 P-51Ds manufactured at Inglewood. Triple bazooka-type rocket launchers had previously been fitted.

following day, despite appalling weather conditions. On 6 March the 357th FG shot down twenty German aircraft without loss; already rivalry was building up both between Fighter Squadrons within a Group, and between exponents of the P-51 and the P-47 which, it should be remembered, was engaged in combat missions of equal intensity, as indeed were the P-38 Lightnings.

From mid-February 1944 USAAF Mustangs began to dispense with their olive drab finish and it was discovered that in their base metal finish they flew some 5mph faster because of the reduction of skin friction. Some ground crews applied wax polish to their P-51s to improve speed still further. On 23 March color schemes for individual Squadrons were adopted, and the colored markings were applied to spinners, engine cowlings and fin and rudder. This reflected growing Allied air superiority and the infrequency of German attacks on United Kingdom air bases, where camouflage had previously been advisable for dispersed aircraft.

The 4th Fighter Group shot down its 300th victim on 29 March, and such was the range of the Mustang that strafing forays took place on targets as far away as Munich and Berlin in early April. This was highly dangerous because of the effectiveness of the German flak, and destroying aircraft on the ground was no easy way of acquiring victories. The controversial decision to award a victory for an enemy aircraft

Top left: Arming a P-51 with .5 caliber ammunition.
Top: Generals Auton, Eisenhower, Spaatz, Doolittle and Major General Kepner.
Above: A fine air-to-air shot of a P-51D over England.

In May 1944 the first P-51Ds began to arrive in Great Britain to replace the P-51Bs and Cs in 42 USAAF Squadrons. Some pilots considered the D inferior in performance, which, with 450lb increased weight, it theoretically was. However the difference was marginal and the improved vision and fire-power more than compensated. Even so, some pilots got their ground crews to fit single or twin rear-view mirrors.

From mid-1944 American pilots began to receive the Berger G-suit. This garment automatically constricted blood supply to the lower body and limbs during high rate turns, and enabled the pilot to perform more extreme maneuvers than previously possible without blacking out. The suit was in-flated by the aircraft's vacuum system. It did have the dis-advantage of allowing the pilot to sustain more G than his machine could on occasions, and aircraft were known to return to base after engaging in violent combat with popped rivets and increased dihedral. Some simply disintegrated through being overstressed.

A total of 7956 P-51Ds were produced (6502 at Inglewood and 1454 at Dallas), and 281 were supplied to the RAF as Mustang IVs, while a further 594 P-51Ks also carried the same designation. One P-51D was modified in mid-1944 for deck landing trials to assess the suitability of the type for carrier operations with the United States Navy. The 44-14017 was specially strengthened and fitted with an arrester hook, and with Lieutenant R M Elder USN at the controls, successfully completed landing and takeoff trials on USS *Shangri-La* on 14 November. With 35 knots over the deck the aircraft needed only 250ft of the 855 available to become airborne. The wide-track undercarriage was advantageous, but the pilot's view from the cockpit during the approach was considered in-adequate even with the seat fully raised and the project was terminated.

Four 8th Air Force Groups, each with three Squadrons, were flying the P-51 at the time of the invasion. The 4th FG was based at Debden, the 339th FG at Fowlmere, the 355th FG at Steeple Morden and the 357th FG was still at Leiston. During the night of 5 June the distinctive black and white

stripes of the Allied Expeditionary Air Force were applied to wings and fuselages, and on the following morning 355th FG machines attacked enemy transport and installations west of Paris. Little opposition was encountered from the Luftwaffe initially, and within a week of D-Day P-51Ds began to arrive.

On 2 June 1944 the first shuttle mission to Russia was flown under the command of General Eaker. One hundred and thirty B-17 bombers were escorted to the target after which they and their escorts, the 4th Fighter Group augmented by the 352nd Fighter Group's 486th Fighter Squadron and the Italian-based 15th Air Force's 325th Fighter Group all led by Donald Blakeslee, continued on to land on Russian airfields. After a seven and a half hour flight of 1470 miles during which the marshalling yards at Debreczen in Hungary were attacked, the Mustangs landed at Piryatin airfield. On 6 June the force raided Galati airfield in Rumania and returned to its Russian bases, and on 11 June the return was made to Italian bases via oil installations at Constanta and Giurgiu and the marshalling yards at Smederovo.

Above right: **Major Merle J Gilbertson of 20th Fighter Group in the remains of his P-51.**
Below: **P-51K over the Sind Desert near Karachi.**

Below: **As their bombers return to base, P-51s of 353rd Fighter Group peel off to land at Raydon, Essex.**

On 21 June the second shuttle mission to Russia took place and this time escort was provided by the 8th AF's 357th Fighter Group and the 15th AF's 31st Fighter Group. The synthetic oil plant at Ruhland was attacked and the surviving 64 P-51s again landed at Piryatin after an aerial battle with about thirty German fighters near Brest-Litovsk. A simultaneous 8th raid was also launched against Berlin. On 25 June the planned return journey to Italy was cancelled because of bad weather, but the next day saw the P-51s' departure and return to Italy by way of the marshalling yards at Drohobycz. They were unable to return to the United Kingdom until 5 July, again due to bad weather conditions. Subsequent Operation Frantic missions – as these were known – took place on 7 August with attacks on Polish oil refineries and on 11 September when Chemnitz was attacked.

By July most 8th AF P-38 Lightning Squadrons had converted to the P-51, and shortly before the end of the month the first Luftwaffe jet fighters began to be encountered over Germany. Because of the Messerschmitt Me 163's high speeds, the Mustangs could not catch them except by diving, and during a raid on Magdeburg three were shot down.

On 18 August a rescue took place when First Lieutenant Royce Priest of 355th FG observed Captain Bert Marshall's P-51D force landing in a field near Soissons in France. He landed alongside the wrecked machine and picked up Marshall, on whose lap he sat for the safe return flight to England. Also in August the first Messerschmitt Me 262 jets appeared, and on 11 September the first P-51 fell to the Me's guns. On 7 October Lieutenant Urban Drew of the 376th Fighter Squadron was flying P-51D 44-14164 over Achmer airfield, home of Major Walter Nowotny's Me 262 Kommando, when he saw two taking off. He shot both down. Arado Ar 234 reconnaissance jets began to appear about the same time, and could likewise be shot down if caught unawares by P-51s flying standing patrols above their bases. A special M23 .5in incendiary round with twice the amount of incendiary composition was developed to counter the volatile German jet aircraft. Although the limited flying hours and experience of the average German fighter pilot led to many relatively 'easy' air victories, the skies above Germany were still highly dangerous and flak, particularly at low level, still took its toll.

On 18 September 355th FG Mustangs escorted B-17s to drop supplies to the beleaguered Polish partisans engaged in the Warsaw uprising. As 1944 progressed Donald Blakeslee was grounded, having flown an estimated three times the official limit of 300 combat hours. The USAAF suffered a severe loss on 25 December when Major George E Preddy, Commanding Officer of 228th Fighter Squadron, was shot down and killed by American anti-aircraft fire near Liège in Belgium in his P-51D 44-14906 'Cripes A'Mighty.' He had destroyed two Messerschmitt Me 109s earlier the same day, and shot down a total of 27 enemy aircraft, including six Me 109s in one day on 6 August. By December the 78th Fighter Group was the last 8th AF Group to convert on to the P-51. With the exception of the 56th FG (The Wolfpack) which retained its P-47s until the very end, all fourteen 8th AF Fighter Groups were flying P-51s by VE-Day.

January 1945 saw the continuation of the severe weather which had predominated the winter, and aircraft were lost because of icing, pilot fatigue and landing accidents. It also saw the arrival of the P-51K, a lightened Dallas-manufactured P-51D in which the 11ft 2in Hamilton Standard propeller was replaced by an 11ft 0in diameter lightened Aeroproducts one. Vibration problems arose and only 1500 P-51Ks were built before P-51D production was resumed. However by spring the Allies had won virtually total air superiority over Germany, and by the beginning of April the 4th Fighter Group had destroyed a total of 867 enemy aircraft on the ground and in the air. On 18 March the 359th FG encountered Russian fighters over Berlin for the first time, and during one clash a P-51D of the 353rd FG force landed after being fired at in error. Reichsmarschall Hermann Göring stated in 1945 that, when American bombers came over Berlin with fighter escort, he knew that Germany had lost the war.

Above left: **Three P-51Ds and a P-51B over England.**
Below: **P-51Bs and Ds escorting B-24 Liberators of the 8th Air Force.**

THE 2ND TAF OPERAT

The Americans by no means had a monopoly of Mustangs over Europe between 1943 and 1945. The Second Tactical Air Force of the Royal Air Force was a new command which obtained many of its pilots from the Desert Air Force. The 122nd Wing of 2 TAF was the first to equip with the Mustang, and in late December 1943 65 Squadron received the first of a total of 910 Mustang IIIs finally delivered to the RAF. These did not have the 85 US-gallon fuselage fuel tank and an immediate program of fitting Malcolm Canopies was launched. The Wing consisted of this Squadron along with 19 and 122 Squadrons, and was unfortunate to lose its Wing Leader, Wing Commander R Grant on 28 February 1944 just thirteen days after the Wing's first mission, when he suffered engine failure after takeoff and crashed on the home airdrome of Gravesend. In addition to undertaking tactical ground attack missions, the Wing also provided escorts for returning USAAF bombers but, because of the absence of the fuselage tank, could not reach far into Europe.

On 26 March two Polish Squadrons – 306 (Torunski) and 315 (Deblinski) – exchanged their Spitfire VBs for Mustangs, and 129 Squadron joined them at Coolham in Surrey in early April. These three Squadrons formed 133 Wing and, with 122 they began operations over northern France flying Ranger sorties, bomber escort missions and shipping strikes in the North Sea.

On 15 April 122 Wing moved to Ford on the south coast in readiness for the invasion, and during the build-up period and immediately afterward, both Wings devoted their attention to enemy ground targets, which exacted a heavy toll of pilots and machines. On D-Day itself the Mustangs escorted transport aircraft carrying troops across the Channel, and on 25 June aircraft of 122 Wing flew over to land at B-7 Advanced Landing Ground, and thus were the first to operate from a base on the Continent. The 133 Wing remained in the United Kingdom after the invasion, but continued to operate over occupied Europe. The Commanding Officer of 315 (Polish) Squadron, Wing Commander Eugeniusz Horbaczewski, saw one of his pilots crash land south of Cherbourg shortly after the invasion. He himself landed at a half-completed landing ground nearby, struggled across country to reach the pilot, and flew back with him to the United Kingdom. Horbaczewski was killed on 18 August, by which time he had amassed 16.5 aerial victories and shot down four V-1 flying bombs.

As the Allied armies thrust deeper into France, the Squadrons of 122 Wing followed close behind. On 15 July 19 Squadron suffered casualties to both personnel and aircraft from shelling. The RAF Mustangs again became targets for over-zealous P-47 and P-38 pilots who failed to identify them. To lessen the risk, they adopted a more distinctive type of roundel incorporating white and yellow on their upper wings to augment the invasion stripes which all aircraft carried. Enemy aircraft were met and engaged and in August a series of successful attacks on barges on the Seine with 1000lb bombs was carried out to hinder German plans for the withdrawal of their ground forces; the bridges were already down.

On 28 and 29 September the three component Squadrons of 122 Wing were brought back to the United Kingdom and joined 150 Wing at Matlaske in Norfolk as part of the Air Defence of Great Britain force. From then on they were to escort RAF bombers on daylight raids under the operational control of No 11 and No 13 Groups, and their place in France was taken by 2 TAF Tempest Squadrons. While in France they had destroyed 93 German aircraft and countless ground targets had been dealt with.

As part of the reconnaissance element of 2 TAF, Mustang Is were operated by three Royal Canadian Air Force Squadrons. The 83 Group had 400 Squadron at Redhill and 414 and 430 Squadrons at Gatwick, 84 Group had four RAF Squadrons under its control, 2 and 4 Squadrons at Odiham and 168 and 268 Squadrons at Thruxton. Two out of the three Groups belonging to 2 TAF under the command of Air Marshal Arthur Coningham were equipped with Mustangs.

In November 1943 the RAF Squadrons, with the exception of 268, combined to form 35 (Reconnaissance) Wing based at Sawbridgeworth. Every opportunity was taken by the RAF and RCAF pilots to engage the enemy as well as to photograph him, and in readiness for the invasion a program of systematic reconnaissance began in early 1944. Three Mustang Squadrons trained for Naval Shore Bombardment Spotting carried out this task on D-Day, although two Mustangs fell to Spitfires whose pilots had failed to recognize them.

In June the Mark I Mustangs began to be replaced by Mark IIs and commenced a series of tactical reconnaissance (Tac R) missions which were again interrupted by friendly fighters, but managed to acquire much valuable information. The Mustang was also used by Group Captain Leonard Cheshire VC, DSO and 2 bars, DFC as a target marking aircraft for the pinpoint bombing attacks of 617 Squadron which he commanded. Taking full advantage of the Mustang's maneuverability and range he flew one modified to carry smoke markers to a V-2 rocket site at Siracourt in France in June 1944 and successfully marked it from low level. In July he flew two similar sorties, to Creil and Mimoyecques for marking an ammunition dump and an underground long-range artillery position respectively. Unable to obtain a Mustang from his own Service, Cheshire borrowed one from the USAAF, and when he was posted his successor carried on the tradition.

On 18 June 1944 the Germans launched 22 V-1 (Vergeltungswaffe, or Reprisal weapon) flying bombs at London, and countermeasures were immediately taken. The 122 Wing flew to France later in the month, but 133 Wing was available and was able to use its Mustang IIIs in Operation Diver against the new threat. To augment the Gun Belt stretching from Beachy Head to Dover which was hurriedly deployed by General Sir Frederick Pile, GOC of Anti-Aircraft Command, Mustangs flew standing patrols off Kent over the Channel, and the pilots were vectored on to their targets by a radar controller. At night searchlights were used for target illumination. The V-1s mostly flew at heights between 2–3000ft, and fighters were ordered to fly no lower than 8000ft to allow a margin of safety from the guns which engaged targets crossing the coast at lower altitude. V-1s were small targets and flew at 380mph. Trial and error determined the best technique for dealing with them, which was to approach

ONS

from astern and open fire from 350 yards, whereupon with luck the target would explode and the attacker could fly through the debris unscathed.

A successful exponent of this dangerous art was Warrant Officer Tadeusz Szymanski of 316 (Warszawski) Polish Squadron who destroyed nine V-1s including some whose gyros he caused to topple by formating alongside the flying bomb and gently raising his Mustang's wing tip against the underside of the target's. His Squadron, flown down from Coltishall in Norfolk to augment the defenses along with Meteors, Spitfires and Tempests, destroyed 74 V-1s. Attempts were made to boost the power of the Merlin by using 130-octane fuel, but this caused valves to burn out, and the only way that Mustangs could reliably attack the bombs was by diving to achieve the necessary speed. As the majority of the launching sites were overrun by September 1944, the danger temporarily passed, but V-1s soon began to arrive from the east, and the Diver Belt Gun Box defenses were increased to extend from the Thames Estuary to Great Yarmouth in Norfolk. In all 232 flying bombs were destroyed by Mustangs.

In October 1944 122 and 133 Wings combined to form a seven-squadron unit based at Andrews Field, also known as Great Saling, near Chelmsford in Essex. The seventh squadron was 316 from Coltishall. From Andrews Field they provided escorts for RAF day bombing attacks and in December they were joined by a further expanded Wing of six RAF Squadrons converted to Mustang IIIs and based at Bentwaters in

Suffolk. This brought the total of RAF Mustangs to nearly 250. The first Messerschmitt Me 262 fell to an RAF Mustang in late March 1945.

In February 1945 the RAF finally obtained the P-51D and called it the Mustang Mark IV; the Americans had received it in the United Kingdom as early as May the previous year. It equipped the third planned Mustang Wing at Hunsdon in Hertfordshire, which never reached full strength by the time hostilities ended. Most Mustang IVs flew in bare metal finish, and carried the red, white and blue upper wing roundels introduced on 3 January 1945. The first RAF Squadron to receive the Mustang IV was 303 (Kosciuszko) Polish Squadron, and the RAF eventually received 281 P-51Ds and the later K version both of which carried the Mark IV designation.

This Mustang re-equipped two Mustang III Squadrons which had flown their earlier Marks as escorts to Mosquito and Beaufighter shipping strikes off the Norwegian coast. These operations were flown at sea level, and involved a round trip of some 1000 miles from the airdrome at Peterhead near Aberdeen. Two RAF Mustang Squadrons were involved, 19 and 65 Squadrons from 122 Wing. Over Norway they met spirited opposition from the Luftwaffe, many of whose experienced pilots were sent there for rest and recuperation. These operations subjected the Mustang pilots to great strain, since even momentary failure of the Merlin would mean the aircraft hitting the sea, and the quality of the opposition awaiting them was more predictable than over the skies of Germany where, by this stage in the war, many German fighter pilots had very little flying experience. In August 1944 the USAAF's 4th Fighter Group participated in several sorties, but the bulk of this flying was done by the RAF until the end of the war. On 16 April 1945 Mustang IVs of 611 Squadron encountered Russian fighters over Berlin. When the German High Command surrendered unconditionally on 7 May 1945, the sixteen RAF Mustang Squadrons had some 320 aircraft available and the USAAF about 1600 in Europe.

Below: **Group Captain Leonard Cheshire, VC, DSO, DFC used P-51s to pinpoint targets on bombing raids.**

Below: **Relaxing at an advanced landing ground following the Normandy invasion.**

ITALIAN OPERATIONS

In November 1943 the United States 15th Air Force was designated the Mediterranean theater strategic bomber force, and relied initially upon three P-38 Lightning Groups and subsequently one P-47 Thunderbolt Group as fighter escort in the 306th Fighter Wing. The 15th Air Force had been created on 1 November 1943 under the command of Major General James H Doolittle. The 12th Air Force with which it operated was a tactical formation which had been instituted in August 1942, as the American counterpart to the RAF's Desert Air Force, to provide support for the US 5th Army. In December 1943 it was incorporated into the newly-formed Mediterranean Allied Air Forces. With the expansion of the bomber force new escort groups were soon needed, and on 2 April 1944 the 31st Fighter Group received its first P-51Bs as replacements for the Spitfires previously used. Two weeks later they flew to Rumania on their first escort operation, and on 21 April the 31st FG escorted a raid on the Ploesti oil refineries north of Bucharest, during the course of which they shot down seventeen enemy aircraft. The 31st was commanded by Major James Thorsen. In May the second 15th AF Mustang Group, the 52nd, received its machines, and the 325th exchanged its P-47s shortly afterward to form the third. It was the last-mentioned Fighter Group – the Checkertails – which helped escort the first shuttle mission to Russian bases on 2 June 1944. On the day the Allied invasion was launched along the French Channel coast, the 325th escorted their bombers on the raid on Galati in Rumania.

The 52nd Fighter Group succeeded in shooting down thirteen German fighters without loss during a raid on Munich three days later, and the 31st Fighter Group took part in the second shuttle mission, along with P-38s, on 21 June 1944. During their short stay in Russia and before the return journey to San Severo was made, they took part in an aerial battle over Poland in which the Mustangs engaged a force of 41 German aircraft, mainly Junkers Ju87s, and shot down 27 confirmed.

In June 1944 the 332nd Fighter Group received its first Mustangs. This unit was an all-Negro one and its red-tailed and spinnered P-51s were based at Foggia. During July, August and September much ground strafing was carried out, and on 31 August the 52nd FG was sent to attack the Luftwaffe airfield at Reghin in Rumania, and destroyed over 150 enemy machines as the Mustangs flew pass after pass over the devastated area. In three days (30 August–1 September) 193 P-51s claimed a total of 211 enemy aircraft destroyed and a further 131 damaged on four Rumanian airfields. The 325th FG attacked another airfield at Ecka in Yugoslavia on 10 September and destroyed forty aircraft. During a strafing attack by the 31st FG a rescue similar to the ones carried out by Royce Priest and Eugeniusz Horbaczewski took place when Lieutenant Charles E Wilson force-landed his P-51 after it was damaged when a train he was attacking exploded. Major Wyatt P Exum landed nearby and picked him up.

During the autumn and winter of 1944 opposition in the air over the Balkans declined, although the P-51 Groups continued to harry ground targets, but on 14 March 1945 the 325th was involved in a great air battle over Hungary with 35

Focke Wulf Fw 190s. Two P-51s were lost for the destruction of seventeen of the enemy. Ten days later all four Mustang Groups combined to escort a bomber force to Berlin and back – a round trip of over 1500 miles. On the return journey Colonel William Daniel, Commanding Officer of 308th FS of the 31st FG, engaged a Messerschmitt Me 262 and shot it down, while six others were shot down on the same day, three by the 332nd FG. This Group also claimed thirteen enemy aircraft destroyed in a fight near Linz in Austria.

In March 1944 260 Squadron RAF exchanged its P-40 Kittyhawks for Mustang IIIs. This Desert Air Force Squadron was based at Cutella in the south of Italy and collected its machines

from Casablanca. In May the Squadron attacked and breached the Pescara dam, and the resulting floods enabled the British 8th Army to provide support for the US 5th Army, because the former's right flank was protected by the water. July saw the equipping of 112 and 213 Squadrons with Mustangs, and ground attack missions were flown for both armies. The 112 Squadron had flown Kittyhawks and continued to display on its Mustangs the sharks' teeth insignia carried on its predecessors'. In September 249 Squadron and 5 Squadron South African Air Force received Mustangs and 3 Squadron RAAF equipped with them in November. The 112, 213 and 249 Squadrons were all re-equipped with Mustang IVs.

All six squadrons operated over the Balkans, primarily engaged in ground support tasks. To this end they carried two 1000lb bombs, thereby doubling the recommended bomb load, but the wings of the Mustang were strong enough to carry the extra weight. Rocket projectiles were also fitted and used to good effect. However, as the Americans had found, there was little opposition in the sky, and after the last winter of the war it was apparent that the enemy in Europe was defeated.

Below: **Lieutenant General Carl Spaatz (right) debriefs an Italian-based American bomber crew just returned from a mission over Austria.**

CHINA-BURMA-INDIA

The Mustang's first appearance in India was with the 311th Fighter Group of the United States 10th Air Force in October 1943. This consisted of 528, 529 and 530th Fighter Squadrons. The Group had 40 A-36A dive bombers divided between two squadrons, and the third was equipped with P-51A Allison Mustangs. It operated from Dinjan and flew missions against the Japanese in northern Burma from northeast India, and protected the air route to China, where P-51Bs were to equip the United States 14th Air Force, which was commanded by Major General Claire L Chennault. He had raised the American Volunteer Group in November 1940 in the United States which flew under the operational control of the Chinese Air Force from December 1941 until 4 July 1942, when it was finally incorporated into the 23rd Fighter Group. In this period, flying Curtiss P-40B and E Warhawks, the AVG destroyed 286 Japanese aircraft. This included 6.5 shot down by the then Captain James Howard. The air route took Allied transport 'over the Hump' with essential supplies and the P-51's range was put to good use.

The P-51As of 530th FS deployed south to Kurmitola in Bengal, from where they escorted B-25 Mitchell and B-24 Liberator bombers in attacks on Rangoon. To provide sufficient range two 75 US-gallon drop tanks were carried. Losses were high however; in November Colonel Harry Melton, the commander of the 311th FG, was lost, and the heavily laden P-51As were found to be at a disadvantage when confronted by Japanese Nakajima Ki-43 Oscar and Nakajima Ki-44 Tojo fighters. The attack during which he was lost was aimed at the home airfield of the Japanese 64th Sentai, which provided fighter defense for the area. During the winter of 1943 enemy lines of communication continued to be attacked, and escort was provided for aerial supply missions to Chinese forces moving southward down the Hukawng Valley. In early March 1944 the Group also began operations in support of Merrill's Marauders in the same area. During these operations the ground forces made use of Army Air Force Forward Air Controllers to call down air strikes just ahead of the troops, with notable accuracy and success. The Japanese retaliated by trying to destroy the 311th FG's base but their air attacks were repulsed.

The P-51As also equipped two Air Commando Units which were employed to provide air support for Major General Orde Wingate's Chindits who operated behind Japanese lines. Their tasks included carrying a 1000lb bomb or triple rocket launchers mounted beneath each wing for ground attack, and a cable was sometimes trailed to destroy Japanese telephone and power lines. These Mustangs operated under difficult conditions from rough strips and performed most useful work.

In April 1944 the first Merlin-engined P-51Bs began to arrive to equip the 311th FG at Dinjan, but the bulk of Mustang production was directed toward Europe. In May 1944 one squadron of the Group was sent to Dohazari to disrupt attempts made by the Japanese to resupply their troops at

Right: **P-51s with distinctive recognition markings over the Chin Hills in Burma, on a mission to destroy Japanese supply depots.**

THEATER OPERATIONS

Myitkina and Imphal. In four days it shot down 24 Japanese aircraft without losing a single Mustang, a sign of the increasing American air superiority.

In China the 23rd Fighter Group had been re-equipped with Merlin-engined Mustangs by December 1944 and the 311th FG moved these from India to begin operating from an advanced landing ground at Hsian in Northern China. Here as everywhere else conditions were spartan and all supplies had to come by air. Much improvisation and the use of coolie labor enabled the fighters to keep flying. Modifications included the fitting of two 250lb bomb racks outboard of the 75 US-gallon drop tanks, provision for eighteen antipersonnel bombs on racks outboard of three 100lb bomb mountings beneath each wing and a total of four 75 US-gallon drop tanks which, including the capacity of the 85 US-gallon fuselage tank, provided a range of 2700 miles. With this extreme range Japanese targets could be attacked which had previously been immune. The 311th FG – known as the Yellow Scorpions – rotated its squadrons through Hsian, and on 24 December 1944 the 530th FS carried out a spectacular attack on Tsinan airfield, destroying some eighty Japanese aircraft on this and two subsequent raids.

The 23rd Fighter Group based at Kweilin also carried out constant strafing and bombing attacks both on shipping and land targets, as well as escorting medium-range American bombers. The Group was joined by the 118th Tactical Reconnaissance Squadron in mid-1944, which soon began to develop a skip-bombing technique not normally included in the

Above: **A P-51 of the Flying Tigers with triple rocket launchers.**
Above right: **Col Tex Hill, CO of 23rd Fighter Group and his P-51 at Kweilin, China.**
Right: **Curtiss P-40 Warhawk as used by the AVG. The P-51 superseded the P-40.**

repertoire of a reconnaissance unit. On 8 December thirteen Mustangs successfully raided Hong Kong harbor using 500lb bombs, and on the return journey shot up the Japanese airfield at Tok Pak Uk.

Major John C Herbst – known as Pappy because of his relatively advanced years – commanded the 74th FS of the 23rd FG. He flew a P-51B (43-7060) 'Tommy's Dad,' and between July 1944 and February 1945 he shot down twenty Japanese aircraft to add to his single German victory from North Africa, and thus became the highest scoring American pilot in the theater. Another successful exponent of the P-51 was Colonel Ed McComas, who shot down fourteen.

The Royal Air Force intended to use Mustang IVs in Burma, but the war ended before the several hundred which were shipped to India and assembled at Dum Dum airfield near Calcutta could be brought into action. The Mustang – of which there were never more than 500 in the CBI theater – had again proved its versatility in far from ideal conditions and, as in Europe, had used its great range for escorting bombers and transports as well as reaching far behind enemy lines. And it still had one more important part to play in the Southwest Pacific.

THE PACIFIC

Not until late 1944 did General George C Kenney, Commander of the United States 5th Air Force in the Southwest Pacific area, receive any Mustangs. The first were F-6D reconnaissance aircraft which were assigned to the 82nd Tac R Squadron of the 71st Reconnaissance Group, stationed at San Jose Field at Mindoro in the Philippines. On 11 January 1945 Captain William A Shomo was leading a pair of F-6Ds with First Lieutenant Paul N Lipscomb as his wingman on a reconnaissance mission to Japanese airfields in North Luzon. As they drew near to their target area they spotted a formation of enemy aircraft consisting of a single Mitsubishi G4M Betty bomber containing, presumably, some eminent Japanese since it was escorted by no less than twelve Kawasaki Ki-61 Tony fighters. Despite the enemy's numerical superiority, the two American pilots turned to attack, and in the ensuing melee Captain Shomo shot down the bomber and six fighters, while his wingman dispatched a further four. For his bravery and success Shomo was awarded the Congressional Medal of Honor.

In January 1945 the Third Air Commando Group received its first P-51Ds. By this time there was not much Japanese air activity over the Philippines, and the squadrons of the Group were able to pursue their primary task of low-level ground attack on Japanese tactical targets and communications.

On 19 February 1945 United States Marines invaded the island of Iwo Jima, and a 36-day battle of unparalleled ferocity began. The Japanese had about 23,000 soldiers on the island, well dug in, and with a complex of tunnels from which they would emerge to attack the American rear. When the battle was over American dead numbered 6821 and only 1083 Japanese were taken prisoner. No sooner had a foothold been gained than Seabees (Construction Battalions) moved in to establish a landing ground for the P-51Ds of the 15th and 21st

FGs. These units were to escort the B-29 Superfortress bombers of the United States Twentieth Bomber Command on their raids against the Japanese homeland. The B-29s had already launched raids on Japan from their bases at Saipan and Tinian in the Marianas, but without fighter escort.

On 6 March the 15th FG arrived on the South Field of Iwo Jima, and on 15 March the 21st FG joined them. At a cost of the most appalling USMC casualty figures, a base was now available from which the P-51s could escort the bombers along the 700 or so miles to Japan; but before the first escort mission was flown, the Mustangs provided air support for the Marines both on the island and on others nearby. The Japanese were still offering resistance, and on occasions the North Field airstrip came under attack and American Squadron personnel were killed. The fields themselves consisted of volcanic rock whose dust, in addition to causing visibility problems after the slipstream of aircraft taxying and taking off had created swirling clouds of it, also acted as a fine abrasive and clogged filters. As ever, the ground crews soldiered on in thoroughly unpleasant, sometimes dangerous but unspectacular conditions, to ensure that their machines were on top line, as they did in all other theaters.

On 7 April the first escort mission to Japan was flown when 96 P-51Ds from the six component squadrons of both Fighter Groups took off and set course to rendezvous with a force of over 100 B-29s. The Mustangs carried two 110 US-gallon metal drop tanks pressurized by the aircraft's vacuum pump, but even so they had little time to loiter over their target, the Nakajima aircraft factory in the capital city, Tokyo. To ease navigation problems an escort B-29 was provided on both legs, and only one P-51 was lost on this first raid. Due to the vast distances involved and the unpredictability of the weather, special weather flights preceded the main force, and

Above: Fifth Air Force 35th Fighter Group aircraft taxi out in the Philippines.
Left: 45th Fighter Squadron, 15th Fighter Group armorers replenish a P-51's guns.
Below: P-51D prepares to take off from Iwo Jima.
Bottom: 'Bore-sighting' a 41st Fighter Squadron P-51s guns at Clark Field, Luzon in 1945.

the B-29 shepherd aircraft carried life rafts in case an American pilot was forced to come down in the sea. If he did so, his chances of survival were good, since the United States Navy had pre-positioned submarines to pick him up along the route. All of this must have been very reassuring to the pilot of a single-engined fighter when faced with flights of many hours duration over the Pacific Ocean. Both Groups encountered strong enemy resistance on the first raid, but shot down 21 Japanese aircraft for the loss of only three B-29s.

On 16 April the first strafing attack was launched on the Japanese home island of Kyushu. This was another flight of nearly 800 miles each way and was successful. In another raid four days later Major James B Tapp of the 15th FG shot down his fifth enemy aircraft over Japan and achieved 'ace' status when his and the 21st FG were sent to attack airfields at Yokosuka and Atgui. In May the 506th Fighter Group added its P-51Ds to those of the other two Groups and on one of its first missions with them on 1 June 1945 was unfortunate to encounter a vast frontal system reaching from sea level to well over 20,000ft. A total of 148 Mustangs took off to escort a B-29 force to Osaka, but two hours later they flew into the towering clouds associated with this front. In the ensuing turbulence and zero visibility collisions occurred, aircraft broke up, pilots became completely disoriented as their instruments toppled and airframes iced up. The squadrons were hopelessly

split up; under thirty picked up their formation and continued toward their rendezvous with the bombers off Japan, over ninety aborted and returned to Iwo Jima and some 25 were lost. This was the greatest air disaster to befall the Americans in this theater. The Groups consolidated and continued to harass Japanese industry and airfields. Opposition became increasingly stubborn and large numbers of fighters met the attackers in the closing months of the war. At 0815 hours local time on 6 August 1945 the first atomic bomb exploded over Hiroshima, and on 9 August the second was dropped over Nagasaki. The war was over.

The Mustang had flown distances which no one just under five years earlier would have believed possible for a single-engined fighter, or its pilots; sometimes over eight hours elapsed before a weary fighter pilot in his early twenties would bring his aircraft over the fence at 110mph and feel the reassuring rumble of ground beneath his wheels. In the intervening war years the Mustang had destroyed 4950 enemy aircraft in the air and a further 4131 on the ground.

Right: **Republic P-47 Thunderbolt, Lockheed P-38 Lightning and P-51D Mustang.**
Below right: **Major Robert W Moore, CO of a P-51 squadron on Iwo Jima.**
Below: **P-51D and B-29 Superfortress rendezvous off the Japanese coast, July 1945.**

PROTOTYPES AND PO

The development of the P-51 from the Allison-engined A version via the B, C and D had been accompanied by a steady increase in weight; the P-51A weighed 6433lb empty and the P-51D 7125lb. By way of comparison, a Spitfire V weighed only 5050lb. With a view to producing a lighter machine, Edgar Schmued led a group of engineers from North American to Great Britain in early 1943 to study British design techniques. As a result of their findings, North American proposed a lighter version and a contract for three prototypes was approved in July. These were designated XP-51F, G and J. The first incorporated a new laminar flow wing and components were redesigned and lightered. A new and lighter undercarriage was housed in a wing which had a straighter leading edge, the canopy was extended and the oil cooler was replaced by a heat exchanger. A three-bladed Aeroproducts propeller with hollow blades was fitted to the standard 1450hp Packard Merlin V-1650 7 engine of the P-51D. The fuselage fuel tank was omitted and the armament reduced to four .5in Brownings. A weight saving of 1300lb had been intended, and when the first P-51F took to the air on 14 February 1944 it weighed 5635lb empty, which represented a weight reduction of 1490lb. Not surprisingly its performance was considerably enhanced, and the P-51F added 30mph to its predecessor's maximum speed of 437mph. The RAF had requested one for evaluation and received one of the three produced in June, which became FR 409. Had it been accepted it would have become the Mustang V, but the machine was not without vices and no further examples were built.

The P-51G carried a Rolls-Royce Merlin 100 engine with a five-bladed British Rotol propeller. Two were produced and one (FR 410) was supplied to the RAF who obtained a maximum speed of just under 500mph from it at 20,000ft, a height to which it could climb in a breathtaking 3.4 minutes.

The P-51J reverted to the Allison V-1710-119 engine and performed well, but again only two were built. It was from experience with the P-51F that the lightweight production model, the P-51H, was developed. The H version was powered by a 1380hp Packard Merlin V-1650-9 with water injection and driving a four-bladed constant speed Aeroproducts propeller, which gave it a speed of 487mph at 25,000ft. To improve directional stability the fin was enlarged and the dorsal strake which had been omitted on the F was replaced. The D-type canopy was fitted and the two 105 US-gallon wing tanks were augmented by a 50 US-gallon fuselage one. The weight saving on the P-51D was in the region of 1000lb and the armament fit was either four or six .50in Brownings. Only 555 P-51Hs were built before the end of the war brought construction to a halt, and only a few had reached the Pacific theater by then.

A planned P-51L would have carried an uprated Packard Merlin V-1650-11 but the project was cancelled and the last P-51 produced was the M, an H without water injection, of which a single example was built at Dallas in September 1945.

Perhaps the most interesting project which arose during the war was for a long-range escort fighter consisting of two P-51H fuselages joined together. This design was prompted by

TWAR

Above: Air-to-air view of the lightweight production P-51H.
Above right: One of three P-51Fs supplied to the RAF.
Below: Prototype lightweight XP-51F showing the enlarged canopy.

the desire to reduce pilot fatigue during prolonged flights in the Pacific Theater, and the prospect of doubling the crew of an already proven aircraft obviated the time-consuming and costly development program of a completely new type. When North American suggested the idea as the XP-82, the USAAF accepted and four prototypes were ordered on 7 January 1944. The first flight took place in Los Angeles on 15 April 1945.

In the XP-82 Twin Mustang two P-51H fuselages were joined by a common center-wing section and inboard horizontal stabilizer; the outer stabilizers were deleted. The pilot of the combination sat in the port fuselage and the second pilot in the starboard. The former had a full range of instruments and the latter sufficient to take over should the need arise, or to act as navigator. The armament of six .5in Brownings was housed in the center section of the wing, and the outer wings carried pylons for one 1000lb bomb or 310 US-gallon drop tanks. Interval tanks housed 576 US-gallons which, with drop tanks, gave a maximum range of some 4000 miles.

The P-82B of early 1945 was the first production model and was powered by two 1380hp Packard Merlin V-1650-9 engines with propellers rotating in an inward direction. Some were converted into P-82C and D night fighter versions as a replacement for the Northrop P-61 Black Widow, and the P-82E was a long-range escort fighter with Allison V-1710 engines and autopilot. The F was a photographic reconnaissance and night fighter variant carrying a pod for the AN/APG-28 radar beneath its center section. This arrived in squadron service in 1948; in July 1947 the US Army Air Force had changed its name to the United States Air Force and in June 1948 the USAF changed the designation P (Pursuit) to F (Fighter). So the P-82F became the F-82F and both this and the F-51 saw action in Korea.

The TP-51D was a two-seater trainer version of the P-51D and ten were built. Several war weary P-51Bs with WW on their tails, had been converted unofficially into two-seaters, some with additional Malcolm hoods, but the large blister canopy of the D provided sufficient room for a second seat if the radio was moved into the rear fuselage. The TP-51Ds maximum all-up weight was 11,300lb.

With the cessation of hostilities in 1945 production was run down; in September the North American plant at Dallas ceased P-51 production and in November Inglewood followed suit. The United Kingdom-based squadrons departed and in East Anglia many former Mustang bases reverted to farmland. In America P-51s were available on the war-surplus market at one-fifteenth of their original production cost, but other

Above: **Twin Mustang in flight.**
Below: **Twin Mustang – the F-82 showing its substantial armament.**

Above: **TP-51 – the two-seater trainer version of which ten were produced. It was used to train pilots for service in the Pacific.**

Above: **Australian license-built CA-17 Mustang 20 series aircraft equipped the RAAF after 1945.**

models remained in first-line USAF service to until the 1950s. The Air National Guard fighter squadrons were equipped with Ds and Hs for a decade postwar, while Mustang IVs flew with the RAF until May 1947.

While American production ceased, Australia was still producing P-51Ds under license as CA-17 Mustang 20s at the Commonwealth Aircraft Corporation near Melbourne. Tooling-up had begun in February 1945, and on 29 April the first CA-17 was airborne. Two hundred were eventually built, some with 1450hp Merlin 68 engines known as Mustang 21s, while the 22 was a PR version, and the 23 carried British-built Merlin engines. A further 298 were provided by the United

States under Lend-Lease agreements. Mustangs were flown by three regular RAAF squadrons in early 1946.

As part of the occupation forces in Japan the 81st Wing consisted of 76, 77 and 82 Squadrons, and the Mustang equipped the five reserve squadrons of the Citizen Air Force in Australia until the late 1950s. Canada also continued to fly the Mustang for a few years after the war had ended, ordering 130 between 1947 and 1951 for use with the Royal Canadian Auxiliary Air Force; the Royal New Zealand Air Force acquired thirty in 1951 to equip the Territorial Air Force.

Mustangs continued to serve in many air forces after the war. The United States had supplied 50 P-51Ds to the Chinese

Above: **F-51D of the Italian Air Force resting on perforated steel plate sheets.**

Nationalist Air Force before Japan surrendered, and they obtained many more from surplus USAF stocks before withdrawing to Formosa. The Chinese Communists captured some which were left behind on the mainland, but the Nationalists had two F-51D and one RF-51D Squadrons in December 1954.

The Royal Swedish Air Force evaluated two P-51Bs and two P-51Ds (including one belonging to the US 8th AFs 339th FG) which had infringed Sweden's neutral air space during the war, and had been interned. Impressed by the aircraft, they ordered 157 P-51Ds as the J26, which were supplied between April 1945 and March 1948. From surplus Swedish stocks the Dominican Air Force obtained 42 in 1952, which flew as fighter bombers until 1978. Such longevity says a great deal for the strength of the design.

Israel received 25 between November 1952 and the spring of 1953 from the same source, and flew them until 1960; during the battles of 1956 they flew ground attack missions against the Egyptians. The Nicaraguan Air Force also bought 26 ex-Swedish P-51Ds in November 1954 and operated them for eleven years.

Under the terms of the Rio Pact, the United States supplied Mustangs to several countries in the Caribbean and South America in the immediate postwar years. Cuba operated some until 1960 and the Guatemalan and Haitian Air Forces received a few. The latter retains six to this day, while the former operated theirs until 1972. Uruguay acquired 25 P-51Ds in 1950 and flew them for ten years. The Air Forces of El Salvador, Honduras and Bolivia also flew small numbers.

The Armée de l'Air of France received P-51Ds for its 33rd Reconnaissance Wing in February 1945. Switzerland purchased some 140 in 1948 and operated them for ten years, and

Below: **This P-51D Mustang (N991R) was modified for air racing which has developed since the war as a popular pastime.**

Below: **P-51D photographed at an air display in England. P-51Ds were bought up cheaply after World War II.**

Above: **P-51D (N10601) photographed at Dulles Airport, Washington DC.**

Italy obtained 48 in the same year and flew them for a similar period, finally selling some to Somalia. The Royal Netherlands Air Force flew Mustangs postwar in the Dutch East Indies where forty were flown by 121 and 122 Squadrons against Indonesian forces in 1948–49. With the advent of peace the Dutch handed over their remaining stocks to their former enemies, who still operate some. The Philippine and South Korean Air Forces also acquired small numbers.

In the same era the American National Air Races were revived and large numbers of surplus P-51s were enthusiastically adopted by air racing pilots who recognized the aircraft's potential at once. The Bendix Trophy Race of 1946 was won by Paul Mantz in NX 1202, a P-51C conversion which covered the 2048 miles from Van Nuys in California to Cleveland Municipal Airport at an average speed of 435.5mph, and second and third places were also taken by P-51Cs. Throughout the late 1940s Mustangs battled with P-38 Lightnings and F-6 Corsairs, ever improving their power output. The 1949 Bendix Trophy

was won by Joe De Bona's F-6C conversion at a speed of 470.1mph; like Paul Mantz he had fitted a 'wet wing,' in which all available internal space had been converted into a fuel reservoir. The Korean War effectively brought air racing to a stop in 1950, and not until the early 1960s did it enjoy a revival when P-51s again proved their worth in races held at Reno, Nevada in 1964. The following year saw Reno established as the home of American air racing when the National Championship Air Races were held there. The contestants were now mainly P-51Ds, again heavily modified. In 1975 one P-51D appeared powered by a 2445hp Rolls-Royce Griffon 57 engine with a de Havilland six-bladed contra-rotating propeller. In the United Kingdom Charles Masefield flew a P-51D to win the 1967 King's Cup Air Race, and won several other races in the same year.

Below: **A P-51D in the markings of the 83rd Fighter Squadron of the 78th Fighter Group, 8th Air Force.**

Below: **P-51D (N6306T) postwar at Reading, Pennsylvania. Air racing was revived again after the Korean War.**

KOREA AND AFTER

On 25 June 1950 the North Koreans crossed the 38th parallel and invaded South Korea, thus beginning the Korean War. The nearest United Nations air forces were based in Japan, where the Royal Australian Air Force's 77 Squadron was still stationed at Iwakuni – although its two sister squadrons had been withdrawn to Australia only the previous year. On 2 July they flew their first operational mission escorting USAF B-29 bombers over the North. The 77 Squadron was sent to South Korea and ultimately moved into the North. Until April 1951 saw the re-equipping of the Squadron with Meteor F.8s it flew many ground attack missions over inhospitable mountainous terrain which offered little chance of a successful forced landing, and the old vulnerability of the liquid-cooled engine to ground fire was rediscovered.

The South African Air Force also flew P-51Ds in the Korean War although it had not operated the type previously. Having converted at Johnson Air Force Base near Tokyo, its single squadron – 2 (Cheetah) Squadron – flew its first operation on 19 November 1950 attached to the USAF's 18th Fighter Bomber Group, and continued to fly P-51s until January 1953. It also engaged in low-level operations and lost nearly sixty Mustangs to enemy ground fire. In addition to the hostile environment, the piston-engined fighters had to contend with Russian-built MiG-15 jets and the United States rated the all-volunteer South African Squadron's efforts so highly that it was awarded a Presidential Unit Citation for 'extraordinary heroism.'

The United States Air Force had, of course, retained F-51s postwar, and both these and the F-82 Twin Mustang were available when the Korean War broke out. The 347th (All-Weather) Fighter Group was based at Itazuke in Japan and in June 1950 consisted of the 4th, 68th and 339th Fighter Squadrons. On 27 June an F-82G piloted by Lieutenant William G Hudson of 68th FS scored the first American aerial victory of the war by shooting down a North Korean Yak-9 fighter during a mission providing top cover for the evacuation of Americans near Seoul in South Korea. Four others were dispatched in the same fight.

The F-51D was flown by the 8th, 35th and 49th Fighter Bomber Groups during the early days of the war and the 18th FB Group operated it until January 1953. The 45th Tactical Reconnaissance Squadron flew RF-51s from September 1950 until the Armistice in July 1953. Altogether the Americans employed some 250 F-51Ds in the ground-attack role and, as did all the UN Mustang Squadrons, suffered very heavy losses. But the Mustang was the only aircraft available in quantity which had the necessary range and endurance and could carry sufficient weapons to inflict damage. Various combinations of bombs and 5in HVAR RPs in multiples of three were carried, along with the effective battery of six .5in Brownings. There was still a use for the piston-engined fighter in the jet age, and the American F-80 Shooting Stars were not as well suited to low-level operations. Major Louis J Sebille, Commanding Officer of the 67th FS, won a posthumous Congressional Medal of Honor in an F-51D on 5 August 1950 when, mortally wounded, he continued to press home an attack on ground forces near Pusan and finally crashed his aircraft straight into his objective.

Above: An F-51D releases its napalm over a North Korean target in August 1951.
Top: As his family watches, Captain Johnnie Gosnell taxies his F-82 in Japan.

Above: Ilyushin Il-2 falls to the guns of an F-51 flown by Lt-Col Ralph D Saltman.
Below: South African Cheetah Squadron aircraft returns from a mission.

The Korean War really saw the demise of the F-51 as a combat aircraft, however, and the one attempt to convert it into a counterinsurgency machine did not lead to its adoption. The Trans-Florida Aviation Company of Sarasota undertook a program of F-51D conversion in 1961. The D was given a second seat and called the Cavalier 2000. It was aimed at providing an executive aircraft capable of high-speed cruising over long ranges, with an element of excitement lacking in more pedestrian civil aircraft designs. For instance, the executive could subject his client to up to +9G at speeds not exceeding 490mph, and he could cruise at 424mph at 30,000ft. The Cavalier's twin wing-tip tanks held a total capacity of 220 US-gallons which gave a range of 2000 miles, and 400lb of luggage could be stored in the former gun bays in the wings. Considering the aircraft's origins, a high degree of comfort was provided. The Cavalier's full instrument panel was arranged in vertical stacks and automatic heat controls were fitted to reduce the risk of overheating inherent in all liquid-cooled engines while taxying. For those already owning Mustangs a conversion kit was provided, and a choice of tanks allowed a variety of ranges. The late Ormond Haydon-Baillie flew a Cavalier at air displays in the United Kingdom in the 1970s but was killed when he crashed in Germany.

When it became apparent that the United States was likely to become involved in Southeast Asia in 1967, a counter-insurgency version of the Cavalier was proposed by the manufacturers. A 1760hp British Merlin 620 replaced the 1595hp Packard Merlin V-1650-7 of the Cavalier, but the Hamilton Standard four-bladed constant speed propeller was retained, as were the tip tanks. Provision was made for 4000lb of under-wing stores and for six .5in Brownings. The P-51H type tail fin was fitted and an ejector seat was standard. The Mustang II was a two-seat version and the Turbo Mustang III, a private venture, carried a Rolls-Royce Dart 510 turboprop driving a Dowty-Rotol propeller in a very slender engine cowling. This version dispensed with the characteristic ventral radiator duct, and in clean configuration attained 540mph. In 1971 a new turbo version, the Enforcer, was produced by the renamed Cavalier Aircraft Corporation and had a 2535shp Lycoming T-55-L-9 turbine engine.

The United States Air Force adopted none of these designs. The Mustang now flies in peaceful skies, and its airworthiness nearly forty years after the first P-51 flew is a tribute to the design of a warplane which, by the very nature of its work, was not expected to last. While so many military aircraft were scrapped postwar, of which no examples remain, the Mustang is quite well represented. In the United States the Confederate Air Force still flies a number, including one F-82B, and when the USAF released its last ones in 1957, a P-51H (44-74936) of the West Virginia ANG was put on display at the Air Force Museum at Wright-Patterson Field. However only four P-51B and C examples appear to remain in the United States. An ex-RCAF P-51D is held at Duxford by the Imperial War Museum in the United Kingdom, appropriately in the markings of a machine flown by the 78th Fighter Group of the US 8th Air Force from that airdrome in the war and bearing the serial number 44-72258.

APPENDICES

1. Comparative data tables - Various marks of P-51

Engine	P-51A Allison V-1710-81	P-51B Packard Merlin V-1650-3	P-51D PM V-1650-7	P-51H PM V-1650-9	F-82G 2 × Allison V-1710-145
Horsepower	1,200	1,620	1,695	2,218	1,600 each
Wing span	37ft 0.25in	37ft 25in	37ft 0.25in	37ft	51ft 7in
Length	32ft 2.5in	32ft 3in	32ft 3.25in	33ft 4in	42ft 2.5in
Height	13ft 8in	13ft 8in	13ft 8in	13ft 8in	13ft 9.5in
Maximum speed (mph)	390 at 20,000ft	440 at 30,000ft	437 at 25,000ft	487 at 25,000ft	460 at 21,000ft
Maximum ceiling (ft)	31,350	42,000	41,900	41,600	28,300
Weight empty (lb)	6,433	6,840	7,125	6,585	15,997
Weight loaded (lb)	10,600	11,200	12,100	11,500	25,891
Range internal (miles)	750	550	950	755	2,240
Range drop tanks (miles)	2,350	2,200	2,080	1,530	4,000
Rate of climb (mins)	9.1 to 20,000ft	7 to 20,000ft	7.3 to 20,000ft	5 to 15,000ft	
Armament – guns	4 × 0.5in Browning	4 × 0.5in Browning	6 × 0.5in	6 × 0.5in	various
Armament – bombs/RP	2 × 500lb	2 × 1,000lb	or 6 × 5in RP		

2. Order of battle of USAAF 8th Air Force, UK, 1944

1st Air Division 67th Fighter Wing

Group	Squadrons	Identification	Cowling	Spinner	Tailplane	Base
20 FG	55 FS	KI			black triangle	
	77 FS	LC	black and white vertical bars and spinner		black circle	Kingscliffe
	79 FS	MC			black square	
352 FG	328 FS	PE			red rudder	
	486 FS	P2	blue	blue	yellow rudder	Bodney
	487 FS	HO			blue rudder	
356 FG	359 FS	OC			yellow rudder	
	360 FS	PI	red and blue checkers	red and blue checkers	red rudder, black bar	Martlesham Heath
	361 FS	QI			blue rudder	
359 FG	368 FS	CV			yellow	
	369 FS	IV	green	green	red	East Wretham
	370 FS	CS			blue	
364 FG	383 FS	N2			black circle	
	384 FS	5Y	blue and white band behind spinner		black square	Honington
	385 FS	5E			black triangle	
364 Group Scouting Force		5E (9H wef March 1945)		red	red leading edges	

2nd Air Division 65th Fighter Wing

Group	Squadrons	Identification	Cowling	Spinner	Tailplane	Base
4 FG	334 FS	QP			red	
	335 FS	WD	red	red	white	Debden/Steeple Morden
	336 FS	VF			blue	
355 FG	354 FS	WR	red band behind white		red	
	357 FS	OS	blue band behind white		blue	Steeple Morden
	358 FS	YF	yellow band behind white		yellow	
361 FG	374 FS	B7			red	
	375 FS	E2	yellow	yellow	blue	Bottisham/Little Walden
	376 FS	E9			yellow	
479 FG	434 FS	L2			red	
	435 FS	J2	silver	silver	yellow	Wattisham
	436 FS	9B			black	
355 Group Scouting Force		WR	green and white cowling band		silver	

3rd Air Division 66th Fighter Wing

Group	Squadrons	Identification	Cowling and Spinner	Tailplane	Base
55 FG	38 FS	CG	green and yellow checkers and band	red	Wormingford
	338 FS	CL		green	
	343 FS	CY		yellow	
78 FG	82 FS	MX	black and white checkers	red	Duxford
	83 FS	WZ		black	
	84 FS	HL		white (edged red)	
339 FG	503 FS	D7	red and white checkered cowling	red	Fowlmere
	504 FS	5Q		green	
	505 FS	6N		yellow	
353 FG	350 FS	LH	yellow and black checkered cowling	yellow	Raydon
	351 FS	YJ		silver	
	352 FS	5X		black	
357 FG	362 FS	G4	red and yellow checkered band	silver	Leiston
	363 FS	B6		red	
	364 FS	C5		yellow	
55 Group Scouting Force		CL	green and yellow checkers and band	red and white checkers	

496 Fighter Training
Group (555 FS)   C7
7 Photographic Reconnaissance Group from January 1945   red rudder

3. Order of Battle of other USAAF Air Forces
(listing component squadrons and identification letters where known)

Air Force	Group	Component Squadrons	Identification
5th	15 FG	78 FS	
	21 FG	45 FS	
		46 FS	
	506 FG	457 FS	
		485 FS	
9th	354 FG	353 FS	FT
	100 FW	355 FS	GQ
		356 FS	AJ
	363 FG	380 FS	A9
		381 FS	5M
		382 FS	C3
10th	311 FG	528 FS	
		529 FS	
		530 FS	
12th	52 FG		
14th	23 FG	74 FS	
	75 FS		
15th	31 FG	307 FS	M2
		308 FS	WZ
		309 FS	HL
	325 FG	317 FS	
		318 FS	
		319 FS	
	332 FG	99 FS	
		100 FS	
		301 FS	
		302 FS	

Bibliography

The Army Air Forces in WW2: Combat Chronology, Kit Carter and Robert Mueller, Office of Air Force History HQ USAF.
The Army Air Forces in World War II, edited by Wesley Craven and James Cate, University of Chicago Press.
World War II Fighter Conflict, Alfred Price, Macdonald and Jane's.
The Mighty Eighth, Roger Freeman, Military Book Society.
Airfields of the Eighth, Roger Freeman, After the Battle.

P-51 Bomber Escort, William Hess, Pan/Ballantyne.
Mustang at War, Roger Freeman, Ian Allan.
The North American Mustang, M J Hardy, David and Charles.
2nd TAF, Christopher Shores, Osprey.
The North American P-51B and C, Richard Atkins, Profile Publications.
Classic Aircraft – Fighters, Bill Gunston, Hamlyn.
Camouflages and Markings, James Goulding and Robert Jones, Doubleday & Co, NY

Two Cavalier Mustangs leave Sarasota after being accepted by the USAF.

B·29
SUPERFORTRESS

John Pimlott

Below: A standard B-29 runs up its R-3350 engines.

INTRODUCTION

At 0816 on 6 August 1945 the Japanese city of Hiroshima ceased to exist. A 9000lb bomb, nicknamed 'Little Boy,' had, in less than a millisecond, produced an explosion equivalent to 20,000 tons of TNT, generating a flash of heat and a blast wave which ignited and then flattened the target area, killing approximately 78,000 people and injuring a further 51,000. It was the first atomic strike, constituting the dawn of a new and terrible era in warfare whereby heavier-than-air machines could literally tear the heart out of an enemy state, destroying with relative ease its capacity and will to wage war. The Hiroshima raid, together with another against Nagasaki three days later, was carried out by an American B-29 'Superfortress' bomber of the 509th Composite Group from Tinian in the Marianas Islands of the Central Pacific. Its actions on that August morning ensured the aircraft type a permanent place in history. The B-29 became an instrument of death of unparalleled proportions, the ultimate equipment in man's constant search for methods of mass destruction.

In truth the B-29 was neither designed nor contemplated specifically for the atomic mission. The aircraft had its origins in the period between the two world wars, when men were recovering from the terrible destruction, both physical and moral, which had characterized the Great War of 1914–18, and were trying desperately to understand how the trends and developments of that conflict might affect the future of war. The most important of these developments was undoubtedly that of air power, for although the conquest of the air dated back to the exploits of Orville and Wilbur Wright on 17 December 1903, it had taken World War I for military principles and roles to become established. During that conflict intrepid pilots of many nations had shown the capabilities of their machines, initially in reconnaissance, then in air-to-air combat and finally, in the spring of 1917, in what became known as strategic bombing. On 13 June and 7 July 1917 German Gotha bombers, operating from bases in occupied Belgium, had flown virtually unopposed over London and killed about 250 civilians through aerial bombardment. Public reaction in the English capital was dramatic: mobs ran riot in the streets, people decided not to turn up for work in the highly-vulnerable munitions factories and the government of David Lloyd George came under tremendous political pressure to organize some sort of air defense.

The government's reaction was typically British, for in the immediate aftermath of the raids a special committee was set up to investigate what had happened and to recommend ways of preventing any repetition. This committee, chaired by the South African soldier and statesman Jan Christiaan Smuts, reported in considerable haste, probably without fully considering the implications of their findings, and made a number of gloomy forecasts. To Smuts the Gotha raids represented a preview of future war, when the bombing of enemy cities would 'become the principal operations of war, to which the older forms of military and naval operations may become secondary and subordinate.' Although he did initiate a

Left: In-flight photo shows the clean aerodynamic lines of a standard B-29.
Above: Surviving B-29 of the 'Confederate Air Force'; marked as 497th BG, 73rd BW.
Far left: The first strategic bomber: a Gotha GVb in 1917.
Left center: Cottages destroyed by a Zeppelin raid, King's Lynn, 1915.
Below left: Searchlights over the Embankment, London, in 1918.
Below: Bomb damage in London: Odhams' printing house, destroyed 28 January 1918.

Above: **Brigadier General 'Billy' Mitchell in the cockpit of a Morse pursuit plane.**

complex air defense system around London which was in fact quite effective by 1918, he went on to recommend that the only real form of defense was the mounting of a strategic counteroffensive against German cities. He had problems in persuading people to accept this theory at first, but after a series of new German raids in early 1918 which included the dropping of one-ton bombs on London, political and military leaders alike decided to take their response to the heart of Germany itself. On 1 April 1918 the Royal Air Force came into existence as an autonomous service, charged solely with the mounting of a strategic bombing campaign against the enemy state.

In the event, the war ended in armistice before this bombing force could really be organized, and although a few raids were carried out against cities such as Mannheim, Frankfurt and Koblenz and plans were well advanced for hitting Berlin in the spring of 1919, strategic bombing as a policy of war was left as little more than a theory, untested and unproven but frighteningly persuasive. From the evidence of the German attacks on London it seemed that bombers could penetrate air-defense systems with impunity, drop their bombs when and where they liked, undermining the morale of the civilian population and destroying the factories upon which the state depended in fighting modern, technological war. The problems encountered by the Germans in sustaining their offensive – problems of navigation, weather and unreliable aircraft – were conveniently ignored, as were the signs of growing air defense capability shown by the anti-aircraft guns and interceptor fighters of Britain in 1918. To many people, Smuts was right. In the event of future war, military and naval campaigns would be relatively unimportant; the decisive operations would be carried out by waves of bombers flying freely over vulnerable heartland targets.

It was not in everyone's interests to believe such stories, and in most of the modern states of the world army and navy leaders fought hard to undermine and discredit the ideas of their air colleagues. In Britain this took the form of attempts, throughout the 1920s and early 1930s, to disband the RAF as a separate service, thereby returning air power back into the hands of the other two arms. In other states, notably America, it was manifested by a conscious policy of preventing autonomy from developing at all. Despite the theories of people such as Giulio Douhet in Italy, Sir Hugh Trenchard in Britain and Brigadier General William ('Billy') Mitchell in America,

by the early 1930s a paradoxical situation had arisen. Few air forces were organized for strategic bombing but the idea itself had both caught and terrified the public imagination. It was not until the 1930s had produced the specter of fascism in Europe, particularly that associated with National Socialism in Germany, that the politicians of the 'Free World' began to stir. To many commentators, they were almost too late.

One of the most vociferous of these commentators was Billy Mitchell, for although he was to die in February 1936, he had laid the groundwork of strategic bombing in America. An air commander with the American Expeditionary Force in France in 1917–18, he had been deeply impressed by the potential of aerial bombardment on the proposed RAF pattern and had returned to the United States intent upon gaining strategic autonomy for what was then a divided air corps, tied inextricably to providing tactical support to land and naval forces. To Mitchell strategic bombing was a natural war policy for the United States; the country was isolated between two immense oceans, making response to any attack upon her interests overseas dependent upon a long and costly process of preparing and dispatching military or naval forces to the scene of action. By comparison aircraft could provide an immediate response, appearing almost instantaneously over the enemy state to threaten or even carry out aerial bombardment. A fleet of bombers was therefore cheaper and more effective than a fleet of vulnerable battleships or a large, slow-moving army.

Mitchell did not succeed in his self-appointed task – he was in fact court-martialled and forced to resign his commission 'for five years' in 1925 after having made a particularly heated public attack upon his superiors – but he did manage to influence enough members of the next generation of American air officers to ensure that his ideas did not die with him. They were tacitly supported by a continuing trend of improvement in aeronautical engineering and aircraft design in America which at least made sure that if Mitchell's theories were ever accepted by the strategists and planners in Washington, the necessary equipment would be available.

Well to the forefront in the field of aerial technology during this period was the Boeing Aircraft Company of Seattle, Washington, which produced a series of innovatory designs for long-range bombers, based in part upon their experience and expertise in the field of commercial airliners. In 1930 Boeing produced what became known as the B-9, the world's first all-metal, twin-engined, monoplane bomber, and when an experimental model was tested by the Army Air Corps (AAC) at Wright Field, Dayton, Ohio, in April 1931 Army planners were sufficiently impressed to order six for further evaluation. With a top speed of 188mph at 6000ft and a bomb-load capacity of 2000lb, the B-9 was the beginning of the development trend which was to produce the B-29 nine years later.

Boeing was not the only company in the arena, and in July 1932 the Glenn L Martin Company of Baltimore, Maryland, improved significantly upon the performance of the B-9. Their B-10 all-metal, twin-engined, monoplane bomber, introducing the innovation of a retractable undercarriage, reached 197mph. Three months later, with new engines fitted, this speed was pushed over the 200mph mark and the Army gained permission to purchase 48 of the type. In 1934 one of Mitchell's most able disciples, Lieutenant Colonel Henry ('Hap') Arnold, led a flight of B-10s nonstop from Juneau, Alaska, to Seattle, illustrating the potential for long-range bombing and national defense which such aircraft possessed. It may be presumed that the lessons were not entirely wasted, for it was about this time that the AAC planners began to put forward specifications for even more modern designs. One of these, issued in 1934, was satisfied by the B-18 from the Douglas Aircraft Company of Santa Monica, California, and 133 examples of this twin-engined monoplane, capable of carrying 4400lb of bombs over 2000 miles at 217mph, were ordered in January 1936.

Meanwhile the Boeing designers had not been idle. In the summer of 1934 they produced an experimental four-engined machine, known as the XB-15, to satisfy a very optimistic Army demand, Project A, for a long-range bomber capable of carrying 2000lb over something like 5000 miles. This attempt to produce an aircraft which would extend the capability of the AAC beyond the realms of national defense into those of strategic bombing proper had disappointing results – the XB-15 was far too heavy for the available engines and only managed 197mph – but Boeing had learned a great deal. They were now well ahead of their rivals in four-engined design and its problems, so when the Army toned down its specifications to the more modest range of 2000 miles, the Company was ready with a design, having already produced a mockup at their own expense. This became the highly successful B-17 'Flying Fortress' and, despite a prototype crash on 30 October 1935, this design was the only truly modern bomber in the AAC inventory when America found herself at war in late 1941. Much of the technological knowledge which was to be devoted to the B-29 design came from the manufacture of this aircraft.

Thus by the mid-1930s the AAC had begun to acquire the equipment necessary for the implementation of Mitchell's ideas, but as yet they lacked the political backing to expand their forces and to plan their future strategy. This gradually developed as events in Europe unfolded toward war, for although many Americans were intent upon a policy of isolation from affairs abroad, certain incidents were beginning to penetrate their protective shell. Many of these involved air power, for while the AAC had been slowly building up its design base, other states, particularly Germany, had been rearming and testing their new equipment in combat. On 26 April 1937 elements of the German Condor Legion, supporting General Franco's forces in the Spanish Civil War, bombed the Basque town of Guernica in a raid which sent shivers of apprehension through the people of Europe. The peripheral shock waves even reached Washington, and when the obvious potential of the Luftwaffe was added to the known successes of Japanese air power over Chinese cities, President Franklin D Roosevelt began to consider the question of American defense. He was particularly concerned about the apparent paralysis of Britain and France in their dealings with an expan-

Above: **Brigadier General William 'Billy' Mitchell.**

sionist Hitler, recognizing that this arose in large measure from the fears of Luftwaffe raids upon their respective cities. Intent upon preventing a similar situation in America, in January 1937 Roosevelt requested an appropriation of $300 million from Congress to enable the AAC to build up its strength, ostensibly as a deterrent. This request was granted on 3 April and the AAC planners were given the green light.

Time was not wasted. Even while Congress was deliberating, Arnold – by now a major general and acting head of the AAC – had consulted the famous airman Charles A Lindbergh about the current state of German aeronautical engineering. Lindbergh, recently returned from a detailed tour of Luftwaffe factories and bases, was convinced that Germany was well ahead of her potential European rivals. He was able to persuade Arnold that the AAC must look very seriously indeed at the future of aerial technology if America was not to be left far behind. As a result Lindbergh was appointed to a special committee, chaired by Brigadier General W G Kilner, which was directed to examine and report on the long-term needs of the AAC. A report was produced in late June 1939 which recommended the immediate initiation of plans to develop several new long-range medium and heavy bombers. Official consideration of these suggestions was hastened considerably by the outbreak of war in Europe on 1 September. On 10 November Arnold felt bold enough to request authority to contract major aircraft companies for studies of a Very Long-Range (VLR) bomber, capable of carrying any future war well beyond the shores of America. Approval was granted on 2 December and AAC engineering officers under Captain Donald L Putt of Material Command at Wright Field began to prepare their official specification. The B-29 was about to be conceived.

Below: **Mitchell (center, with stick) and staff, Koblenz, 1919.**

DEVELOPMENT

The official letter, containing Request for Data R-40B and Specification XC-218, arrived on the desk of Philip G Johnson, President of the Boeing Company, on 5 February 1940. It was an ambitious proposal, calling for a bomber with a range of 5333 miles yet with a bigger bomb load and higher speed than the B-17. Moreover initial designs had to be submitted within thirty days.

Fortunately the Boeing Company was well prepared. After the failure of the XB-15 in 1934 the drawings had not been scrapped but worked upon, at the Company's expense, to produce plans for Model 316. The B-17 had been improved, at least on paper, to become Model 322. Further Company specifications had been produced in 1939 and in December of that year, again at their own expense, a full-scale mockup of Model 341 had been produced, envisaging wing loadings as high as 64lb per sq ft, a twelve-man crew and an ability to carry 2000lb of bombs over distances in excess of 5000 miles. This was remarkably close to Specification XC-218 and the design, slightly reworked, was submitted to the AAC within the set deadline. At the same time, similar designs were produced by the Douglas, Lockheed and Consolidated aircraft companies. As it turned out, all were asked to resubmit in April, after

incorporating into their designs such items as leakproof fuel tanks and armor protection, found by the combatants in Europe at the time to be of paramount importance.

The new bids were evaluated in May 1940 by a special AAC Board under Colonel Oliver P Echols of Material Command and two designs were initially favored, those of Lockheed and Boeing, with the latter, now known as Model 345, receiving unofficial preference. It was an impressive design, contemplating a pressurized aircraft (the first of its kind for purely military use) capable of carrying one ton of bombs over the stipulated 5333 miles at a cruising speed of about 290mph. It was to have four engines, a twelve-man crew and a tricycle undercarriage (again, an innovation for a heavy bomber) with double wheels all round. It was to be defended by four retractable turrets, each mounting twin 0.5in machine guns, and a tail turret with twin machine guns and a 20mm cannon. The wing span was to be an awesome 141ft 2in, the length 93ft and the weight 97,700lb. Colonel Echols' Board gave it the AAC designation XB-29.

Below: **B-29As in various stages of production at the Boeing factory in Renton, Washington, 1944.**

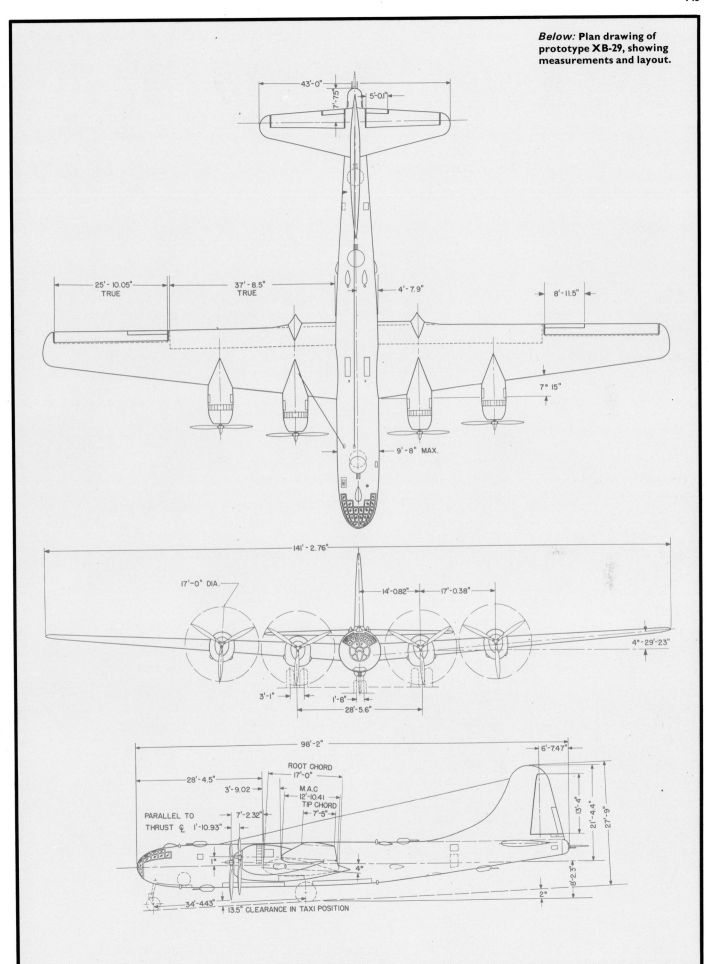

Below: **Plan drawing of prototype XB-29, showing measurements and layout.**

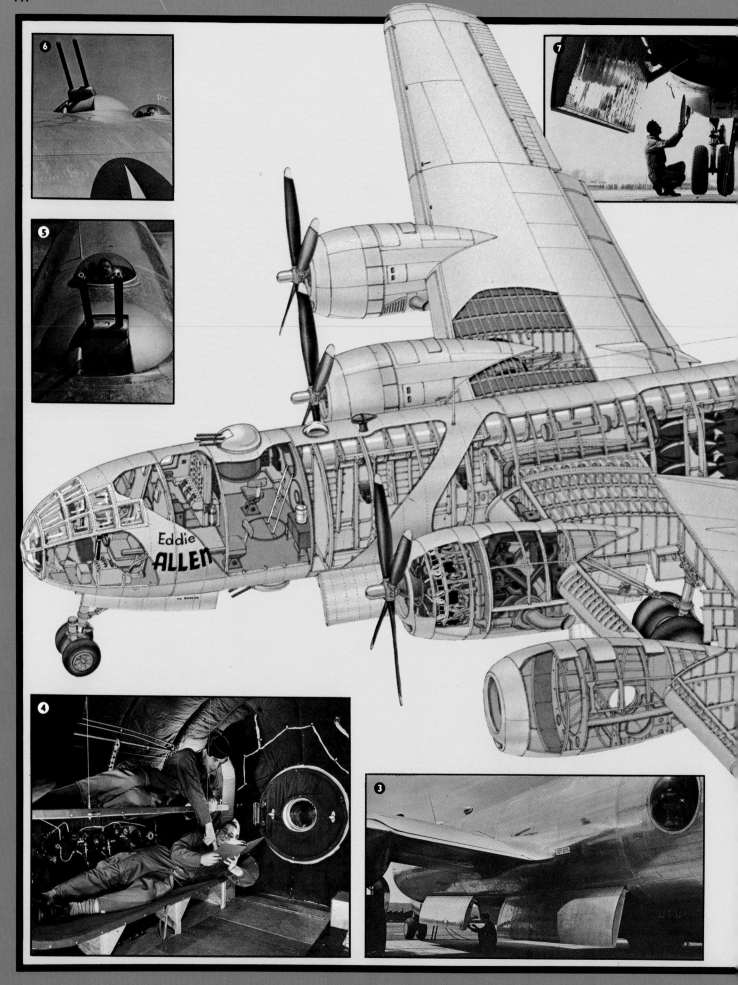

Eddie
ALLEN

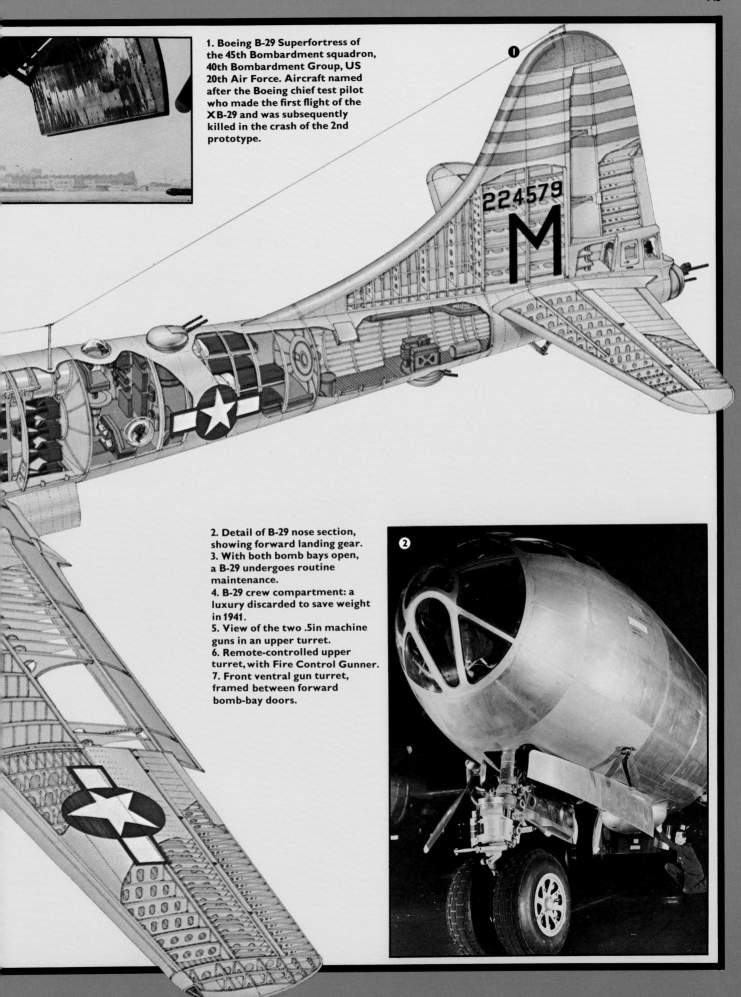

1. Boeing B-29 Superfortress of the 45th Bombardment squadron, 40th Bombardment Group, US 20th Air Force. Aircraft named after the Boeing chief test pilot who made the first flight of the XB-29 and was subsequently killed in the crash of the 2nd prototype.

2. Detail of B-29 nose section, showing forward landing gear.
3. With both bomb bays open, a B-29 undergoes routine maintenance.
4. B-29 crew compartment: a luxury discarded to save weight in 1941.
5. View of the two .5in machine guns in an upper turret.
6. Remote-controlled upper turret, with Fire Control Gunner.
7. Front ventral gun turret, framed between forward bomb-bay doors.

224579
M

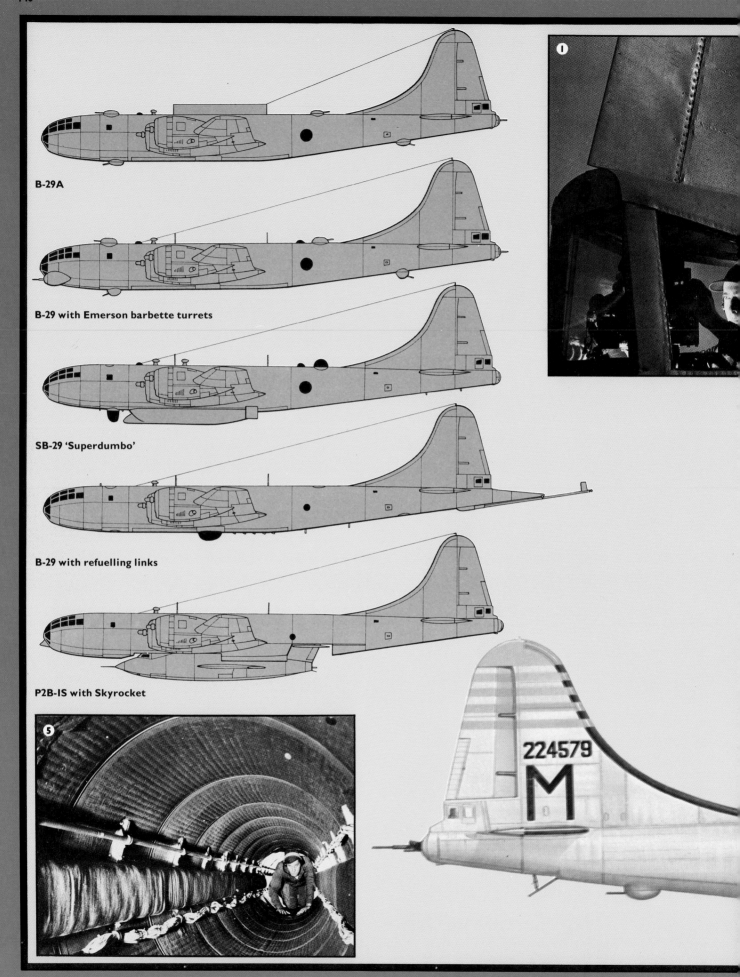

B-29A

B-29 with Emerson barbette turrets

SB-29 'Superdumbo'

B-29 with refuelling links

P2B-IS with Skyrocket

224579
M

1. Tail gunner shows the sighting and firing mechanism for his weapons.
2. Typical tail-gun array – one 20mm cannon and two .5in machine guns.
3. General layout of the gun-control system on a standard B-29.
4. B-29 *Eddie Allen*, 40th BG, 58th BW.
5. Pressurized tunnel linking forward and mid-plane crew areas of a B-29.

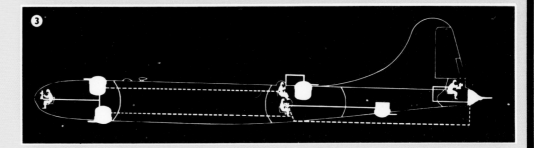

On 4 June 1940 Arnold authorized both Boeing and Lockheed to produce mockups of their designs for wind-tunnel tests and to deliver prototypes to the Wright Field testing center for evaluation. Such was the preparedness of the Boeing Company that it completed preliminary designs by 24 August, enabling Arnold to contract officially for two XB-29 prototypes (at a cost of $3,615,095) on 6 September. Full-scale mockups were ready by late November and when AAC engineering officers visited Seattle they were so impressed that a third prototype was added to the order. By this time Lockheed had decided to withdraw from the competition (their XB-30 never in fact flew), and although the second contract was transferred to Consolidated and the XB-32 – which was eventually to be produced as the B-32 'Dominator' – Boeing were so far advanced that their design was virtually assured of success.

This did not mean that the production of the XB-29 was straightforward: far from it. The design was so advanced and, in some respects, almost revolutionary, that problems were sure to arise. The first of these concerned the wing, for Boeing were, to all intents and purposes, attempting to achieve a technological breakthrough. The difficulty was air resistance, for in an aircraft as heavy as the XB-29 the load borne by each square foot of wing surface was astronomical by contemporary standards. Although it was perfectly feasible that the aircraft, with 1736sq ft of wing area, would fly, its landing speed would be prohibitively high. Boeing designers got around the problem by developing huge flaps, covering 332sq ft of wing area so that, in effect, almost one-sixth of the wings could be lowered to reduce landing speeds. It gave the aircraft a distinctively long, thin wing which, at first glance, looked incapable of supporting the machine in the air and which many airmen distrusted on sight. What they could not see, however, were the immensely strong trusses, constructed in a web-like pattern out of flat pieces of sheet metal, which Boeing engineers had specially developed. The result was a robust aircraft, the clean lines of which were considerably enhanced by the decision to countersink all rivet heads until they lay flush with the aluminum alloy skin surfaces. In the end the XB-29 looked rather like a long, smooth cigar.

Another problem concerned pressurization, for although a cabin supercharger of proven design was available (Boeing had already used it in their commercial Stratoliner of the 1930s), the principle was endangered by the obvious need to open bomb bays during high-altitude flight. Again the designers came up with a solution, this time by producing two areas of pressurization – the extensively glazed control cabin at the front and the gunners' area amidships – connected by a tunnel, big enough at 34in diameter for a man to crawl through, but totally separate from the non-pressurized bomb bays. A third compartment in the tail, unconnected to the others, housed the rear gunner. It was another distinctive feature of the aircraft and rendered its legend even more memorable.

However, not all the problems could be solved at Seattle, for certain areas of design were outside the full control of the Boeing Company. The most important of these concerned the engines, which were chosen by the AAC. They favored the Wright Aeronautical Corporation's R-3350 (the number refers to the total displacement in cubic inches), an eighteen-cylinder air-cooled radial engine, capable of producing 2200bhp at takeoff, and turning a three-bladed 17ft diameter propeller.

Left: **B-29s under inspection at Marietta, Georgia, before delivery to Bombardment Squadrons.**

Unfortunately, although this had been designed and tested in 1937, achieving the desired power through the addition of a pair of General Electric B-11 exhaust-driven turbo-superchargers automatically regulated by a Minneapolis-Honeywell electronic system, the engine had not been put into production. In mid-1940 only one example existed, necessitating a speed of production which was to cause persistent problems.

In addition, as work on the prototypes progressed, the AAC insisted upon a phenomenal number of design changes, totalling nearly 900 between mid-1940 and late 1942, in the light of lessons emerging from the war in Europe. The most significant of these concerned the armament of the XB-29, for although the original retractable turrets supplied by Sperry were satisfactory, in late 1941 the firm of General Electric came up with a revolutionary new design. Centered upon a small computer which could correct automatically for range, altitude, air speed and temperature, it produced a central control mechanism which would enable any gunner (except the man in the tail) to take over more than one of the four 0.5in turrets at one time. Thus a gunner without a target could pass control of his turret over to a colleague who was tracking an enemy aircraft. In addition, as the whole system was remote controlled anyway, it was possible for the gunners (again, with the exception of the man in the tail) to be physically removed from their guns, so escaping the noise and vibrations of combat. The concept was too good to ignore, and Boeing were directed to incorporate it regardless of the time-loss involved. Unfortunately such sophistication required a lot of electrical power, necessitating the addition of a large number of specially-designed generators to the aircraft. This delayed production still further and, rather ominously, increased the weight of the aircraft to 105,000lb, even after such luxuries as auxiliary crew bunks and cabin soundproofing had been dispensed with.

Nevertheless, as early as May 1941, before any of the prototypes had even been test flown, the AAC – soon to be renamed the Army Air Force (AAF) – ordered 250 of what now became the B-29. Boeing immediately expanded its work force, opened a new factory at Wichita, Kansas, and, following an increase in the order to 500 after the Japanese air attack on Pearl Harbor had catapulted America into the war, started to subcontract parts of the production process. The Fisher Division of General Motors was charged with producing all the necessary castings, forgings and stampings and both the Bell Aircraft Corporation and North American Aviation were contracted to produce B-29 subassemblies. Factories at Marietta, Georgia, and Kansas City, were constructed to assemble the aircraft in their final form.

All this took place in early 1942 and the B-29 had yet to take to the air. Because of all the problems and delays it was not until early September that the first prototype was finally wheeled out of the factory at Seattle to begin taxi tests. Boeing's chief test pilot, Edmund T ('Eddie') Allen – winner of the 1939 Chanute Award for services to aeronautical sciences – ran the engines up initially on 9 September, and lifted the aircraft off the ground in three short hops of about 15ft altitude six days later. He was not completely satisfied with the engines – according to estimates at the time they could barely last an hour before becoming dangerously overheated – but on 21 September 1942 XB-29 Number One took off on a 75-minute flight. Allen was impressed, as was the AAF project officer, Donald Putt (now a Colonel) when he took it up next day. He scribbled his impressions as he flew, noting that it was 'unbelievable for such a large plane to be so easy on controls . . ., easier to fly than B-17 . . ., faster than any previous heavy bomber . . ., control forces very light . . ., stall characteristics remarkable for heavy plane . . .' These impressions were reinforced on 2 December when, after eighteen hours flight-testing time had been accrued, the prototype was taken up to 25,000ft for the first time. It was clear that the aircraft had the potential to meet the exacting terms of Specification XC-218.

This was a false dawn, soon to be darkened by persistent examples of engine failure. On 28 December the number one R-3350 of the prototype caught fire, forcing Allen to return prematurely to Boeing Field. Two days later, during the maiden flight of XB-29 Number Two, a similar occurrence led to a suspension of further tests. They were renewed on 18 February 1943, only to end in disaster as a double engine fire in the second prototype led to the death of Allen and the entire test crew. It began to look as if Boeing were suffering from a prototype jinx.

Arnold ordered an immediate investigation into the accident, which soon discovered that the fault lay in the hurried production of the R-3350s – an inevitable by-product of the original choice of engine for which no one could really be held to blame. Nevertheless, with further testing of the XB-29

now virtually stopped, the VLR concept was taking on the appearance of an illusion. Something had to be done very quickly indeed to prevent a cancellation of the entire project and with it an end to the strategic dreams of the AAF. Arnold was well aware of this and in mid-April 1943 he set up what was known as the 'B-29 Special Project' under the command of Brigadier General Kenneth B Wolfe. He was told to take charge of the entire B-29 program, including production, flight testing and crew training, with a view to combat commitment by the end of the year. It was a tall order, nearly cut short on 29 May when the third XB-29 prototype was saved from disaster by the opportune discovery, just before takeoff, that the aerilon cables had been connected the wrong way round. However, the wider events of the war, particularly in the Pacific, were demanding the commitment of ever-larger forces. The role to be played by the B-29 was under intense discussion even while the prototypes were being tested.

Above right: **B-29s take shape in the huge, purpose-built hanger at Wichita, Kansas.**
Below: **Early production B-29 takes off from Boeing Field, Wichita, the new plant expanded for B-29 production.**

PREPARING FOR COM

President Roosevelt had long been interested in the possibility of bombing Japan. Before Pearl Harbor he had often discussed with his more immediate advisers plans for providing long-range bombers for the Chinese leader Chiang Kai-shek so that he could retaliate for the air attacks which had been mounted against his cities since the beginning of the Sino–Japanese war in 1937. One of these proposals had almost come to fruition in December 1940 when, on the advice of the Secretary of State Cordell Hull and Secretary of the Treasury Henry Morgenthau, Roosevelt had actually promised to transfer some of the new B-17s to Chinese hands on the express understanding that they would be used against Japanese cities. It was only after General George Marshall, Chief of Staff to the Army, had pointed out that there were barely enough B-17s for American needs that the idea was dropped. Chiang Kai-

shek had to be satisfied with 100 fighter planes instead, but the incident showed how Roosevelt's mind was working. It was therefore no surprise that he returned to the theme of bombing Japan almost immediately after Pearl Harbor.

Unfortunately, despite the growing interest in Mitchell's ideas and the development of the B-17, the AAF – for too long the Cinderella of the services – was in no position to mount an immediate campaign. In accordance with the strategic principles laid down at the Anglo–American Arcadia Conference in Washington (22 December 1941 – 14 January 1942), the emphasis was to be placed upon defeating the Axis powers in Europe first, after which the Allies would be able to devote their full strength against Japan. Given the political realities of the time, particularly the fact that Germany was threatening the territorial integrity of the Allied homelands far more than

Below: **Standard B-29 on crew-familiarization flight, 1944.**

Japan was, this was probably quite sensible. However it did mean that the products of American war industry were channelled across the Atlantic rather than the Pacific. Thus, for example, the majority of B-17s produced in 1942 were sent to build up the 8th Army Air Force stationed in England, and few found their way to the Pacific theater.

Even if large numbers of B-17s had been available, they could hardly have achieved a great deal against the Japanese homeland for the simple reason of geography. During the extraordinary run of Japanese successes between December 1941 and June 1942 all the Pacific bases capable of sustaining bomber formations within range of Japan – the Philippines, Wake, Guam, the Dutch East Indies – had all been lost by the Allies, leaving the Americans with very few options indeed if Roosevelt's demands for action were to be met. One possi-

bility was explored by Colonel James H Doolittle on 18 April 1942 when he led a surprise raid on Tokyo by specially-modified B-25 carrier-borne bombers, but the enterprise was extremely costly. Not only were all sixteen of the bombers lost, but the people of China, to whom the surviving crews turned for aid after baling out of their stricken craft, suffered terribly when the Japanese mounted a land offensive to capture all territory within flying range of their home islands.

Doolittle's raid did boost Allied morale at a difficult time in the war, however, and probably made Roosevelt all the more determined to initiate a more permanent bombing campaign, resurrecting his former ideas about basing the aircraft in China. He began by authorizing an airlift of supplies from India, over the Hump of the Himalayas, to bolster Chiang Kai-shek's forces. By January 1943, at the Casablanca Conference of Allied leaders, he was openly discussing sending '200 to 300 planes' to China, including heavy bombers. It was envisaged that the latter aircraft, which, given the state of development of the B-29 at the time, must have been B-17s or B-24 Liberators, would be based in eastern India, merely using Chinese bases to refuel on their long haul to Japan. However problems of supply – sufficient transport aircraft were just not available to support a bombing campaign in such adverse geographical conditions – coupled with the fact that neither the B-17 nor the B-24 really had the ranges to make the journeys involved, prevented any further action being taken. Moreover, with the gradual build-up of air operations against Germany and the plans for an invasion of occupied Europe taking strategic precedence, the resources, even of a mobilized America, could not satisfy the demands of a two-front war in this way.

The picture began to change in August 1943 when, at the Quadrant Conference at Quebec, Arnold submitted an 'Air Plan for the defeat of Japan.' This document contained the first reference in strategic policy to the B-29. Up to that time a rather vague proposal for committing the new bombers to Europe had existed – it was envisaged that twelve groups would be stationed in Northern Ireland and twelve near Cairo, Egypt – but Arnold's plan was much more specific. He proposed the deployment of the 58th Bombardment Wing (Very Heavy), newly activated under Wolfe's command and organized to contain four groups of B-29s, to the China, Burma, India (CBI) theater by the end of the year. Following Mitchell's beliefs on strategic bombing almost to the letter, Arnold expressed confidence that once the B-29 was available in sufficient numbers (he envisaged a total deployment of 780 in the CBI), the bombers could bring Japan to her knees in something like six months through the destruction of her war industries. They were to be stationed permanently in China, possibly around Chengtu in the south-center of the country, with supplies of fuel, bombs and spares being flown in from eastern India. Full-scale operations, involving the full total of B-29s, would probably not begin much before October 1944, but this could mean that Japan would be defeated, without the need for a costly seaborne invasion, by mid-1945, a date

already projected by the Combined Chiefs of Staff as the end of the war.

Roosevelt was delighted with the concept and followed it up, despite the fact that both the Joint Plans Committee and the Joint Logistics Committee rejected Arnold's plan as strategically unfeasible. He passed the proposal on to Lieutenant General Joseph W ('Vinegar Joe') Stilwell, Chiang Kai-shek's acerbic American Chief of Staff, for evaluation, and was even more delighted when he suggested a return to the President's original plan of eight months earlier. Instead of basing the B-29s in China, Stilwell proposed that they should be maintained in eastern India, merely staging through Chengtu in the process or aftermath of the raids. This had obvious advantages. The raids could begin at the earliest possible date as a complex base facility would not need to be constructed in China and the airfields in India would not be particularly vulnerable to a surprise Japanese land offensive. Also the thorny problem of supply would be simplified, especially if the B-29s themselves could be used to carry fuel, bombs and spares to build up the dumps at Chengtu. The Joint Chiefs of Staff were still not completely convinced, but Roosevelt soon made sure that they had no choice in the matter. On 10 November 1943 he sought, and gained, the co-operation of the British in the provision of bases around Calcutta and persuaded Chiang Kai-shek to begin the construction, with American engineering help, of five new airfields around Chengtu. The B-29 appeared at last to have a strategic role.

However, things rarely go smoothly in wartime and this was no exception. As early as October 1943 Arnold had become concerned about the speed with which the President was preparing his strategy, particularly as he was frequently discussing the first raids being mounted on 1 January 1944. Arnold was forced to inform him that B-29 deployment could not

Below: Roosevelt (second from left, seated) and Churchill (right, seated) with advisers, Quebec, August 1943.

Below: Roosevelt and Churchill brief war correspondents and service officers, Casablanca, January 1943.

Below: Four views of Wichita-built B-29, serial number 293869, as it is prepared for squadron delivery.

really begin much before March or April of that year, with the campaign itself commencing on 1 May at the earliest. Roosevelt was bitterly disappointed, chiefly because such delays could well be seen as breaking promises made to China, but he could do little about it. The enormously complex job of preparing the new bombers for combat could simply not be rushed, even under the pressures of war.

First of all, an entirely new command structure had to be set up to ensure that the program of crew training was carried out and that the bombers, once deployed, were capable of performing their strategic task. Arnold began the process in late November 1943, moving Wolfe yet again, this time to the command of a new formation, XX Bomber Command, which would take responsibility for mounting the campaign. The Command was assigned two Bombardment Wings, each of four groups of B-29s – the 58th, the command of which was now transferred from Wolfe to his erstwhile deputy, Colonel Leonard ('Jake') Harmon, and the 73rd, newly-activated under Colonel Thomas H Chapman. Headquarters were set up conveniently close to the B-29 factory at Wichita and responsibility for crew training delegated to Colonel La Verne G ('Blondie') Saunders of the Second Army Air Force. He moved into four airfields in Kansas – Smoky Hill, Pratt, Great Bend and Walker – and began his onerous task.

The crew training program was one of the most complicated aspects of the B-29 story. By late 1943 the size of a typical crew had been settled as eleven, the original Boeing specification of twelve having been reduced by the introduction of the General Electric gun system, which dispensed with the services of one turret gunner. Five members of each crew were officers (the aircraft commander, pilot, bombardier, navigator and flight engineer – although the last-named post did become an enlisted man's responsibility as the war progressed), and six were enlisted men (the radio operator, radar operator, Central Fire Control gunner, left gunner, right gunner and tailgunner), and all required some degree of specialist training. It usually took something like 27

weeks to produce a fully-fledged pilot, fifteen to train a navigator and twelve to produce a competent gunner, and all this had to take place before the men could be brought together and trained specifically for the B-29. Even using the revised deployment schedule put forward by Arnold there was not enough time available to start from scratch, so volunteers were called for among B-24 crews recently returned to America from operations in Europe and North Africa. Even then the problems were by no means solved. The B-29 was a complex piece of machinery, bigger and faster than the B-24 and with more sophisticated equipment on board, necessitating a fairly lengthy process of crew integration before combat deployment could begin. The whole affair was not helped by a unique policy decision to provide each B-29 with two crews, presumably in deference to the enormous distances which would have to be flown once the campaign began.

Saunders thus faced a tremendous task in late 1943, and it is to his credit that enough crews were available when the 58th Bombardment Wing left America for the CBI a few months later. There can be no doubt that the training was of a sketchy nature, partly because of the very tight time schedules involved, but also because of a chronic shortage of B-29s throughout the training period. Crews slowly began to arrive at the Kansas bases in November 1943, fully expecting to be introduced immediately to the new bomber that they had heard so much about. They were invariably disappointed – in fact some of the gunners did not even see a B-29 until early 1944 – and had to be satisfied instead with simulated training on rather tired B-17s. This did at least enable a degree of crew integration to take place – the aircraft commanders, pilots and flight engineers were usually trained for five weeks as separate teams to ensure that they worked together during the complicated and dangerous period of takeoff – but by the end of December a mere 67 pilots had managed to fly a B-29, and very few crews had even been brought together as a complete team. Even those who had were restricted in their training, for the B-17s that were used for formation-flying practice

Right: The Tokyo Raid of 18 April 1942: one of Doolittle's modified B-25s takes off from USS *Hornet.*
Below: B-29B, used for training commanders, pilots and flight engineers, 1944.

Above: Lt Gen Joseph ('Vinegar Joe') Stilwell, Burma, 1943.
Above left: Stilwell (center) at a planning conference, 1944.
Left: Navigator briefs commander and pilot prior to takeoff on training flight.

Above: **Head-on view of production B-29 shows length of wing and tricycle undercarriage (B-17s and B-29s in background).**

could barely reach 20,000ft altitude, 8000ft below that envisaged as the operating height of the B-29. The whole production program for the aircraft appeared to have become bogged down.

The main reason for this sorry state of affairs is fairly easy to isolate in retrospect, for Boeing was being asked to produce an almost revolutionary aircraft in an impossibly short time, and their job was not made any easier by the constant call for modifications as the lessons of air combat, particularly in Europe, were assessed. Thus although a total of 97 B-29s had been produced by mid-January 1944, only sixteen were flyable and none had been issued to the 58th Bombardment Wing. They were all in AAF modification centers, chiefly at Marietta, Georgia, undergoing a series of improvements and changes which sometimes took sixty days to complete.

The most important, if not the most time consuming, of these modifications concerned the engines. In the aftermath of the prototype crash in February 1943, the R-3350 had been further developed and improved by the Wright engineers, but problems remained. Some of these were solved by the replacement of the original R-3350-13 packs on the prototypes with R-3350-21 models on the early production aircraft, and this had at least reduced the risk of engine fires spreading to the highly-inflammable aluminum-covered wings. Accidents continued at an alarming rate – between February 1943 and September 1944 something like nineteen B-29s are known to have been lost to engine fires – and yet another R-3350 model, the 23, was developed. Unfortunately these were not ready to be fitted to the aircraft as they came off the production line at Wichita, so they had to be added at the modification centers. At the same time the three-bladed propellers of the XB-29s were replaced by four-bladed ones of 16ft 7in diameter. These were Hamilton Standard Hydromatic propellers, with constant-speed governors and hydraulic operation for pitch control and feathering. They represented an improvement in design, but, of course, took time to provide and fit.

Meanwhile, AAF engineers had to check out the condition of the B-29s to make them combat-ready. They were helped by civilian specialists in certain key areas, notably the General Electric gun system. The comments of one of these men, Philip J Klass, illustrates the immense nature of their task:

The condition of the General Electric system was pretty horrible, and I assume that was true for many others. Wires interconnecting aircraft cables made by newly-trained workers sometimes ran to the wrong pins on connectors. Whoever stripped the insulation off sometimes nicked four or five of the seven strands of wire, and left the connection hanging by only a couple. There were blobs of solder shorting out adjacent pins or sockets in the connectors. We did the best we could to assure that the turret system was operable, but we lacked the time to inspect every wire and every connector, and we could only hope they would hang together. (Quoted by David D Anderton, *B-29 Superfortress at War* Ian Allen, 1978.)

Similar problems were experienced with the radar systems, for the AN/APQ-13 bombing-navigational aid, based upon the British-designed H2S system which provided a blurred but useful radar map of the ground as the aircraft flew over, was a complex piece of kit. The radome, containing a 30in radar antenna, was situated between the two bomb bays on the early B-29s and was particularly vulnerable to dirt and general misuse, so had to be carefully checked. Finally certain combat modifications were added to the list, including the addition of extra fuel tanks for the journey out to India and, as supply problems loomed nearer, special dollies and mounts in the bomb bays so that each B-29 could take a spare engine with it. It was all a lengthy business and it soon began to look as if Arnold's revised promise of 150 bombers in the CBI by mid-April 1944 was not going to be realized.

Faced with this possibility, Arnold made a personal visit to Marietta in mid-February, only to be assured that all would be ready by 10 March when deployment could begin. He planned accordingly and it was not until he and one of his assistants, Major General B E Meyer, arrived at Salina on 9 March to supervise the departure of the B-29s that the full extent of the delays became apparent. The modification program was in complete chaos, with not one of the bombers fully combat-ready or even likely to be so in the immediate future. Appalled at the lack of organization and efficiency, Arnold directed Meyer to take charge, demanding a full report on the state of readiness of every B-29 by the following morning. The resultant burst of frenetic activity – known to those involved as the 'Battle of Kansas' or 'Kansas Blitz' – was remarkable in its achievements. Beginning in mid-March as many technicians and specialists as possible were drafted into the modification centers to work flat out to satisfy the delivery deadline of mid-April. Work went on round-the-clock, often in extremely adverse weather conditions, but the first B-29 was ready by

the end of the month. Others quickly followed, until 150 of them had been handed over to the XX Bomber Command by 15 April.

As soon as the aircraft were received, Wolfe assigned them to squadrons within the 58th Bombardment Wing (the 73rd had not been detailed for the CBI until later in 1944), and they took off for India. It was an enormous journey, covering some 11,530 miles and involving stops at Marrakech, Cairo, Karachi and Calcutta. One B-29 even flew to England first in an attempt to confuse Axis intelligence about the actual theater of operations. The speed of modification and preparation soon began to tell and a number of accidents occurred. These culminated in the week 15–22 April, when a total of five B-29s crashed near Karachi, all from overheated engines. The bombers were immediately grounded while an investigation was mounted.

The results – basically that the R-3350s had not been designed to operate in ground temperatures in excess of 115

degrees Fahrenheit – were wired back to America and the Wright engineers yet again tried to sort out the problems. They concluded that the fault lay in the exhaust valves on the rear row of cylinders which were literally melting under pressure, and to correct it they designed new engine baffles to direct a blast of cooling air onto the stricken area. They also improved the flow of oil to the rear cylinders by installing crossover tubes from the intake to the exhaust port of the five top cylinders on both the front and rear rows. It was a patch-up job, but it did seem to work. B-29 flights were resumed and by 8 May 1944, only just outside the schedule originally put forward by Arnold the previous October, 148 of the bombers had reached Marrakech, with 130 of them actually on their airfields in India. It had been a long and difficult road, but the B-29 was about to enter the war. It was probably fortunate that the commanders and crews of the 58th Bombardment Wing could not see into the future, for their problems were only just beginning.

Below: **B-29 radar operator prepares his AN/APQ-13 bombing-navigational receiver equipment.**

Below: **The worker adjusting the rudder acts as a useful yardstick for the height of a B-29 tail fin.**

THE RAIDS FROM CHIN

As the B-29s arrived in eastern India the four Bombardment Groups of the 58th Bombardment Wing were assigned their base locations. The headquarters of the 58th BW, together with the four Bombardment Squadrons of the 40th BG (the 25th, 44th, 45th and 395th) were allocated an airfield at Chakulia, the 444th BG (676th, 677th, 678th and 679th BS) went to Charra; the 462nd BG (768th, 769th, 770th and 771st BS) to Piardoba; and the 468th BG (792nd, 793rd, 794th and 795th BS) to Kharagpur, the latter having already been chosen by Wolfe as the headquarters of XX Bomber Command as a whole. All of these bases, lying to the west of Calcutta, had originally been established in 1942–43 for B-24 Liberators, but engineering difficulties had delayed their being fully prepared for the B-29s, so conditions were poor. The runways were still in the process of being lengthened (from 6000 to 7200ft), and although this did not prevent the movement of the big bombers, it did curtail fully-loaded takeoffs and so impose delays. In fact the 444th BG had only been assigned Charra base as a temporary expedient, for their permanent field at Dudhkundi was not prepared at all. They did not make the move until late May, after which Charra became a transport base for the C-87s and C-46s which formed part of XX Bomber Command's transport fleet.

A similar picture emerged when Wolfe and Saunders (who had taken over command of the 58th BW from Harmon before deployment from America began) flew over the Hump in a pair of B-29s on 24 April to inspect the forward bases around Chengtu. These too were not fully prepared, for although construction work had begun at four sites in the area – Kwanghan, Kuinglai, Hsinching and Pengshan – as early as November 1943, progress had been slow in such remote locations. In the event, the runways and base facilities were literally built by hand, with local Chinese farmers providing the labor. A local village quota of work had been imposed – it was set at fifty workers per 100 households – and by January 1944 some 200,000 people had contributed to the program. They achieved a great deal, supervised and aided by American military construction teams specially flown in, and by 1 May all four bases could just about be used by the B-29s but, once again, conditions were far from ideal. Still, by early May there was cause for some satisfaction. Against tremendous odds 148 B-29s had arrived in the CBI and rudimentary bases were available. It showed what could be achieved under the pressures of war.

It was those same pressures which imposed impossible strains upon the entire project, as Wolfe was soon to discover.

A

Above: Heavy equipment, needed to level the runways around Chengtu, is brought in by air in pieces to be reassembled on the ground.
Below: Chinese laborers survey one of the first B-29s to reach Chengtu – *Eileen* of 444th BG, 58th BW.

He was now part of a command structure which afforded to the AAF an unprecedented degree of operational freedom, equivalent in effect to the air force autonomy so eagerly sought by Mitchell in the 1920s. This had come about as a direct result of the B-29 program, for as word of the new bomber and its capabilities spread, every theater and air force commander in the Far East requested control of its operations. In January 1944, when deployment to the CBI was obvious, Major General Claire L Chennault, commanding 14th USAAF in China, even wrote to Roosevelt with his plea, seeing in the B-29 an answer to his problem of containing and then destroying Japanese air power in his theater. He was backed up by Joseph Stilwell who, although envisaging the B-29s being used primarily against ground rather than air targets, insisted that according to precedent, all air units should be controlled by the senior commander on the spot. Similar requests followed from Admiral Chester Nimitz in the Central Pacific, General Douglas MacArthur in the Southwest Pacific

and even Lord Louis Mountbatten, British Commander in Chief of South-East Asia Command (SEAC). It began to look as if the potential of the new bombers was never going to be realized as they would not be able to escape a plethora of conflicting tactical demands.

Arnold, realizing the dangers, had approached the problem with skill, taking as his yardstick the fact that naval forces did not suffer from the same demands, being controlled from Washington by Admiral Ernest King, a member of the Joint Chiefs of Staff. They were regarded as global forces, affecting all theaters as a whole rather than each individually, and this was the precedent which Arnold used when requesting B-29 autonomy. Armed with support from King, he approached the President, and on 4 April 1944 he authorized the establishment of a special strategic command to be known as 20th Air Force. Commanded by Arnold at JCS level, it was given a specific objective which could have been penned by Mitchell himself. Under the operational codename 'Matterhorn,' the B-29s were to begin 'the earliest possible progressive destruction and dislocation of the Japanese military, industrial and economic systems and to undermine the morale of the Japanese people to a point where their capacity for war is decisively defeated.' Furthermore, it was laid down that the bombers were to be used by no one but Arnold. It was argued that he alone enjoyed the information and expertise needed to appreciate their global nature. He could assign the B-29s to local commanders in a tactical emergency, but at all times the operations were strictly under his control.

This was an extremely significant step for the AAF, pointing the way to an autonomous future, but it did impose tremendous pressure upon the B-29 commanders in the CBI. For once the principle of a strategic role had been established, it was imperative that concrete results should be provided as soon as possible. This meant not only that operations had to begin immediately, but also that they should be seen to succeed. Wolfe suddenly found himself in a very difficult position, under pressure from Arnold to begin the bombing of Japan but faced with an ever-growing mountain of problems in the field.

The most important of these was the persistent one of supply. From the beginning it had been specified that XX BC would be virtually self-sufficient within the CBI, providing its own transport facilities without imposing upon those of other forces in the area. This proved impossible in practice, as the

Above: A manually-operated water pump emphasizes the enormous difficulties of base construction in China.

Above: A Rajputana Rifles soldier guards newly-arrived B-29s in eastern India.
Left: Gangs of Chinese laborers - provided by quota from surrounding villages - prepare one of the Chengtu bases.
Below: B-29s arrive at one of the bases in eastern India; the runway is still being lengthened.

logistics administrators in the theater were quick to discover. Even before the 58th BW arrived in India, the preparation of air bases and build up of stocks had required the provision of 20,000 troop places and 200,000 tons of dry cargo space in a supply system which was already under considerable pressure. The CBI at the best of times did not enjoy priority of shipping or stores, coming a very poor third behind Europe and the Pacific, and an extra burden like the bombing campaign nearly caused it to collapse. Special priorities had to be established in February 1944, but even then a significant proportion of equipment had to be 'borrowed' from the British or diverted from airfields in Assam or the highly important Ledo Road project. Understandably, a number of local commanders began to voice their misgivings.

Nor did the situation improve once the 58th BW arrived, for although they were accompanied by their own fleet of transport aircraft, including a number of converted B-24s (known in their new role as C-87s), it soon became apparent that these were insufficient for the build up of supplies around Chengtu. If the bases in China were to be used at all, they had to contain vast quantities of fuel, bombs and spares, all of which had to be flown in first from eastern India. Some transports were diverted from Air Transport Command in the CBI to help out – a decision which did nothing to quieten complaints from local commanders – but the process was lengthy. In the end the B-29s performed the bulk of the operation, particularly in the transportation of fuel. Following an idea originally mooted in Washington by the Matterhorn planners, selected numbers of bombers were stripped of their armaments systems (except for the guns in the tail) and given as many auxiliary fuel tanks as possible, tied into a special fuel

Below: **Lt Gen Henry H Arnold (left) inspects P-40 Flying Tigers pursuit planes with Brig Gen Claire L Chennault, China, 1943.**

design which incorporated an off-loading manifold. These aircraft could lift seven tons of high-octane at a time, but it was not particularly cost effective. Even on a good day, it took two gallons of fuel burned by the delivery aircraft to transport one gallon to Chengtu. On a bad day, with head winds and diversions to avoid bad weather over the Himalayas, this could rise to twelve gallons for every one delivered.

The results were depressing. Wolfe had been ordered by Arnold to mount the first B-29 operation against Japan on or before 1 May, but as the transport fleet had only managed to deliver 1400 tons of supplies to Chengtu by then, further delays were inevitable. The situation was hindered even more by the launching of the Japanese 'Ichi Go' offensive in central China, which took place on 19 April. The Japanese plan was to attack Honan and then strike south and west toward Changsha and a series of 14th USAAF bases around Kweilin and Liuchow which they imagined were going to be used by the B-29s. Indeed some thought had been devoted to this idea by the American commanders, but it was dropped when the vulnerability of the eastern bases was realized. One big disadvantage of Chengtu was that it was too far west, necessitating long overflights of Japanese-occupied territory in China before the Japanese home islands could be attacked, and even then only bringing the southern island of Kyushu within B-29 range. Kweilin and Liuchow did in fact fall to the Japanese in November 1944, but the real disruption to the B-29s was the problem of supply. As the Japanese offensive gathered pace in late April and early May, Stilwell withdrew the Air Transport Command contingent from Wolfe's operations, slowing the build up at Chengtu still further.

Meanwhile, Arnold was pressing for action of some description and, despite the paucity of supplies, Wolfe felt obliged to act. The Hump route was in fact so dangerous and difficult that each time a B-29 flew the 1000 miles involved it counted as a combat mission (and was usually signified as such by the painting of a camel on the aircraft nose). After tremendous transport efforts sufficient stocks were built up to order a 'shakedown' raid. This took place on 5 June and the target was the Makasan railroad yard at Bangkok, Thailand. The raid was a disaster. Some 98 B-29s took off from eastern India on what was a 2000-mile round trip, but fourteen aborted before reaching the target, mostly because of engine problems. The aircraft were supposed to fly in four-plane diamond formations, but this was never fully achieved. The target was overcast, necessitating bombing by radar. The formations became so confused that aircraft dropped their loads at altitudes anywhere between 17–27,000ft instead of the envisaged 22–25,000ft. A mere eighteen bombs landed in the target area; five B-29s crashed on landing and a further 42 were forced to put down at bases which were not their own as fuel ran out. It was an extremely inauspicious start to a campaign which was supposed to be decisive.

The pressure on Wolfe did not ease, for Arnold was now insisting upon a raid against Japan, the first since Doolittle's attack over two years previously. After more tremendous efforts, enough supplies were stockpiled to enable 68 B-29s to take off on 14 June against the Imperial Iron and Steel Works at Yawata, on the island of Kyushu. Some 47 of the bombers made it to the target, this time arriving during the hours of darkness, but results were if anything even worse. Only one hit was recorded and that was three-quarters of a mile from

Left: **Chennault (right) receives a decoration from Chiang Kai-shek.**
Right: **Chennault (left) with Maj Gen A C Wedemeyer, C in C China Theater, 1944.**
Below: **B-29s of 468th BG, 58th BW, attack targets near Rangoon.**

the aiming point. In addition a further six B-29s were destroyed in accidents and one – the first of many – went down to enemy fire. The XX BC was quite clearly failing to carry out its strategic role.

Nevertheless this did not prevent the Yawata raid being hailed as almost a victory in the United States, and the resultant glare of publicity merely heightened Arnold's desire for more attacks. On 16 June he ordered Wolfe to send the B-29s 'the length and breadth of the Japanese Empire.' With fuel stocks at Chengtu down to less than 5000 gallons this was clearly impossible since it took 8800 gallons to send just one B-29 against Japan. Wolfe had no hesitation in saying so, an action which led to his recall to Washington on 4 July. He was promoted and reassigned, leaving Saunders in temporary command in the CBI.

While awaiting Wolfe's replacement, Saunders continued the bombing operations as and when he could. On 7 July eighteen B-29s paid a return visit to Kyushu, dropping bombs (fairly ineffectively) on targets at Sasebo, Nagasaki, Omura and Yawata. Two days later 72 of the bombers flew against a steel-making complex at Anshan in Manchuria. Four aircraft were lost on the latter raid and results were poor, affecting less than eight percent of the industrial facility. This picture was repeated on the night of 10–11 August when 56 B-29s, staging through British air bases at Ceylon, hit oil storage tanks at Palembang in Borneo. It was almost as if the campaign was drifting from target to target, with no real purpose or long-term aim. This undoubtedly reflected the command vacuum at Kharagpur, but the fact that some of the raids took place in the day while others were at night implied a lack of operational control and combat technique. To put it bluntly, Matterhorn had stagnated.

All this changed on 29 August when Wolfe's replacement, Major General Curtis E LeMay, arrived in the CBI. A forceful personality and superb air leader, LeMay had received praise (and accelerated promotion) for his handling of the 3rd Bombardment Division of the 8th AAF in Europe, and Arnold was confident that he could inject some life into XX BC. He was not to be disappointed, for although the first B-29 raid experienced by LeMay against Anshan on 8 September was by far the most successful to date, with relatively few abortions and a reasonable bombing pattern, he was not slow to impose a number of sweeping changes upon the Command. In the sphere of operational technique, he began by replacing the four-plane diamond formation by one of twelve aircraft grouped in a defensive box along the lines used by the B-17s in Europe. This he regarded as imperative if his second reform was to stand any chance of success, for he now insisted upon daylight, precision attacks at all times, again on the European pattern, to make sure that tactical expertise could be gained. In order to achieve the best results from such tactics he also introduced the concept of lead crews who would bear responsibility for finding and marking the target area, an idea which RAF Bomber Command, with its Pathfinder Squadrons, had found exceptionally useful over Germany. Finally, having witnessed some of the problems facing the B-29 crews over Anshan, LeMay ordered that in future both the bombardier and radar operator should control the bombing run, so that whoever had sight of the target at the critical moment could release the bombs. It was hoped that this would save confusion should the target be covered in patchy cloud or haze, conditions which were common in the Far East.

Complementary to these operational changes was a radical reorganization of the 58th BW, designed to simplify and rationalize its basic structure. The prevailing system of four Bombardment Groups, each of four squadrons with seven

B-29s per squadron, was scrapped and the junior squadron from each group (the 395th, 679th, 771st and 795th BS) was disbanded. This left each group with three squadrons of ten B-29s each, an organization which, it was argued, would be easier to administer and control.

It obviously took time for these changes to have any effect – another raid against Anshan on 26 September failed to prove much one way or another – but very gradually things began to improve. On 25 October, for example, an attack upon the Omura aircraft factory on Kyushu showed signs of success, particularly in the use of a two-to-one mixture of high explosive and incendiary bombs. This was repeated on 11 November when the Chinese city of Nanking, occupied by the Japanese since 1937, suffered substantial damage. Practical problems of supply and aircraft accidents were still conspiring to prevent the concentration of force and effort which strategic bombing required to be effective, and these were joined by the new menace of growing Japanese resistance. On 21 November Omura was revisited and the B-29s met solid opposition from interceptor fighters and light bombers (the latter being used to drop phosphorous explosives into the B-29 formations) and six of the Superfortresses failed to return. A similar loss rate occurred on 7 December over the Manchurian Aircraft Company plant at Mukden. In fact B-29 losses were soon reaching prohibitively high levels. When losses from all causes – accident, enemy interception and, in September particularly, Japanese air raids on the Chengtu bases –

Left: **Major General Curtis E LeMay.**
Below left: **B-29s of 468th BG, 58th BW hit the Omura aircraft factory on Kyushu, October 1944.**
Below: **B-29 of 468th BG over Yawata, July 1944 (note fires in areas of coke ovens, furnaces and shipyards).**

were added together at the end of 1944, they came to the sobering total of 147. In other words, the equivalent of the entire B-29 strength in the CBI on 1 May had been wiped out in something like eight months.

It was apparent that despite LeMay's leadership the raids were too expensive and would have to be stopped. A pointer to the future was perhaps provided on the 18 December when 94 B-29s, operating in a tactical emergency as the Japanese approached Kunming, hit the enemy supply base at Hankow in a low-level fire raid, but by then it was too late. Soon after this attack a decision was made by the JCS to phase out the Chengtu operations and instead to concentrate all the B-29s on the newly-captured Marianas Islands in the central Pacific.

The last raid out of China was flown on 15 January 1945, but that too was tactical in concept, against targets in Formosa to divert Japanese attention away from the landings at Luzon. Thereafter the 58th BW withdrew to its bases in India, and although it was not officially redeployed to the Marianas until February, it did little in its last few weeks of CBI existence. A few minor raids in support of ground forces culminated in an attack against oil storage facilities in Singapore on 29 March and then the campaign ended. In strategic terms it had achieved nothing, for only 49 missions, involving 3058 aircraft sorties, had been flown and only 11,477 tons of bombs had been dropped. As the official USAF historians concluded postwar, the China missions 'did little to hasten the Japanese surrender or to justify the lavish expenditure poured out in their behalf.' Matterhorn had failed, but the experience gained in the process was to be of inestimable value as the B-29s built up their operations from the far more convenient and logical base of the Marianas. The big bombers still had something to prove, but still had to find a role.

EARLY RAIDS FROM M

The Marianas Chain, consisting principally of the islands of Saipan, Tinian and Guam, lies in the central Pacific, occupying a 500-mile arc between latitudes 13 and 21 degrees north. In the context of World War II, it appeared to be an ideal base from which to launch B-29 raids against Japan. The islands were about 1500 miles south-southeast of Tokyo, a range which the B-29s could just about manage. They were relatively invulnerable to enemy counterattack and, most important of all, they could be put on a direct supply route from the United States. In short, they seemed to offer solutions to the majority of B-29 problems experienced in the CBI, except for one crucial factor. When strategic deployment of XX BC was discussed in 1943, the Marianas were firmly under Japanese control.

Suggestions for the seizure of the Marianas were initially put forward by Admiral Ernest King at the Anglo-American Trident Conference in Washington in May 1943, but no action was taken then or two months later at Quebec. With Allied forces locked in a vicious struggle in the Solomons and New Guinea, plans for the occupation of such distant targets must have seemed premature. Instead the AAF planners were obliged to adopt the CBI deployment of the B-29s as put forward by Arnold at Quebec, with all its attendant problems. It was not until September 1943 that the potential of the Marianas as a bomber base was fully realized, and it was this which prompted Arnold to approach the Joint Planning Staff with new ideas. On 4 October he pressed officially for 'the seizure of the Marianas at the earliest possible date, with the establishment of heavy bomber bases as the primary mission.'

This proposal was placed before the Combined Chiefs of Staff at the Cairo Conference in December and after lengthy discussions they decided to incorporate it into an overall offensive Pacific strategy for the coming year. This envisaged two main Allied drives across the ocean toward Japan, one through the center under Nimitz and one from the southwest under MacArthur. Nimitz, whose drive was seen as the more important, was directed to make plans accordingly. He pro-

Below: **Spare R-3350 engines are overhauled in front of a B-29 of 19th BG, 314th BW, Guam, 1945.**

ARIANAS

posed a concentration on nine separate islands – Kavieng, Kwajalein, Manus, Eniwetok, Mortlock, Truk, Saipan, Guam and Tinian – the seizure of which would drive a wedge deep into the enemy defenses and open the way to Japan itself, hopefully by the end of 1944. In the event, Truk was by-passed and left to 'wither on the vine,' enabling the other operations to take place ahead of schedule. As early as March 1944, the JCS was able to set the Marianas invasion for 15 June.

The first of the islands in the chain to be attacked was Saipan. On 11 June a four-day naval and air bombardment began softening up the defenses for an assault landing. On the 15th, the 2nd and 4th Marine Divisions stormed ashore. They were reinforced 24 hours later by the 27th Army Division. After heavy fighting which cost over 3000 American lives (by comparison, the Japanese lost nearly 24,000) the island was effectively cleared by 9 July. This enabled the invasions of Guam and Tinian to go ahead on 20 and 23 July respectively, these islands were declared clear on 9 August. The Americans now had potential bomber bases within range of the entire Japanese mainland.

Before the B-29s could begin operations airfields and support facilities had to be built. Construction work started on Saipan as early as 24 June, while the battle was still raging for possession of the island. Naval Construction Battalions, the celebrated 'Seabees,' concentrated initially upon a former Japanese airstrip called Aslito, soon to be renamed Isley Field after Navy Commander Robert H Isely (unfortunately his name was misspelled at some point and the incorrect version stuck). When the Seabees arrived, Aslito was a short coral strip, just about capable of handling fighter aircraft, and was being used by P-47 Thunderbolts of the 19th Fighter Squadron. They had something like ninety days to transform it into a bomber base for the entire 73rd BW, recently ordered to the Marianas instead of the CBI. As the wing contained the usual four Bombardment Groups (the 497th, 498th, 499th and 500th), each of three squadrons of ten B-29s per squadron, Isley had to be big, with at least two runways, paved to 9000ft and a plethora of support facilities. It was an enormous task and had not been fully completed when the first B-29 touched down on 12 October. Only one runway was capable of taking the bomber – and that was paved to only 6000ft – and there was a total absence of hardstands or buildings. It looked like Chengtu all over again.

Left below: **B-29s of 29th BG, 314th BW assume combat formation after taking off from Guam, June 1945.**
Below: **The bomb-bay doors of this B-29 were hydraulically operated; most crews preferred the more instantaneous electrical system in combat.**

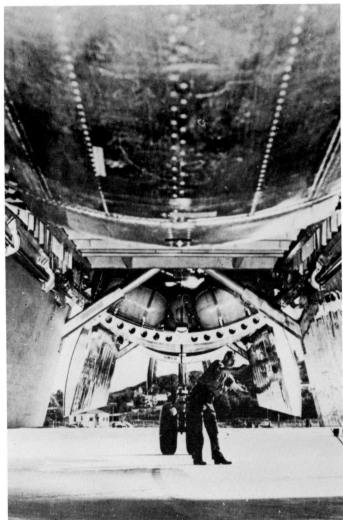

The B-29 which arrived on 12 October was piloted by Major General Haywood S Hansell Jr, a man who had been Arnold's chief of staff at 20th AF until August 1944, when he was directed to take command of the newly-activated XX1 Bomber Command, formed specifically for the Marianas operations. His command consisted entirely of the 73rd BW. Another three BWs were still in the process of being formed and the first would not be ready much before the end of the year, and the bombers began to arrive on 18 October. The first was piloted by Brigadier General Emmett (Rosie) O'Donnell, who had replaced Chapman as commander of 73rd BW back in March. By 22 November over 100 aircraft had arrived on Saipan, directly from their training bases.

By that time Hansell had already begun to prepare his forces for their primary mission, that of destroying the Japanese capability to continue the war. Before leaving America he had been told by the JCS that the top priority for the Marianas-based bombers was to destroy the aircraft industry of Japan, and they had supported his preference for high-altitude, daylight precision attacks. However, it was soon apparent that the skill required for such attacks to be successful was not available among the inexperienced crews of 73rd BW. In late October and early November a series of tactical shakedown raids were mounted from Saipan and almost immediately the CBI pattern of problems re-emerged. On 27 October, 18 B-29s were sent against Japanese force targets on Truk; four aborted because of the inevitable engine failures, combat formations were scrappy and the results were officially described as 'poor to fair.' A similar pattern was repeated in two further raids against Truk on 30 October and 2 November. Furthermore, as the Japanese realized what was going on, they added the complication of low-level air raids from Iwo Jima on Isley Field, damaging several B-29s on 2 November. Hansell reacted by ordering retaliatory strikes against Iwo Jima on 5 and 11 November, but again the results were poor. The parallels between these raids and the early ones from Chengtu were obvious to all; the B-29s, beset with problems, were in danger of being dissipated in tactical missions and even then were not enjoying much success.

The outcome was familiar, for Arnold, so acutely aware that the entire autonomous future of the AAF was riding on the Marianas' B-29s now that the Chengtu raids were beginning to fail, pressed Hansell for attacks upon Japan as soon as possible. Hansell, like Wolfe before him in the CBI, was not really ready to oblige. The Saipan base was incomplete (some of the maintenance facilities did not actually arrive until April 1945), the B-29s were experiencing all the usual problems of overheating engines, and the air crews were finding it difficult to settle down to combat conditions. This was due in large measure to Hansell's insistence upon high-altitude, daylight precision attacks, for these presupposed a high level of crew expertise, particularly in formation flying and self-defense. Unfortunately the 73rd BW had done the bulk of its training on radar bombing, with each aircraft having a certain degree of choice about altitude and bombing runs. This had implied that night raids would be flown, so escaping from the danger of enemy interception. When Hansell had announced his choice of tactics the training schedule had been changed, with the result that few crews were really adept at anything. Far from being the surgeon's scalpel which Hansell envisaged and precision bombing required, the 73rd BW was just about capable of becoming a bludgeon, but only if mechanical problems allowed. Arnold seemed incapable of appreciating this.

All this should have been apparent during the shakedown raids against Truk and Iwo Jima and, when this was not the case, it should have become glaringly obvious once the raids against Japan began. The first raid was scheduled for 17 November but the weather, in a preview of problems to come, closed in, grounding the bombers for a week. This breathing space was quite useful from a maintenance point of view – the 73rd BW mechanics used it to fit extemporized cooling baffles to the R-3350s – but it did not prevent the usual run of problems when 111 B-29s finally took off on 24 November. Their target was the Nakajima Aircraft Company's Musashi engine plant, just outside Tokyo, which produced about thirty percent of the engines needed by the Japanese Air Force. It was the first visit to Tokyo by American bombers since Doolittle's raid and was conducted in a glare of publicity.

Above right: Captain R S Steakley in RB-29 *Tokyo Rose* was the first reconnaissance pilot over Tokyo in 1944; hence his DFC.
Above far right: Results of a B-29 fire raid on Hamamatsu, 17 June 1945. Whole blocks of the city have been razed.
Below: B-29s of 497th BG, 73rd BW, prepare for takeoff, late 1944.

1. Kawasaki Ki-45 'Nick' twin-engined fighter dives beneath a B-29 of 497th BG, 73rd BW, over Japan.

2. Sergeant J R Krantz, a waist gunner in 497th BG B-29 *American Maid*, hanging outside the aircraft after a depressurization accident over Japan. He was recovered by his crew colleagues.

3. A typical eleven-man crew pose before an untypical B-29, the nose of which has been severed by a runaway propeller.

The raid began badly as seventeen B-29s aborted due to engine failure and things did not improve as the remainder approached the target at altitudes of 27–32,000ft, for they hit a weather phenomenon at that time unknown – the jet stream. Over Japan, particularly during the winter months, winds of exceptionally high speed roar out of the west at almost exactly the altitudes used by the B-29s. The bombers were therefore bowled along at anything up to 450mph, formations were disrupted and accurate bombing was impossible. To cap it all, the Nakajima plant was covered in patchy cloud and only 24 B-29s dropped their bombs in roughly the right place; the rest merely unloaded over the general urban complex of Tokyo. The target was hardly touched and although the Japanese defenses were poor, one B-29 was deliberately rammed by a fighter aircraft and destroyed. It was not a good start.

Over the next few weeks, Musashi was to be revisited no less than ten times by high-flying B-29s, and their overall lack of success acts as an indication of Hansell's failure. Only ten percent of the damage caused was within the 130 acres of plant area and only two percent of the bomb tonnage dropped actually hit buildings. The Japanese work force suffered only 220 fatalities, a figure which was in fact lower than that suffered by the B-29s, for with forty bombers lost on the eleven raids as a whole, 440 airmen failed to return. The final irony was that in one raid carried out by naval fighters and bombers from Vice-Admiral Marc A Mitscher's Task Force 58 in early February 1945, far more damage was done to Musashi than in all the B-29 strikes put together. A similarly depressing picture emerged from raids against the Mitsubishi engine plant at Nagoya in mid-December. Although the actual damage caused was greater than at Musashi, with some seventeen percent of the complex gutted, B-29 losses to enemy defenses had begun to mount until, by the end of 1944, they were averaging four or five per mission. With eleven men on board each aircraft, few of whom were likely to survive even if they bailed out because the Japanese population felt little sympathy for their plight, the defeat of Japan through aerial bombardment was beginning to seem very expensive indeed. On the precedent of the CBI raids earlier in the year, changes of some description were clearly imminent.

They came in early January 1945 when Arnold, dissatisfied with progress, recalled Hansell and moved LeMay from eastern India to take over XXI BC. Hansell continued to direct operations until LeMay's arrival on 20 January. The results did not improve even when, against his beliefs, he authorized an incendiary raid on Nagoya on 3 January in response to pressure from Arnold, who wanted to see if the Hankow success of 18 December could be repeated elsewhere. High-level, daylight bombing had failed, and Hansell laid the blame on the poor training of the 73rd BW as well as on the problems of mechanical breakdown and Japanese defense.

It is worth noting that in two respects Hansell had laid a firm base upon which LeMay could build. The first concerned the B-29 itself, for many of the persistent engine failures could be attributed to its excessive weight. In mid-January 1945, when the abort rate was running at a staggering 23 percent per mission, a weight reduction program was initiated which, through the removal of one of the bomb bay fuel tanks and a cutback on ammunition carried for the 0.5in machine guns, shaved over 6000lb from each aircraft. Performance instantly improved and when this was coupled with a maintenance centralization reform, whereby Hansell's headquarters controlled the entire maintenance operation instead of it being split between the various Bombardment Groups, B-29 endurance began to lengthen. Thereafter engine life was extended from 200–250 hours to 750 hours and the abort rate

gradually declined. By July 1945 it was down to less than seven percent per operation.

LeMay therefore took over a potentially more effective bomber force in the Marianas than he had done in the CBI, and one which was expanding in size. In January the 313th BW (6th, 9th, 504th and 505th BG), commanded by Brigadier General John H Davies, arrived in the islands. He took over the newly-built North Field on Tinian – the biggest bomber base ever constructed, with four parallel, paved runways, each 8500ft long, and all the attendant base facilities. They were ready to join the campaign by early February, taking part in a high-altitude, daylight attack on Kobe on the 4th. This turned out to be one of the last of such attacks, for although LeMay had not imposed tactical changes on his new command immediately, they were not long delayed. After diverting his B-29s to help in the capture of Iwo Jima LeMay issued his new directive on 19 February. Iwo Jima was an essential island base in the bombing campaign as it could be used to house fighter squadrons capable of escorting the B-29s to Japan as well as act as a useful emergency landing ground midway between the Marianas and the targets. The directive introduced the concept of incendiary raids, placing them above attacks on the aircraft industry in the list of priorities. Mindful of Hansell's failure in producing a precise scalpel, LeMay was accepting the facts of life. Owing to crew inexperience and rushed B-29 development, a bludgeon was all that could be fashioned in the short time available. In crude but simple terms, LeMay was arguing that if the B-29s could not hit the factories exactly, they should be used to burn out the towns which contained and supported them. It was a crucial decision.

These new tactics, still carried out at high altitude and in daylight, were tested in two raids against Tokyo on 25 February and 4 March. The material damage caused was substantial by the record of the recent past – on 25 February alone nearly 28,000 buildings were gutted when 172 B-29s unloaded

Below: 'T - Square - 2': a B-29 of 498th BG, 73rd BW, flies over Tokyo suburbs at low level, May 1945.

Above: **The last raid on Kobe, 5th June 1945; after this the target was not deemed worth revisiting.**

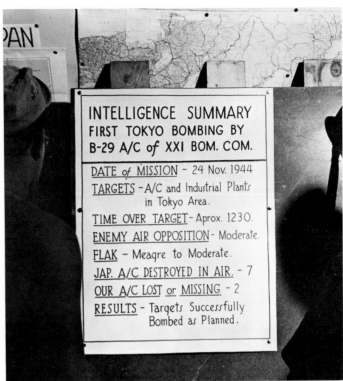

INTELLIGENCE SUMMARY
FIRST TOKYO BOMBING BY
B-29 A/C of XXI BOM. COM.

DATE of MISSION - 24 Nov. 1944
TARGETS - A/C and Industrial Plants
in Tokyo Area.
TIME OVER TARGET - Aprox. 1230.
ENEMY AIR OPPOSITION - Moderate.
FLAK - Meagre to Moderate.
JAP. A/C DESTROYED IN AIR. - 7
OUR A/C LOST or MISSING - 2
RESULTS - Targets Successfully
Bombed as Planned.

Above: **Intelligence summary informs ground crews of the first B-29 raid on Tokyo, 24 November 1944.**

450 tons of incendiaries. It was obvious though that far more could be achieved, particularly if concentrated bombing patterns emerged. LeMay analyzed the results carefully and came to three important conclusions, that the effects of the jet stream, cloud cover and high operating altitudes were to blame for the failures. All could be countered, he argued, if high-altitude, daylight attacks were phased out and replaced by low-level, high-intensity incendiary raids, possibly at night. He therefore ordered all the B-29s to be stripped of their General Electric gun systems, leaving only the armament in the tail for defense, loaded up with incendiaries and brought down to an operating altitude of 5–6000ft. This would escape the worst of the jet stream, get the bombers below most of the cloud cover and, as the B-29s would no longer have to struggle up to 30,000ft or above, would save on fuel and engine strain. The air crews were understandably wary because they liked the apparent safety of height and computerized gun systems, but LeMay was of the opinion that the Japanese defenses would be caught unawares, having been organized by now to deal only with high-altitude attacks. Anyway, if the raids could be flown at night, the protection of darkness would undoubtedly reduce casualties. It was a bold approach to the problem, reminiscent of the RAF reaction to daylight losses and lack of results over Germany in 1940–42.

The first raid to use these new techniques was scheduled for the night of 9–10 March against the entire urban complex of Tokyo. As yet another Bombardment Wing had arrived in the Marianas – the 314th (19th, 29th, 39th and 330th BG) under Brigadier General Thomas S Power, stationed at North Field on Guam – LeMay was able to deploy a large number of B-29s. A total of 279 arrived over the target, led by special pathfinder crews who marked a central aiming point, and in a raid which lasted for two hours early on the morning of 10 March the center of Tokyo was devastated. High ground winds gusting up to 28mph fanned the incendiary bursts into a fire-storm of terrifying proportions, sixteen square miles of urban build-

ings were destroyed and nearly 84,000 people died. It was a crippling bludgeon blow to the body, as distinct from the industrial heart of the enemy. Although the loss of fourteen B-29s implied that LeMay's beliefs about ineffective Japanese defenses were wrong, the big bombers had at last begun to make their mark.

Nor was this a purely fortuitous result, for over the next few nights the pattern was successfully repeated, albeit in not quite such a devastating fashion. On 11–12 March 285 B-29s dropped 1700 tons of incendiaries on Nagoya, levelling two square miles of the city for the loss of only one of their number; on 13–14 March eight square miles of Osaka disappeared in a sea of flame; on 16–17 March three square miles of Kobe were gutted; and on 19–20 March, in a return visit to Nagoya, a further three square miles were added to the list of devastation. In all over 120,000 Japanese civilians died in less than two weeks, a relatively small number of B-29s were lost (twenty including those shot down over Tokyo) and the entire strategic bombing project was justified. Arnold was naturally ecstatic and ordered the raids to continue. Unfortunately by 20 March XXI BC had run out of incendiaries (some high-explosive ordnance had been used against both Kobe and Nagoya as stocks ran down) and a pause had to be imposed. Nevertheless the B-29 now had a viable strategic role which could be used to prove the need for future air force autonomy. Up to this time the arguments had been based upon the interwar theories of Mitchell – that the manned bomber could fly with relative impunity over the enemy homeland to destroy precise targets of industrial importance – but the fire raids provided a proven alternative. Using napalm and incendiary clusters, bombers could now impose a high degree of damage on the enemy state. Mitchell had favored the scalpel. The B-29 experience suggested that a bludgeon was all that could be developed under the pressures and problems of war. By 20 March 1945 this had become a highly effective bludgeon, but one which had yet to defeat the enemy single-handed.

THE DESTRUCTION OF

As LeMay awaited the arrival of new incendiary stocks in late March, he was able to devote the B-29s to tactical support missions over the island of Kyushu, designed to prevent Japanese aircraft stationed there from interfering with the imminent invasion of Okinawa. Plans for such support had been finalized on 7 March, before the fire raids began, and it had been decided that the bombers should concentrate upon airfield and support facilities on Kyushu. The first raid took place on 27 March, five days before the Okinawa assault went in, when 151 B-29s hit airstrips at Tachiari and Oita as well as an aircraft plant at Omura. In a series of follow-up strikes all known airfields on Kyushu were destroyed, but the B-29s were ordered to continue their operations throughout April and early May in a desperate attempt to stop kamikaze suicide strikes being launched from Kyushu against American naval forces around Okinawa. In the event, the kamikazes continued to attack, using temporary airstrips in remote locations, and by 11 May Nimitz was forced to admit that the B-29s could not achieve a great deal more. He therefore released them for other operations.

In fact LeMay had never committed his entire force to these strikes – by April 1945 he had over 700 B-29s under his command – and had been able to issue a new fire-raid directive in early April. This gave high priority to the destruction of the aircraft-engine factories at Musashi and Nagoya, but designated selected urban areas for incendiary strikes. These were to be concentrated in the six major cities of Japan – Tokyo, Nagoya, Osaka, Kawasaki, Kobe and Yokohama – with the aim of destroying them and demoralizing their civilian populations.

The raids began on 13 April when 327 B-29s, following the pattern of the earlier incendiary strikes, dropped 2100 tons onto Tokyo's arsenal area and burned out about eleven square miles of the city. Japanese defenses were better organized to deal with night area raids by this time, and seven of the bombers were shot down. Even when these were joined by a further thirteen B-29s, destroyed on 15 April over Tokyo, Kawasaki and Yokohama, the results far outweighed the losses. In addition by mid-April XXI BC had received yet another Bombardment Wing, the 58th, redeployed from the now defunct XX BC in the CBI to West Field on Tinian, and LeMay was able to use 500 bombers in one raid for the first time. He was now of the firm opinion that Japan could be defeated, using air power alone, within six months.

With this aim in mind, he initiated a new series of sustained fire raids in May, beginning on the 14th when 472 B-29s gutted three square miles around and within the Mitsubishi engine factory at Nagoya. Two nights later, a return visit to the city devastated a further four square miles and the first signs of civilian panic began to appear as 170,000 terrified people fled into the surrounding countryside. On 23 and 25 May the B-29s concentrated yet again on Tokyo, and although bomber losses began to rise alarmingly (43 were lost on these two raids alone), the Japanese capital was rapidly becoming a fire-scorched desert. By the end of the month over fifty percent of the city area, some 56 square miles, had been destroyed.

However, the losses were worrying, and in an attempt to confuse the enemy defenses as well as to lure Japanese fighters into an air battle they could not possibly win, a change of tactics was ordered on 29 May. Reverting temporarily to daylight, high-altitude attacks, 454 B-29s appeared over Yokohama escorted by P-51 Mustang fighters from Iwo Jima. The result was a ferocious 'dog-fight' which effectively drew the teeth of the Japanese defending aircraft as 26 were destroyed for the loss of four B-29s and three P-51s. Thereafter, as the Japanese began to hoard what aircraft they had left for a massive, last ditch suicide strike against any Allied invasion force which approached the home islands, air defense of the cities seemed to decline in priority. By June 1945 LeMay was able to report that air interception had lessened considerably and that the B-29s had virtual control of Japanese airspace. This was reflected by the fact that on 5 June the B-29s were able to attack Kobe with such devastating effect that the city was subsequently crossed off the target list as not worth revisiting. Osaka followed suit within ten days. By the end of the month the six major cities in LeMay's April directive had been effectively destroyed, with 105.6 of their combined 257.2 square miles completely devastated. It was an impressive record, particularly when its announcement coincided with the first anniversary of the B-29 strikes upon Japan.

This success, coupled with the ever-growing strength of XXI BC, enabled LeMay to vary his bombing tactics considerably, so increasing Japanese defensive confusion and adding to the general destruction of the enemy. Experiments had in fact begun as early as 7 April, when LeMay had authorized a series of selective high-level precision strikes, using the more experienced crews, and the results were spectacular. The targets were the seemingly indestructible aircraft-engine plants at Musashi and Nagoya. On 7 April 153 B-29s hit the Nagoya complex with about 600 tons of high-explosives, destroying something like ninety percent of the surviving facilities. Five days later 93 B-29s did the same to the Nakajima factory at Musashi. The Japanese aircraft-engine industry had virtually ceased to exist.

JAPAN

Below left: Incendiary bombs rain down on dockyard facilities at Osaka, 1 June 1945.
Right: The unseen results of the incendiary raids: Japanese school children practice their fire drill.
Below: B-29s of 498th BG, 73rd BW show AN/APQ-13 radomes extended as well as the intermediate tail-fin markings of April 1945.

Such results encouraged LeMay to devote a substantial force of bombers to specific high-priority targets. He chose to concentrate upon Japan's ailing oil-producing and storage facilities and gave the task of their destruction to the newly-arrived 315th BW (16th, 331st, 501st and 502nd BG), commanded by Brigadier General Frank Armstrong and stationed on Northwest Field, Guam. This wing was in fact unique, for it was equipped entirely with the only true variant of the B-29 ever manufactured – the B-29B. Produced at the Bell Aircraft Company's plant at Marietta, Georgia, these aircraft were actually stripped-down versions of the normal B-29, bereft of the General Electric gun system and a variety of other components in order to save weight and increase bomb-carrying capacity. The resultant unladen weight of 69,000lb was a vast improvement, lessening the strain on engines and airframe and enabling the payload to be increased from 12,000 to 18,000lb of ordnance. In addition the B-29Bs were equipped with the new AN/APQ-7 'Eagle' radar sets which gave a much clearer presentation of ground images through a wing-shaped radome slung beneath the fuselage. The crews of the 315th had undergone intensive training for low-altitude, nighttime pathfinder missions, so their navigation and bomb-aiming skills were good. These were proved between 26 June and 10 August when, in a series of strikes against carefully selected targets, they effectively destroyed the oil stocks and production facilities of Japan.

As a final variation of usage LeMay also contributed his B-29s to the extensive mining of Japanese home waters, something which many historians have seen as one of the most decisive campaigns in the Pacific War. Between 27 March and 10 August aircraft, principally of the 313th BW, dropped nearly 13,000 acoustic and magnetic mines in the western approaches to the narrow Shimonoseki strait and the Inland Sea, as well as around the harbors of Hiroshima, Kure, Tokyo, Nagoya, Tokuyama, Aki and Noda. The results were dramatic. All Japanese coastal shipping came to a standstill in April and then, when merchant vessels were ordered to break through the blockade in May, 85 ships totalling 213,000 tons were sunk. After the war was over the United States Strategic Bombing Survey, set up to assess the contribution of aerial bombardment to victory, credited the B-29s with 9.3 percent of the total Japanese shipping loss of 8,900,000 tons.

Meanwhile LeMay had not dispensed with incendiary raids, issuing a new directive in mid-June which specified 58 smaller Japanese cities, all with populations of between 100,000 and 200,000, as the targets. On 17 June 450 B-29s flew low-level, night area raids against Kagashima, Omuta, Hamamatsu and Yokkaichi, following them up two nights later with attacks upon Toyohashi, Fukuoka and Shizuoka. The damage was substantial, particularly as by now the bombers were virtually unchallenged in their flights over Japan. Then in late June yet another new technique was introduced. Special leaflets, warning of forthcoming attacks, were dropped over Japanese cities and every third night thereafter the specified urban areas were devastated. The civilian population, faced with this constant proof of American power, began to show signs of panic and the Imperial Cabinet for the first time explored the possibilities of a negotiated end to hostilities. The B-29 had become a highly versatile and awesome weapon of strategic war, and by the beginning of August LeMay was running short of worthwhile targets.

The fact remains, that, despite these continuous and damaging blows to the body of the enemy state, the fire raids, precision strikes and mining operations carried out by the B-29s did not produce the unconditional surrender which the AAF planners had promised. They were certainly contributing enormously to the process of weakening the enemy, but the Allied leaders were still faced with the apparent need to invade the Japanese home islands. It was estimated that this operation would extend the war well into 1946 and probably cost the lives of a million Allied soldiers. It was this above all else that led to the decision in July 1945 to use the new and untested atomic weapons. As the B-29 was the only aircraft capable of acting as a delivery platform, it was about to make its most significant contribution to the history of war.

Experiments in atomic fission had been conducted in a variety of countries before World War II, notably in Germany where the chemist Otto Hahn had described a feasible process of neutron bombardment in 1938, but it was not until the enormous industrial and economic potential of the United States had been mobilized in 1942 that the real work of producing a bomb began. Although this work, carried out under the codename Project Manhattan, did not reach fruition until 1945, it was clear from quite early on that all that

Below: **A veteran B-29 –** *Look Homeward Angel* **of 6th BG, 313th BW – after a forced landing on Okinawa, August 1945.**

was needed was time, and as early as July 1943 Arnold was requested to provide specially-modified B-29s for flight and bomb-drop tests. Few of the AAF officers involved were told anything beyond the existence of a new weapon. Operating in conditions of enormous secrecy, a team of technical experts was gradually brought together at Wright Field. In December 1943 one of the early production B-29s was withdrawn from the 58th BW and the modification program began.

At first the AAF team could only be provided with very rough dimensions for the new weapon since at this stage even the Manhattan scientists were not sure what it would look like, and attention was concentrated initially upon the bomb bays alone. Aware of the potentially delicate nature of the intended load, the technicians fitted a new H-frame, hoist, carrier assembly and release unit to the B-29. The first drop tests, using dummy bombs of roughly the right dimensions, took place at Muroc, California, on 28 February 1944. These led to the fitting of an entirely new suspension mechanism to

the B-29, while the scientists used the information provided to add several new design features to the projected weapon. Tests resumed in June 1944 and after even more modifications a contract was awarded to a firm in Omaha, Nebraska, to produce a further three of the redesigned B-29s. By this time the scientists were able to provide more accurate dimensions for two types of bomb. One, dependent for its chain reaction upon uranium and nicknamed 'Little Boy,' would be 28in in diameter, 120in long and weigh about 9000lb. The other, using plutonium and called 'Fat Man,' would be 60in in diameter, 128in long and weigh about 10,000lb. Fortunately both these weapons could be lifted and delivered by the modified B-29s; by August the Omaha firm had completed a total of 46 'atomic bombers.'

Meanwhile a special air crew training program had been initiated under the command of Colonel Paul W Tibbetts Jr, a veteran of B-17 operations in Europe and North Africa who was already familiar with the B-29, having been involved in

Above: **B-29s of 29th BG, 314th BW on the long haul over the vastness of the Pacific to targets in Japan.**
Right: **Colonel Paul Tibbetts, commander of 509th CG, poses before** *Enola Gay* **just prior to takeoff for Hiroshima, 6 August 1945.**

Above: **B-29 *Enola Gay* of 509th CG. Note distinctive tail-fin marking and masked side blister.**

flight testing the machine for over a year. He gathered around him a hand-picked and highly competent staff and in September 1944 took command of the newly-activated 509th Composite Group at a remote air base near Wendover, Utah. The 509th, unique in B-29 history as it contained only one Bombardment Squadron – the 393rd under Major Charles W Sweeney – was a completely self-sufficient unit. It was surrounded in secrecy, with its own engineer, material and troop squadrons as well as a military police contingent. Training began immediately, with test drops of bomb models from high altitude over Inyokern, California, and long overwater navigation flights to Batista Field in Cuba. The 509th was ready for deployment overseas by spring 1945, with the vast majority of its officers and men completely ignorant of its intended role.

Commanders in the Pacific theater were informed of the potential of atomic weapons in February and March 1945, and engineering officers attached to the 509th gained LeMay's full co-operation. Although the unit was to be part of XXI BC in the Marianas its operations were to be strictly controlled from a far higher level of command. Elements of the 509th began to move out from Wendover in early May, and by July the bombers and their support elements were established at North Field, Tinian, the superb, four-runway base only recently completed for the 313th BW. Further bomb-drop tests and long-distance training flights were carried out, causing wry amusement to the battle-hardened veterans of XXI BC, and the modified B-29s were prepared for action. Some were subjected to even more modification when Curtiss electric propellers were fitted. These had reversible pitch to add braking power and sported special blade cuffs which increased airflow, much of which was fed back into the R-3350 engines to aid cooling.

The unit arrived on station only just in time, for early on 16 July the Manhattan scientists test-exploded their first atomic device at Alamogordo in the New Mexico Desert. It was an awe-inspiring success, producing an enormous ball of fire and blast wave which devastated the test site. The news was sent immediately to President Harry S Truman, at that time in Potsdam for the Allied Conference on the future of a now-peaceful Europe. He was fully briefed about potential casual-

ties should Japan be invaded, and had no hesitation in authorizing the use of the new weapons. On 24 July a mission directive was sent to General Carl A Spaatz, commander of the newly-formed US Strategic Air Forces in the Pacific. It ordered the 509th to 'deliver its first special bomb as soon as weather will permit visual bombing after 3 August 1945 on one of the targets: Hiroshima, Kokura, Niigata and Nagasaki.'

Components of 'Little Boy,' the first bomb to be used, had begun to arrive at Tinian on 29 July and by 2 August everything was ready for the attack. That afternoon LeMay's staff made out the necessary field order, specifying Hiroshima as the primary target, with Kokura and Nagasaki as alternatives should bad weather prevent a visual drop. The raid was set to take place on 6 August and Tibbets, who had decided some time before that he would command the attacking B-29, spent the intervening days preparing his crew and aircraft. After the last of their training flights, he directed the unit sign writer to paint his mother's name, *Enola Gay*, beneath the pilot's cabin on the port side of the fuselage.

On 6 August three special reconnaissance F-13As took off from Tinian at 0145 hours to report weather conditions over the primary and secondary targets. Tibbets followed in *Enola Gay* an hour later and during the long outward journey he was cleared for Hiroshima. As Navy weapons expert Captain William Parsons armed the bomb – it had been decided not to do this on the ground at North Field in case of accident – the target was approached and the aiming-point sighted. Once 'Little Boy' had left the bomb bay at 0815, Tibbets pulled the B-29 sharply away in a 155 degree turn to escape the glare and blast he had been warned to expect. His rear-gunner, Technical Sergeant George (Bob) Caron, witnessed the instantaneous death of 78,000 Japanese people, the destruction of some 48,000 buildings and the dawn of a new age.

Despite its devastation the raid did not lead to an immediate Japanese surrender. Poor communications between the remains of Hiroshima and Tokyo, coupled with an understandable lack of comprehension among the Japanese leaders, resulted in a series of cabinet meetings but a lack of consensus about surrender. By 8 August there had still been no official reaction, and the Americans were forced to prepare the plutonium 'Fat Man' – the only remaining atomic device in existence – for a second raid. It was loaded into a B-29 called *Bock's Car*, named after its commander Captain Frederick C

Bock but to be flown on this mission by Major Sweeney. The primary target was specified as Kokura, with Nagasaki as an alternative.

This raid did not run quite as smoothly as the first. As Sweeney approached Kokura early on 9 August, the city was protected by patchy cloud and despite three separate bombing runs the bombardier could not pinpoint the specified aiming feature. Running low on fuel, Sweeney turned for Nagasaki. A few minutes before 1100 hours, the B-29 swung over the new target, also covered with cloud, and released 'Fat Man' on a fleeting sight of the aiming point. A few seconds later Nagasaki disappeared under the now-familiar fire-ball and mushroom cloud. An estimated 35,000 people died.

The Japanese government, rocked by these two demonstrations of American power as well as a Soviet declaration of war on 9 August, realized that the end had come. After consultations with the Emperor, acceptance of Allied terms was wired to the 'Big Three' leaders through Switzerland and Sweden. It took time for the final details to be settled – in fact LeMay's campaign of conventional bombing continued until 14 August, when a record number of 804 B-29s hit targets in Japan – but to all intents and purposes, the war was over. The surrender ceremony took place on 2 September aboard the battleship USS *Missouri* in Tokyo Bay. By that time the bulk of the B-29s had been diverted from errands of death to ones of mercy, dropping food and clothing to the thousands of Allied POWs still in Japanese hands.

Thus, almost exactly three years after its maiden flight, the B-29 had more than justified its costly and difficult development. From the problems of the early months of operations against Japan, the aircraft had rapidly assumed the role of a true strategic bomber, capable of defeating an enemy state virtually on its own. During the Marianas operations, a total of 23,500 individual aircraft sorties had been flown and 170,000 tons of conventional ordnance, as well as two atomic bombs, had been dropped. A total of 371 bombers had been destroyed in the process, but their loss had saved enormous casualties by precluding the need for an invasion of Japan and, as it turned out, had paved the way to USAF autonomy. In 1947 an independent air force was created, based upon the proven ability of atomic-armed bombers to undermine the enemy's capability to wage modern technological war. The B-29s were an integral part of the new Strategic Air Command and although they were quickly superseded by even more powerful aircraft, notably the B-36 and B-50, their war service was far from over. They still had one more campaign to fight.

Left: The awesome mushroom cloud of an atomic explosion; in this case over Nagasaki, 9 August 1945.
Below: Japanese Foreign Minister Mamoru Shigemitsu signs the surrender document on board USS *Missouri*, 2 September 1945.

KOREAN SWANSONG

By 1950 the B-29 was no longer the sophisticated ultra-modern bomber it had seemed eight years earlier. Production had ceased in May 1946, by which time a total of 3960 had been built, and new aircraft, based upon the experiences of World War II and reflecting the new needs of an independent USAF, had begun to appear. Vast numbers of B-29s had been placed in storage. Eighty-eight of these were in fact transferred to the Royal Air Force in 1950, where they became known as 'Washingtons,' and those which remained in USAF Strategic Air Command (SAC) or conventional bombing squadrons rapidly began to look tired and not a little obsolete. Indeed by 1950 they had been redesignated as 'medium' bombers, with their role as the 'very heavy' components of American aerial power being taken over by the B-36 and B-50. Their useful life was clearly nearing its end.

This became irrelevant on 25 June 1950 when North Korean forces, equipped and trained by Communist-Bloc countries, suddenly crossed the 38th parallel into South Korea. A small, bitter war began which was soon to draw in the United States and demand the use of whatever conventional weapons were available. The B-29s of the Far Eastern Air Forces (FEAF), 22 aircraft of the 19th Bomb Group stationed at Anderson Field, Guam, and still a part of 20th Air Force, were the only bombers capable of hitting the Korean peninsula with any effect using conventional ordnance, and their commitment was guaranteed. In the event, they and a number of SAC B-29 Bomb Wings transferred from the United States were to find themselves involved in very little strategic bombing as such, but their contribution over the

next three years to the containment of Communist aggression in Korea was to be significant. Despite persistent problems, not only with the aircraft themselves, but also with the roles they were expected to carry out, the B-29s were to prove to be a useful weapon.

They were not committed immediately, however, for American military involvement in Korea was by no means an inevitable result of the North Korean invasion. Korea as a whole had been freed from Japanese occupation in 1945 by Soviet forces from Manchuria in the north and American forces from the Pacific in the south. To prevent unnecessary friction or confrontation the two nascent superpowers had decided, rather arbitrarily, to meet on the 38th parallel. The outcome had been the development of two entirely separate states; the Democratic People's Republic (North Korea) under Premier Kim II Sung, backed by the Soviets, and the Republic of Korea (South Korea) under Dr Syngman Rhee, ostensibly backed by the United States. The immediate post-war years saw a massive demobilization of American forces and a drift back toward international isolationism. Although the United States was interested in seeing a reunification of Korea through United Nations supervised elections, it was not prepared to insist upon this with force when Kim II Sung refused to co-operate. The last of the American occupying troops left South Korea in June 1949 and the initial reaction to the North Korean attack a year later was merely to protect US nationals caught in the war zone. It was not until the UN Security Council had voted in favor of supplying aid to the South Koreans on 27 June that General MacArthur, com-

Above: Bridges over the Han River, destroyed by B-29s in an attempt to stop the North Korean advance, June 1950.

Above: A reconnaissance RB-29 of 31st SRS, 1950, at the time of the Korean War.

manding US forces in Japan, was authorized to commit units to the defense of Syngman Rhee's embattled troops.

At first President Truman restricted US involvement to air elements only, and on 27 June MacArthur ordered General George E Stratemeyer, Commander in Chief of FEAF, to employ his aircraft against any targets of value, particularly troop concentrations and supply dumps, between the front line and the 38th parallel in an attempt to blunt the North Korean advance. When the B-29s flew their first combat mission of this new war, therefore, they were committed to tactical support of the South Korean Army, a role for which they had not been specifically designed. As a result they were thrown into a conflict which was so confused that more formalized and planned bombing policies were impossible to work out. On 28 June four aircraft of the 19th BG flew over Korea, searching for and destroying targets of opportunity on rail routes to the north of Seoul, the already-fallen South Korean capital. A more definite policy seemed to be emerging

the next day, when, on direct orders from MacArthur, a further nine B-29s began to hit North Korean airfields, but the pressures of a fast-moving war doomed this campaign to an early grave. As North Korean forces concentrated on the Han River in preparation for a major push southward, the bombers were diverted to attacking them, with predictably poor results. This was to be a constantly recurring pattern over the next three years, as the USAF planners on the one hand searched for a role which the B-29s could carry out consistently, while the land commanders on the other insisted upon tactical close support whenever the situation demanded. It was to result in a basic misuse of the strategic bomber and an inconclusive end to the B-29s combat career.

At least the USAF could attempt an independent line, and one of the first steps in this direction was the setting up of a command structure to control B-29 operations. This took place on 8 July when a special FEAF Bomber Command was authorized under Major General Emmett O'Donnell, the

Below: B-29s of SAC 22nd BW fly toward their targets in Korea, September 1950.

Above: **B-29s of SAC 22nd BW release 500lb bombs over Korean targets, September 1950.**

erstwhile leader of the 73rd BW in the Marianas. He established his headquarters at Yokata, Japan, and in addition to the 19th BG, was given two Bomb Wings – the 22nd and 92nd – transferred temporarily from SAC on 3 July by USAF Chief of Staff General Hoyt S Vandenberg. Together with six RB-29 long-range reconnaissance aircraft belonging to SAC's 31st Strategic Reconnaissance Squadron on Okinawa, 24 weather-reconnaissance WB-29s and four SB-29 'Superdumbo' rescue machines, this gave O'Donnell a theoretical strength of approximately 100 aircraft. Unfortunately his first brief came from MacArthur who directed him to use them north of the Han River, principally against targets of opportunity on the battlefield. This role should have been carried out by fighter bombers.

Understandably the results were disappointing and by 18 July Vandenberg was complaining to MacArthur that this was no way to treat the B-29s. MacArthur agreed and diverted the bombers to interdiction raids nearer the 38th parallel, designed to cut off the North Koreans in the south from their sources of supply. This was still not a worthy role for the strategic bombers, but at least it was a more formalized approach to their use. Interdiction Campaign No 1 was duly initiated on 4 August and O'Donnell was for the first time given definite target priorities. Between 4 and 10 August the B-29s hit a variety of marshalling yards and rail complexes in North Korea in an attempt to disrupt supplies, but once again the results were poor, chiefly because of a lack of prestrike intelligence information. As a result between 12 and 20 August the emphasis was shifted to a number of strategic road and rail bridges north of the 37th parallel. The majority of these were destroyed, even though they were of extremely strong construction, and the B-29s had to evolve entirely new combat techniques using unsatisfactory weapons. Both the 22nd and 92nd BWs, used to training for atomic strikes at very high altitude and equipped with B-29s which were only capable of delivering 500lb bombs, were not really suited to the

task at all, while the 19th BG, although capable of using 1000 and 2000lb weapons, experienced tremendous problems. One particular railroad bridge at Seoul, assigned to the 19th, in fact took three weeks to knock down, with strikes organized on every single day. Nevertheless by the end of August, O'Donnell could report the complete destruction of 37 of the 44 bridges involved in the campaign, with the remaining seven unusable.

USAF planners have never been entirely satisfied with this emphasis upon tactical strikes, however, preferring a proper strategic bombing campaign against North Korean industry, something which was initially pressed for in early July. Vandenberg offered to send two more SAC Bomb Wings to Japan, the 98th and 307th, and this was probably the deciding factor; in late July he was authorized to begin the necessary planning. SAC Intelligence, using RB-29s of the 31st SRS, quickly earmarked five major industrial centers for attack: the North Korean capital of Pyongyang (a source of armaments and aircraft as well as an important rail center), Wonsan (oil refineries around a major sea port), Hungnam (chemical and metallurgical industries), Chongjin (iron foundries and rail yards) and Rashin (a naval base with oil storage facilities). Other targets of secondary importance were also listed, including five east-coast hydroelectric power complexes. It was obvious that enough targets existed to justify a strategic campaign, particularly as the majority were conveniently concentrated in the northeast. It looked as if the B-29s could be used in their proper role.

The raids began on 30 July when, in three separate but coordinated precision, daylight attacks the Hungnam industrial complex was flattened, and this success was maintained against the other primary targets as enthusiasm for the venture grew in Washington and Tokyo. Indeed by early September O'Donnell was able to report the destruction of all known industrial facilities in the North with the exception of those at Rashin which, after one B-29 raid, had been deleted from the target list by the President himself. As Rashin was only seventeen miles from the Soviet border it was felt that a slight bombing error might escalate the conflict unnecessarily. It was a remarkable achievement nonetheless, justifying the USAF insistence and proving the continued power of the B-29 when assigned the relevant tasks. O'Donnell was already moving on to his secondary targets – the first raid in fact took place on 26 September against the Fusen hydroelectricity plant – when the entire course of the war was dramatically altered. For a variety of reasons the B-29s were never again to hit strategic targets.

The initial cancellation of the strategic campaign came about because most of the targets in North Korea were actually captured by UN forces in October 1950. A bold amphibious landing at Inchon and an advance eastward to Seoul in late September threatened to cut the North Koreans off from their homeland. An Allied offensive from Pusan added to the pressure and the North Koreans began a retreat which, harried by constant air strikes, soon degenerated into a rout. South Korean forces crossed the 38th parallel on 1 October, Pyongyang fell eighteen days later and a general United Nations advance toward the Chinese border on the Yalu River met little opposition. Stratemeyer diverted many of the B-29s to tactical strikes in what appeared to be the dying moments of a successful land campaign; strategic bombing became unnecessary and FEAF Bomber Command was disbanded on 27 October, with the 22nd and 92nd BWs returning to SAC duties in the United States. Victory seemed assured.

However, the war was far from over, for as the UN forces approached the Yalu, Chinese units could be seen massing to

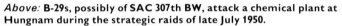

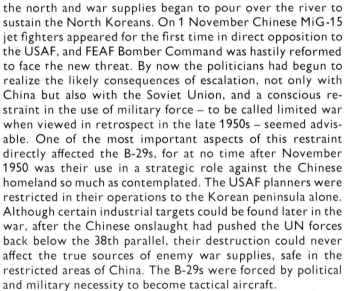

Above: **B-29s, possibly of SAC 307th BW, attack a chemical plant at Hungnam during the strategic raids of late July 1950.**

Above: **B-29 of SAC 98th BW salvoes both bomb bays simultaneously over a North Korean target, 13 July 1951.**

the north and war supplies began to pour over the river to sustain the North Koreans. On 1 November Chinese MiG-15 jet fighters appeared for the first time in direct opposition to the USAF, and FEAF Bomber Command was hastily reformed to face the new threat. By now the politicians had begun to realize the likely consequences of escalation, not only with China but also with the Soviet Union, and a conscious restraint in the use of military force – to be called limited war when viewed in retrospect in the late 1950s – seemed advisable. One of the most important aspects of this restraint directly affected the B-29s, for at no time after November 1950 was their use in a strategic role against the Chinese homeland so much as contemplated. The USAF planners were restricted in their operations to the Korean peninsula alone. Although certain industrial targets could be found later in the war, after the Chinese onslaught had pushed the UN forces back below the 38th parallel, their destruction could never affect the true sources of enemy war supplies, safe in the restricted areas of China. The B-29s were forced by political and military necessity to become tactical aircraft.

This was made obvious as early as November 1950 when O'Donnell was ordered to concentrate his forces against the Yalu bridges which were being used to carry supplies from China into North Korea. Between 8 and 25 November the B-29s hit the southern approaches to these targets (to drop bombs on the northern spans would have been an attack upon Chinese territory) at Sinuiju, Hyesanjin, Uiju, Manpojin and Chongsonjin. Some success was achieved – O'Donnell reported a 65 percent destruction rate – but this was illusory. Many of the broken spans were replaced by pontoons which were only used at night. The small-yield bombs tended not to do the damage which was necessary and the Chinese build up of supplies and troops in the North continued virtually unchecked. In addition the B-29s had begun to suffer casualties; one bomber was shot down and ten others badly damaged during these attacks.

The general lack of effect was felt on 25 November when hordes of Chinese troops fell upon the advancing UN forces and, in a series of extremely costly battles, pushed them back to the 38th parallel. The B-29s, like every other available aircraft, flew close support missions in a desperate attempt to stop the flood, but it was not until the end of December that the line began to stabilize. The situation was now much as it had been before Inchon, with the exception that a strategic bombing campaign was impossible, and the B-29s were soon reverting to the previous emphasis upon interdiction. A sporadic campaign took place against rail targets in the North in late December and early January, but a Communist New Year Offensive, which pushed the Allies even further southward, soon necessitated a return to close support.

As this storm was weathered, again at high cost to the land forces, so the planners began to search for a definite B-29 targeting policy, if only to ensure that the tremendous strike potential of the bombers could be concentrated against worthwhile enemy targets. From the map it was obvious that the key area of Chinese supply build up was in the northwest of Korea, but this was also the area containing MiG bases and anti-aircraft defenses. If the B-29s were to be used, they could not go alone, so in what became known as Interdiction Campaign No 4, instigated in February 1951, they were provided with fighter escorts. The early raids were disastrous. The F-86 Sabre jet fighters, the only aircraft capable of taking on the MiG-15s in a sustained campaign, were not yet fully operational in Korea. The early strikes were escorted by F-80C Shooting Stars and F-84E Thunderjets, neither of which were effective. In addition co-ordination between the bomber and fighter commanders was poor, and it was not unknown for the B-29s to go in alone, with predictable results. By 12 April, with three B-29s shot down and ten badly damaged, Stratemeyer called off the raids and diverted the bombers once again to close support, this time against Communist air bases around the 38th parallel.

Concern over the lack of results in this phase of operations was not alleviated by the fact that new bombing techniques and weapons, designed to solve some of the problems already experienced in interdiction strikes, had been used. Up to early 1951, in the absence of organized enemy defenses, the B-29s had been able to make numerous, unhurried bombing runs against a specific target at altitudes as low as 10,000ft. Once the Chinese became involved and both fighters and anti-aircraft guns appeared, this had become virtually suicidal. The raids on northwest Korea had therefore been put in at 20,000ft with the bombers flying in defensive formations ostensibly escorted by fighters. It was worrying that, even then, they had been a poor match for the enemy defenses.

Similarly, a range of new weapons, designed to improve both hitting power and accuracy, had been seen to fail. These were radio-controlled bombs, dropped from an ordinary B-29 and then guided onto the target by the bombardier. The earlier versions, known as 'Razons' because their controller could alter **R**ange and **AZ**imuth **ON**ly once they left the aircraft, proved to be moderately successful (the 19th BG destroyed fifteen bridges with them in late 1950 and early 1951), but had the disadvantage of being a mere 1000lb each. Given this, the next generation, known as 'Tarzons' and weighing 2000lb each, promised to be an effective addition to the United States' arsenal. Unfortunately they were not. When carried by a B-29 nearly two-thirds of the Tarzon protruded outside the bomb bay and they proved to be unwieldy. In the end they were infinitely more dangerous to the bomber crew than the enemy. They were withdrawn from service in late April 1951 after at least two B-29s had been destroyed trying to ditch their bombs in the sea. The Tarzons, full of unstable RDX explosive from the end of World War II, exploded as soon as they hit the water. All told, thirty of these weapons were dropped over Korea, but as only six bridges were destroyed in the process, they represented yet another dead end in the seemingly endless search for a viable B-29 role.

The important area of northwest Korea was not revisited by the B-29s until the end of December 1951, for, in a decision reminiscent of that made by the 8th AAF in Europe in 1943, USAF planners decided to concentrate upon the destruction of Communist air power before moving on to a more vigorous bombing policy. The B-29s had an important part to play in this new move, for they were to act as bait, attacking Communist air bases throughout the North and forcing the MiGs to enter battle with escorting fighters. Between 13 and 27 October the raids went in, but the results were poor. The Communists took to dispersing their MiG squadrons far and wide, even using temporary grass strips on occasion, so that USAF Intelligence could not keep track of their movements and B-29 losses were heavy. By 27 October five of the bombers had been destroyed and a further twenty badly damaged. The raids were quickly suspended and replaced by nighttime attacks using small numbers of B-29s equipped with Shoran (**SHO**rt **RAN**ge) navigation radar which was used to pinpoint small targets with remarkable accuracy. Some success was achieved and these raids continued for the remainder of the war, although as night fighters and radar-controlled defenses began to be experienced, losses did mount alarmingly. On 10 June 1952, for example, four Shoran B-29s suddenly found themselves being tracked by radar-controlled searchlights over Sinuiju. Night fighters homed in and two of the bombers went down in flames, with a third so badly damaged that it barely reached the UN lines before crash landing. The use of B-29s as night intruder bombers was clearly not the answer.

Meanwhile more concentrated attempts at interdiction had

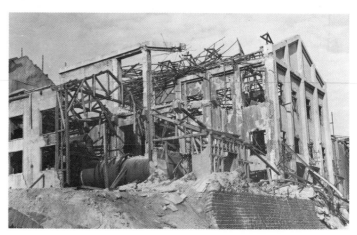

Above: **Aftermath of a B-29 raid on the Chosan nitrogen fertilizer factory, November 1950.**
Top: **Results of a raid on the Chongjin iron foundries, August 1950.**

begun to achieve a small measure of success. On 25 August 1951 35 B-29s of the 19th BG and 98th and 307th BWs had hit the marshalling yards at Rashin (reassigned by Truman to the bombers in light of their importance) in the first of a series of sustained attacks against rail centers. In August and September they concentrated on the north-south rail lines of North Korea with B-29s hitting bridges at Pyongyang, Sonchon, Sunchon, Sinanju and Huichon, but this was soon seen to be indecisive as the Communists quickly repaired or by-passed the break in their supply chain. It was not until more concentrated attacks on specific choke points had been initiated that there was any hope of success. For 44 days, beginning on 26 January 1952, B-29s in close co-operation with other US aircraft dropped nearly 4000 500lb bombs on the one unfortunate village of Wadong where the lateral rail route of North Korea entered a potentially vulnerable defile. Enough damage was inflicted for this new bombing policy to be formalized in early March under the codename Operation Saturate but, again, heavy losses coupled with Communist ingenuity and a lack of suitable targets tended to undermine the effects. The B-29 role had not been found after nearly two years of war.

FEAF planners were well aware of this, and in spring 1952 they proposed the nearest thing they could find to a strategic campaign in a desperate attempt to justify the mounting cost of bomber operations – sustained attacks upon North Korean hydroelectricity facilities. By 28 April the necessary authorization had been gained and four complexes were earmarked for destruction, at Sui-Ho, Fusen, Choshin and Kyosen. The campaign was to be a co-ordinated USAF effort, with the B-29s

Above: **Symbol of air power: a FEAF B-29 flies over an Allied anti-aircraft position, Korea 1952.**

committed to nighttime, Shoran-guided strikes after fighter bombers had gone in during the day. In the event, even the United States Navy contributed with carrier-borne aircraft from Task Force 77 off the coast of Korea. The raids began on 24 June, with the B-29s going in for the first time that night against Choshin. By the 27th it was estimated that nine-tenths of North Korean power supplies had been destroyed.

This success swiftly led to the adoption of a more general bombing policy, based upon the twin characteristics of concentration and co-ordination. The idea was that if selected targets of military importance could be located and then destroyed in a storm of aerial assault, the Communists might be persuaded to agree to an armistice, the negotiations for which had been going on for nearly eighteen months. The first and, as it turned out, the biggest of these raids took place on 11 July against thirty different targets in Pyongyang and the campaign continued over the next few weeks with similar intensive strikes against Sungho-Ri, Choshin, Sindok and Sinuiju. The B-29s contributed to most of these and their gradually-improving nighttime techniques were shown to good effect on 30 September when 45 of them wiped out the Namsan-Ri chemical plant, but enemy defenses were still taking a significant toll. As the raids continued, between November 1952 and January 1953 five B-29s fell victim to night fighters and three more were severely damaged. Only after the deployment of USAF night fighters, especially the F3D-2 Skynight, did losses decrease. Even then it was apparent that the B-29 could never be expected to mount a campaign against North Korea on its own. Only within the protective body of the USAF as a whole could the bomber hope to survive. This fact was reinforced in May 1953, two months before an armistice was eventually signed, when the B-29s could do nothing more than contribute to the successful

destruction of North Korean irrigation dams. The targets were virtually strategic, but the bombers could never have hit them alone.

Thus when the Korean War ended on 27 July 1953, the B-29 was quite obviously an obsolete weapon. Its contribution to the United Nations' cause was undoubtedly significant; in 37 months of conflict over 21,000 aircraft sorties had been flown by the B-29 crews, nearly 167,000 tons of bombs had been dropped and 34 of the bombers had been lost (sixteen to enemy fighters, four to flak and fourteen to other causes). However, the original *raison d'être* of the machine had not been satisfied. This was partly due to a lack of strategic targets caused by the restraints of limited war, but it was also a result of tremendous advances in aerial technology which left the B-29 behind. The aircraft belonged to the 1940s, to an age before the jet fighter, radar-controlled defenses and superpower confrontation. It had more than justified its development in 1945 over the skies of Japan, but by 1950 it was almost an anachronism, awaiting retirement and totally unsuited to the rigors of another war. It is certainly no coincidence that as soon as the Korean War ended the USAF accelerated its program of bomber re-equipment, culminating in the delivery of the first jet-engined B-52s in June 1955. The Superfortress gave way to the Stratofortress and their very names indicate the rapid and far-reaching technological strides which had taken place. The B-29 contributed to containment in Korea, but this was not a fitting end to the aircraft's career. Its true worth lay in 1945, not in 1950. It belonged to the total war conditions of the conflict with Japan, not to the infinitely more subtle and potentially dangerous climate of a Cold War.

APPENDICES

1. B-29 Specifications

A. Normal B-29

Applicable to all 1620 B-29s built by the Boeing Aircraft Company at their Wichita, Kansas, plant between September 1943 and October 1945; to 357 B-29s built by the Bell Aircraft Corporation at Atlanta (Marietta), Georgia, between February 1944 and January 1945; and to 536 B-29s assembled by the Glenn L Martin Company at Omaha, Nebraska, between January 1944 and September 1945.

Span	141ft 2in
Length	99ft
Height	27ft 9in (tail fin)
Wing area	1736 sq ft
Weights	Empty: 70,140lb
	Loaded: 135,000lb with 12,000lb bomb load
Powerpack	Four Wright R-3350-23 Cyclone 18-cylinder radials, each with a pair of General Electric B-11 superchargers to give 2200 brake horsepower at takeoff
Propellers	Four-blade Hamilton Standard Hydromatics (16ft 7in diameter) with constant-speed governors and hydraulic operation for pitch change and feathering. Engine gear ratio was 0.35 (that is, the propeller turned at just over one-third of the engine revolutions, so at 2800 engine rpm the propeller was turning at 980rpm)

(Boeing introduced a new R-3350-41, with baffles and oil crossover pipes for improved cooling, on production block 50; both Martin and Bell followed suit on block 20. All three companies had begun to use R-3350-57 engines by the end of the production run. Both new types of engine continued to use the Hamilton propellers but some B-29s were fitted with Curtiss electric propellers, which enjoyed reversible pitch and blade cooling cuffs, toward the end of World War II)

Maximum range	3250 miles at 25,000ft with full fuel and 5000lb bomb load

(This was raised to 4100 miles under the same load conditions by the addition of auxiliary fuel tanks in the bomb bays of later models)

Practical operational radius	1600 miles, rising to 1800 miles after engine and fuel improvements
Maximum ferry range	5600 miles, rising to 6000 miles after improvements
Maximum speed	375mph at 25,000ft (although speeds in excess of 450mph were recorded in the jet stream over Japan in 1944–45)
Normal cruising speed	200–250mph
Fuel-load capacity	8198 US gallons on early models, carried in four wing-tanks. Increased to 9548 US gallons after the installation of extra tanks in the wing center section on Boeing production block 25. Bell incorporated the same on block 5; all Martin B-29s had them as standard fit. Under operational conditions a B-29 would carry 6988 US gallons only if the semipermanent fuel tanks in one of the two bomb bays were taken out
Rate of climb	38 minutes to 25,000ft at 110,000lb gross weight
Service ceiling	31,850ft
Bomb-load capacity	5000lb over 1600 mile radius at high altitude; 12,000lb over 1600-mile radius at medium altitude; 20,000lb maximum over short distances at low altitude. High explosive and incendiary bombs carried, either exclusively or mixed, depending on type of raid
Armament	Ten 0.5in machine guns and one 20mm cannon. Cannon and two 0.5in in the tail, two 0.5in in each of the four remotely-controlled power turrets (forward and aft dorsal, forward and aft ventral) which made up the General Electric computerized gun system

(The forward dorsal turret was increased to four 0.5in machine guns on Boeing production block 40 to increase forward protection. Bell followed suit on block 10, all Martin B-29s had this as standard fit. Similarly, the 20mm cannon was deleted on Boeing production block 55, Bell block 25 and Martin block 25. Its trajectory, totally different from that of the machine guns, had made aiming difficult in combat conditions)

Crew	Eleven men comprising:
	Aircraft Commander (sometimes termed the Command Pilot)
	Pilot (sometimes termed the Co-Pilot)
	Bombardier
	Navigator
	Flight Engineer
	Radio Operator
	Radar Operator
	Central Fire Control Gunner
	Left Side Gunner
	Right Side Gunner
	Tail Gunner

The first six were housed in the forward pressurized cabin, connected by a 34in diameter tube to the next four in the mid-fuselage pressurized area. The tail gunner, in his own completely separate pressurized turret, was in the rear. The Aircraft Commander, Pilot, Bombardier, Navigator and Flight Engineer were all officers, the remainder enlisted men, although the post of Flight Engineer was gradually opened to suitably qualified enlisted men as World War II progressed

Crew size was occasionally increased to thirteen under World War II operational conditions, with the addition of two radar/radio experts (known as 'Ravens') to man the increasingly sophisticated radar and ECM (electronic countermeasures) equipment

Radar equipment	AN/APN-4 Loran (**LO**ng **RAN**ge) constant-beam navigation aid was fitted on early models, being replaced by a more sophisticated AN/APN-9 system during World War II
	AN/APQ-13 radar bombing-navigational aid in retractable radome located between the two bomb bays. Designed to give a radar image of the ground

(Most operational B-29s carried and distributed 'Chaff,' sometimes called 'Window' – metallic foil strips, cut to the exact wavelength of enemy radar, which would saturate and blur their screens during target approach)

Above right: **Standard B-29 in flight.**
Right: **A B-29 is towed to dispersal.**

B. B-29A

Outwardly there was little noticeable difference between the normal B-29 and the B-29A, the main changes being concentrated in the area of wing construction. Specifications for the B-29A were limited to the 1119 aircraft built at the Boeing plant at Renton, Washington, between January 1944 and May 1946. In the normal B-29 the wing was manufactured as an integral part of the fuselage; in the B-29A a stub center-section was built and then the wing was constructed in seven sections around it. This left room for three wing fuel tanks instead of the normal four, so fuel-load capacity was reduced.

Span	142ft 3in
Length	as normal B-29
Height	as normal B-29
Wing area	1738 sq ft
Weights	Empty: 71,360lb
	Loaded: 135,000lb with 12,000lb bomb load
Engines	as normal B-29, with new R-3350 designs added at much the same time
Propellers	as normal B-29
Maximum range	4000 miles at 25,000ft with full fuel and 5000lb bomb load
Practical operational radius	1800 miles
Maximum ferry range	6000 miles
Maximum speed	as normal B-29
Normal cruising speed	as normal B-29
Fuel-load capacity	9288 US gallons after installation of semipermanent bomb-bay tanks
Rate of climb	as normal B-29
Service ceiling	about 33,000ft
Bomb-load capacity	as normal B-29
Armament	as normal B-29. Four-gun forward dorsal turret installed and 20mm tail cannon deleted on production block 20
Crew	as normal B-29
Radar equipment	as normal B-29

(Some early B-29As were also characterized by the installation of pneumatically operated bomb-bay doors which could be snapped shut in less than a second. Before this the doors had been hydraulically operated, with normal closing speed of seven seconds. By early 1945 all B-29s, normal as well as A and B variants, had pneumatic doors as standard fit)

C. B-29B

Applicable to 311 B-29s built by the Bell Aircraft Corporation at their Marietta plant between January and September 1945. The B-29Bs were basically stripped down versions of the normal B-29, with the General Electric computerized gun system deleted and new radar aids added. Most were issued to the 315th BW in the Marianas in 1945

Span	as normal B-29
Length	as normal B-29
Height	as normal B-29
Wing area	as normal B-29
Weights	Empty: 69,000lb
	Loaded: 137,000lb with 18,000lb bomb load
Powerpack	as normal B-29, although the majority had the R-3350-41 as standard fit
Propellers	as normal B-29
Maximum range	4200 miles at 10,000ft with full fuel and 18,000lb bomb load
Practical operational radius	1800 miles

Maximum ferry range	4000 miles
Maximum speed	364mph at 25,000ft
Normal cruising speed	210–225mph
Fuel-load capacity	6988 US gallons, the bomb-bay tanks not being standard fit
Rate of climb	33 minutes to 20,000ft at 110,000lb gross weight
Service ceiling	32,000ft
Bomb-load capacity	20,000lb (although with a mix of HE and incendiaries, this could be increased to 22,800lb)
Armaments	Two or three 0.5in machine guns in the tail, with provision for two 0.5in in the mid-fuselage pressurized area
Crew	Seven or eight men (the Right and Left Side Gunners were not carried, the Central Fire Control Gunner occasionally acted as an observer and the Bombardier's duties could be taken over by the Radar Operator)
Radar equipment	AN/APQ-7 'Eagle' bombing-navigational aid, housed in retractable radome between the bomb bays and designed to give improved presentation of ground images

D. Boeing 'Washington'

Name applicable to 88 B-29s and B-29As taken out of USAF storage in 1950 and issued to Royal Air Force bombing squadrons under the American military aid to Europe program at the beginning of the Cold War period. Designed to fill the RAF heavy bomber gap between the rapidly aging Avro Lincolns and the still-to-be-developed 'V' bomber jet series. In use between 1950 and early 1958 with Nos 15, 35, 44, 57, 90, 115, 149 and 207 Squadrons, Bomber Command. Specifications as for B-29 and B-29A, except that the RAF usually operated a crew of ten men only, deleting the role of Aircraft Commander, absorbing his duties into those of the Pilot

E. USAAF and USAF operational variants

(a) The atomic B-29s
    Specifications as for normal B-29, but incorporating strengthened bomb bays and suspension systems. Ventral area painted white to minimize glare damage. B-29s of USAF Strategic Air Command all of this type post-1947
(b) F-13A and RB-29 reconnaissance aircraft
    World War II and USAF versions respectively – these were stripped down B-29s with a service ceiling in excess of 35,000ft. Equipped with a plethora of cameras, especially in bomb-bay areas, they were used for pre- and post-operation reconnaissance over both Japan and Korea. Weather reconnaissance versions, used in the Korean War, were designated WB-29s
(c) SB-29A 'Superdumbo'
    Rescue aircraft developed to aid ditched B-29s on the long overwater flights between the Marianas and Japan, 1945. Basic B-29, but with extra crewmen as observers, emergency gear and, most noticeably, a lifeboat slung under the forward fuselage. No armament carried. Continued in use post-World War II

2. Order of Battle, 20th Air Force, 1944–45

Bombardment Wing	Bombardment Groups	Bombardment Squadrons	Date when became operational
58	40	25, 44, 45 (395)	5 June 1944
	444	676, 677, 678 (679)	
	462	768, 769, 770 (771)	
	468	792, 793, 794 (795)	
73	497	869, 870, 871	28 October 1944
	498	873, 874, 875	
	499	877, 878, 879	24 November 1944
	500	881, 882, 883	11 November 1944
313	6	24, 39, 40	27 January 1945
	9	1, 5, 99	25 January 1945
	504	398, 421, 680*	16 January 1945
	505	482, 483, 484	30 December 1944
314	19	28, 30, 93	12 February 1945
	29	6, 43, 52	15 February 1945
	39	60, 61, 62	6 April 1945
	330	457, 458, 459	12 April 1945
315	16	15, 16, 17	16 June 1945
	331	355, 356, 357	1 July 1945
	501	21, 41, 485	16 June 1945
	502	402, 411, 430	30 June 1945
	509 CG	393	1 July 1945

The Bombardment Squadrons of 58th BW in brackets were all disbanded in September–October 1944.

*680 BS did not join 504th BG until June 1945.

A note on aircraft markings

In common with most aircraft types, B-29s were relatively devoid of markings when first issued to individual squadrons. The US national markings, the 'star and bar,' appeared on the top of the port mainplane and beneath the starboard, as well as on both sides of the mid-fuselage section, aft of the gunners' blisters. The manufacturer's hull serial number was painted on both sides of the tail fin. It was not until the aircraft was allocated to its squadron that more distinctive markings, designed to show at a glance what squadron, group and wing it belonged to, began to be applied. The form of these markings appears to have differed in the CBI and Pacific theaters and to have been changed in the latter in early 1945.

The CBI markings

The four Bombardment Groups of 58th BW appear to have used colors and designs to distinguish themselves, and although it is sometimes difficult to be precise, the following list can be compiled from photographic evidence:

Group	Tail marking
40th	Four horizontal tail stripes and tip
444th	Three vertical rudder stripes
462nd	Bellyband, aft of national marking on fuselage
468th	Two diagonal stripes on the rudder

Within each BG, the individual Bombardment Squadrons were distinguished by the color of their group marking – red, green, yellow and blue being the usual ones – perhaps in order of seniority within the group. Thus the 45th BS of 40th BG would have four yellow horizontal stripes and tip to the rudder; the 794th BS of 468th BG, two yellow diagonal rudder stripes. This squadron color was usually repeated on the engine cowls, propeller bosses and blade tips and even, occasionally, the wheel hubs. The aircraft number within the squadron appeared either on the tail or forward fuselage, and it was not unknown for an individual aircraft letter also to be painted on the fin. The 444th BG adopted a diamond tail marking in late 1944 in addition to the rudder stripes, within which the aircraft number appeared.

The Pacific markings

When B-29s arrived in the Marianas a new system of marking appeared, based upon geometric shapes and letters. Throughout the campaign, the Bombardment Wings were distinguished by the following designs:

58th	A triangle
73rd	An uncolored square
313th	A circle
314th	A dark colored square
315th	A diamond
509th	An arrow, pointing forward, within a circle

In addition, each Bombardment Group had its own letter, and although again it is difficult to be precise, the list of these would seem to be:

Bombardment Group	Letter
40th	(C?)
444th	N
462nd	U
468th	S
497th	A
498th	T
499th	V
500th	Z
6th	R
9th	X
504th	E
505th	W
19th	M
29th	O
39th	P
330th	K
16th	B
331st	(H?)
501st	Y
502nd	(J?)

Before about mid-April 1945 a typical fin marking would consist of three separate items, with the BG letter at the top, the BW geometric shape in the center and the individual aircraft number at the bottom. Because of this, many B-29 crews referred to their aircraft by this code. Thus 'Z – square – 50' would denote the B-29 with the squadron number 50, belonging to the 500th BG of 73rd BW

As more aircraft arrived in the Marianas, however, it did become confusing to use such an elaborate code, and in April 1945 the tail markings were ordered to consist just of the BG letter, painted as large as the fin would allow. This gave no indication of BW, so within a few weeks this was altered again to the BG letter within the BW geometric shape, also as large as possible on the tail fin. Thus the letter R within a circle denoted an aircraft of 6th BG of 313th BW; an uncolored M within a dark square one of the 19th BG of 314th BW. Aircraft numbers now appeared on the aircraft nose and engine cowls.

Throughout these changes squadrons appear to have been distinguished by color – red, green and yellow, perhaps in order of seniority – usually on engine cowls, propeller bosses and blade tips.

3. Chain of Command, B-29 Operations, 1944–45

Joint Chiefs of Staff

20th Air Force
(General Henry H Arnold)

US Strategic Air Forces, Pacific (from June 1945)
(General Carl A Spaatz)

XX BC
Lt Gen Kenneth B Wolfe, Nov 1943–July 1944
Maj Gen Curtis E LeMay, Aug 1944–Jan 1945

XXI BC
Maj Gen Haywood S Hansell, Jr
Aug 1944–Jan 1945
Maj Gen Curtis E LeMay,
Jan–Aug 1945

58TH BW
May 1944–April 1945
Brig Gen La Verne G Saunders

58th BW
from April 1945
Brig Gen La Verne
G Saunders

73rd BW
Oct 1944
Brig Gen Emmett
O'Donnell

313th BW
Jan 1945
Brig Gen John
H Davies

314th BW
Apr 1945
Brig Gen
Thomas S Power

315th BW
June 1945
Brig Gen Frank
Armstrong

509th CG
July 1945
Col Paul W
Tibbetts, Jr

4. B-29 Losses, April 1944–August 1945

A. XX Bomber Command

Year and Month	Combat Losses	Non-combat Losses	Total
April 1944	—	7	7
May	—	5	5
June	10	8	18
July	3	5	8
August	14	5	19
September	3	7	10
October	5	16	21
November	19	2	21
December	16	6	22
January 1945	4	3	7
February	4	2	6
March	2	1	3
	80	67	147

B. XXI Bomber Command

Year and Month	Combat Losses	Non-combat Losses	Total
November 1944	4	5	9
December	21	6	27
January 1945	27	—	27
February	26	3	29
March	34	—	34
April	57	1	58
May	88	3	91
June	44	7	51
July	22	5	27
August	11	7	18
	334	37	371

Grand Total for 20th AF 414 combat losses
104 non-combat losses
Another 10 B-29s were lost en route from the USA to combat theaters.
Altogether 528 B-29s were lost, April 1944–August 1945

Below: **P2B-IS (background), used as a launch platform for the Bell X-1A Skyrocket.**

5. Aircraft Strength of 20th Air Force April 1944–August 1945

(Figures include first and second line aircraft)

Year and Month	Aircraft available	Crews available
April 1944	94	143
May	137	222
June	133	226
July	146	224
August	150	221
September	163	221
October	219	287
November	262	391
December	348	484
January 1945	450	579
February	541	688
March	605	778
April	708	870
May	732	880
June	888	1106
July	998	1186
August	1056	1378

6. Bomb Tonnage Dropped by 20th Air Force on Japan June 1944–August 1945

(Atomic bombs not included)

A. XX Bomber Command

Year and Month	High Explosive	Incendiary
June 1944	501	46
July	209	—
August	184	68
September	521	—
October	1023	646
November	1415	215
December	1556	—
January 1945	1584	422
February	1261	604
March	1019	417
	9273	2418

B. XXI Bomber Command

Year and Month	High Explosive	Incendiary
November 1944	343	232
December	1,495	610
January 1945	927	477
February	1,140	1,015
March	3,086	10,761
April	13,209	4,283
May	6,937	17,348
June	9,954	22,588
July	9,388	33,163
August	8,438	12,591
	54,917	103,068

Grand Totals 20th AF dropped   64,190 tons HE
        105,486 tons Incendiaries
on Japan between June 1944 and August 1945

7. B-29s in the Korean War, 1950–53

Units involved

19th Bomb Group of 20th Air Force	operative throughout the campaign.
22nd Bomb Wing of SAC **92nd Bomb Wing of SAC**	transferred to FEAF 3 July and returned to USA 27 October 1950
98th Bomb Wing of SAC **307th Bomb Wing of SAC**	transferred to FEAF 30 July 1950, and returned to USA July 1953
31st Strategic Reconnaissance Squadron of SAC	(renamed 91st SRS on 16 November 1950) operative throughout the campaign using RB-29s

(The terms Bomb Group and Bomb Wing do not appear to have meant the same in 1950 as they did in 1945. Regardless of the nomenclature, each consisted of two squadrons only, so it would seem that whereas 20th AF had maintained the organization, albeit on a reduced scale, of World War II, SAC had taken the Bomb Wing as its basic unit, again on a reduced scale, when formed in 1947. In any event the existence of the two names has caused confusion among writers on the B-29)

Statistics

Aircraft sorties flown	21,000
Tons of bombs dropped	167,000
B-29s lost	34 (16 to enemy fighters 4 to enemy anti-aircraft defenses 14 to other causes, including accident)

Markings

Basic markings were as they had been during World War II, with the addition of the words 'United States Air Force' on both sides of the forward upper fuselage and the letters 'USAF' above the starboard and below the port mainplanes. SAC aircraft carried the SAC crest on the tail fin

Fin markings were the same as the later revisions of the Marianas operations – a letter within a geometric shape. So the 22nd BW carried 'W' within a circle, the 98th BW an 'H' within a square; 31st (91st) SRS an 'X' within a circle

Bibliography

B-29 Superfortress at War, David A Anderton, Ian Allan, 1978

B-29: The Superfortress, Carl Berger, Ballantine Books, 1970

Boeing Aircraft since 1916, Peter M Bowers, Putnam and Company, 1966

The Army Air Forces in World War II, Kit C Carter and Robert Mueller, Combat Chronology, 1941–45 Government Printing Office, Washington, 1975

The Army Air Forces in World War II, Volume Five: 'The Pacific: Matterhorn to Nagasaki', Wesley F Craven and James L Cate, University of Chicago Press, 1953

The US Strategic Bomber, Roger Freeman, Macdonald and Jane's, 1975

Combat Aircraft of World War II, Bill Gunston, Salamander Books, 1978

Air War over Korea, Robert Jackson, Ian Allan, 1975

Ruin from the Air, Gordon Thomas and Max M Witts, Sphere Books, 1978

Below: **SB-29 'Superdumbo' rescue aircraft, with lifeboat slung beneath forward fuselage.**

INDEX

Acknowledgments

The authors and publishers would like to thank the Taylor Picture Library for supplying the photographs and would also like to thank the following for granting permission for their use:
Anglia Aeropics: 124 (bottom right), 125 (bottom left)
Bison Picture Library: 109 (left)
Warren Bodie: 64
Boeing Aircraft Company: 142, 143, 144–145, 156, 157 (center), 161 (bottom), 165 (top left), 165 (bottom), 169 (center), 170–171,
171 (bottom four), 184 (top right), 189
Charles Brown: 24–25
Denis Hughes: 78–79 (top)
Imperial War Museum: 55, 63, 85 (top), 89 (bottom), 96 (top), 109 (right), 138–9 (bottom four), 154 (bottom right)
Lockheed: 26 (bottom), 33 (bottom both), 35 (top)
Martin and Kelman: 104–105
McDonnell Douglas: 14–15, 16–17, 33 (top)
National Archives: 14 (bottom left), 140, 158–159
North American: 72–73, 79 (center), 90–91, 93, 95, 96–97,
114–115, 120–121, 123–124
Robert Hunt Library: 141 (top), 159 (top right), 166 (top)
Michael Ross: 66
Bob Snyder: 37 (bottom and center), 114 (below), 124 (bottom left), 125 (bottom left and top), 139 (top)
Taylor Picture Library: 82, 84, 134–135, 136–137, 138–139 (main picture), 147 (top), 148, 152–153, 156–157, 168 (bottom), 91
USAF: 15 (bottom right), 31 (top), 38 (top), 39 (top), 40–41, 42, 43, 45 (top), 48–49 (all four), 50, 51, 52, 53 (top), 56, 57, 58, 59, 60, 61, 69, 70–71, 74–75, 76–77, 80, 81 (below),
86–87, 89 (top and center), 94 (insert), 98–99, 100, 103–104, 105, 108–109, 110–111, 112–113, 116–117, 118–119, 127 (top three), 128–129, 132, 133, 141 (bottom), 151 (top), 158 (bottom), 177 (bottom left), 163 (bottom), 164–165, 166 (bottom), 167, 168 (top), 169, 170, 171, 172–173, 174–175, 176, 177, 178, 179, 180, 181, 182, 184 (top left), 184–185 (bottom), 186, 187, 188, 196
US Army: 18–19, 23 (top), 126–127, 159 (top left), 163 (top), 183
US Navy: 155
Gordon Williams: 46–47